Old West Swindlers

Old West Swindlers

Laurence J. Yadon
and Robert Barr Smith

PELICAN PUBLISHING COMPANY
Gretna 2011

Library of Congress Cataloging-in-Publication Data

Yadon, Laurence J., 1948-
  Old West swindlers / by Laurence J. Yadon and Robert Barr Smith.
    p. cm.
  Includes bibliographical references and index.
  ISBN 978-1-58980-863-8 (pbk. : alk. paper) 1. Swindlers and
swindling—West (U.S.)—Case studies. I. Smith, Robert B. (Robert Barr), 1933- II. Title.

  HV6698.W47Y33 2011
  364.16'3092278—dc22

                                    2010047568

Printed in the United States of America
Published by Pelican Publishing Company, Inc.
1000 Burmaster Street, Gretna, Louisiana 70053

To our families, who have tolerated cheerfully the immense amount of time we have devoted to this book and not spent with them, and with our occasional requests to "please read this; does it make sense?" They have also put up patiently with our perpetual grumbling, our occasional profanity, and our sometimes vague responses when asked simple questions, our minds being far away in the Old West. If this book has any lasting value, it is as much due to them as to anything we did.

Contents

Preface

This is a book about the sinister side of American enterprise in the making of the West. Real-life confidence men fictionalized in the popular 1973 Paul Newman-Robert Redford movie *The Sting* share space here with financial swindlers who operated on the frontier much as Charles Ponzi and Bernie Madoff did in later times back East. Our goal is to profile a wide cross-section of gaming cheats, grifters, and financial swindlers who operated from Colonial days to the Roaring Twenties.

Thus, cardsharps and other crooked gamblers rub elbows in these pages with counterfeiters, wildcat bankers with no assets other than building leases, corrupt politicians, quacks, land grabbers, mining swindlers, and dishonest railroad barons.

Not everyone profiled here was a criminal. Patrick Henry did not break the law when he tried to buy much of Alabama and Mississippi with nearly worthless state currency. Angry Georgia legislators passed a law insisting on payment in gold or silver, but Henry was not imprisoned. None of the railroad barons who inflated construction costs at taxpayer expense building the transcontinental railroad were ever convicted of anything. Yet each individual profiled here at the very least engaged in "sharp practice," doing things that most people would consider downright dishonest, even if not illegal.

We have again turned to the scholarship of leading historians for these stories, relying upon traditional narratives of events, using standard sources and works of authors generally accepted as reliable. In some instances, we have offered and disclosed factual variations that we deem reliable, based on recent scholarship without extensive comment, since this is a work of popular history rather than academic scholarship. Generally, we reviewed books, magazines, and periodicals available to us as late as January 2010 to develop our narratives. Nevertheless, any errors regarding the contents of this book have been our own.

We hope you enjoy this journey through the making of the American West, as we examine that dark and shadowy place in the American psyche where greed, ingenuity, and unbridled ambition meet larceny.

Prologue:
Slick Cons and Smooth Grifters

Greed. That common human failing gets a lot of people in deep trouble. Some of them steal things; others try to—both are sheer stupidity. The dumbest of the lot are the get-rich-quick, something-for-nothing folks who buy into scams and confidence games. The world is never short of them, to the enrichment and vast amusement of the confidence fraternity. Doc Baggs, one of the most successful charlatans of all time, put it pretty well:

"I am conducting a fair, legitimate business. My mission is to trim suckers."[1]

Or, as another con man cynically said, "Suckers have no business with money anyway."[2]

American swindles began well before the Yazoo land scandal of post-Colonial days. Perhaps the best known today are the Ponzi schemes, named for the originator. Simple enough, these, robbing Peter to pay Paul: the charming promoter induces a series of investors to sink their cash into his scheme, and then uses the money gleaned from later investors to pay off the earlier investors at an exorbitant return. The latest hero of this ancient dodge is of course the egregious Bernie Madoff. He is in prison—Ponzi went to prison too—but there are always more swindlers around.

In the heyday of the con, there was the Pigeon Drop, the Gold Brick, the salted gold mine, the phony diamond mine, the ancient Badger Game—the "you're in bed with my wife" charade—the infallible doctor and faith healer specialties, the Magic Wallet, the Big Store, and a couple of dozen others. Enterprising, trusting Americans bought into lots of them; but they were far from first.

A likeable Frenchman sold the Eiffel Tower—twice. Another

Frenchman named LeMoine convinced sophisticated officials of
the great DeBeers diamond operation that he had discovered how
to produce diamonds artificially. Naturally, DeBeers wanted the
formula for itself—a flood of cheap artificial diamonds would ren-
der the big DeBeers South African mining operation worthless.

In the end, the swindler long gone, DeBeers got the formula—
scribbled on a piece of paper—saying that combining pressure
and heat on carbon would produce diamonds. That was actually
true. Trouble was, it's impossible to concentrate enough heat and
pressure to produce anything marketable.

A smiling Turk once sold the Galata Bridge across the Golden
Horn at Istanbul—again, twice. After World War I, an enterprising
British crook named Ferguson sold the London clock tower known
by the name of its famous bell, Big Ben; supposedly also peddled
Nelson's Column; and even talked a wealthy American out of a substantial "down payment" on Buckingham Palace. Wealthy Americans were his stock in trade; some believed his confidential assurances that Britain was so poor that the government had retained
him to quietly sell off priceless monuments to raise cash.

Eventually, Ferguson moved to the United States and continued peddling public edifices. He supposedly managed to "rent"
the White House for a bargain $10,000 annually to some Eng-
lish tourists. After many successful years, he tried to peddle the
much-sold Brooklyn Bridge to an Australian for a whopping 100
Grand. The Aussie smelled a rat, and Ferguson got five years in
an American prison—which makes one wonder whether he tried
to sell that too.

But the champion public structure salesman was an enterprising New York con man named George Parker, who sold the Brooklyn Bridge as often as twice a week. Sometimes the New York
coppers even had to stop an enterprising buyer from barricading
"his" bridge to collect tolls. The same convincing charlatan sold
many other public structures as well, including Madison Square
Garden and the Statue of Liberty. Somehow he stayed in business
for some forty years.

Steve Brodie was a New York bookie who boasted that he could
jump off the Brooklyn Bridge 135 feet into the river below and survive,

all to win a bet. He did jump and he did survive, to great fanfare in the papers of the day. There are tales—almost surely true—that Brodie substituted a dummy for his own body, since hitting water after falling 135 feet is about like jumping onto concrete. Still, the stunt succeeded, and in the ensuing blizzard of notoriety he opened a saloon, which thrived on its owner's dubious fame.

Brodie's stunt even added his name to the argot of American slang. "Doing a Brodie" (or "pulling a Brodie") came to define any highly dangerous and usually stupid act.

There were also professional fit-throwers, at least one of whom used a green soap to convincingly foam at the mouth. And the "Crying Kid" was only one of many who became adept at falling down on the street and faking serious injury. Perhaps the best was Edward Pape, who parlayed a neck fracture he had suffered as a child into a steady source of income from store owners. The old fracture still looked good on an x-ray.

The glass-eye hoax was also a financial winner. A one-eyed grifter would begin shopping in an upscale store and suddenly announce that he had lost his expensive glass eye and offer a substantial reward for its return. Later in the day, a second "customer" would find it.

"There's a reward for that," said the store manager, but the finder said he had to leave town almost immediately and accepted a small sum from the manager instead. The sucker would then take the glass eye to the owner's hotel, only to find nobody had ever heard of the man. The swindler made only a small profit, but glass eyes were cheap, and the scam could be run several times a day in different stores.

The Classic Fraud

Successful cons get repeated over time. The most famous was the classic fraud called the Cardiff Giant. A New York tobacco-seller called George Hull conceived the idea in October 1869, supposedly to win an argument with a fundamentalist clergyman. The tobacco business must have been good, for the hoax was elaborate and expensive. Hull bought a big block of granite in Iowa and commissioned a talented Chicago stone cutter to carve a giant human figure, which was bashed with a steel-studded board and splashed with acid and other stains for aging.

The granite man was shipped to Cardiff, New York, where Hull's cousin gave it a decent, but quiet burial on his farm. About a year later, two hired well-diggers conveniently uncovered him. Hull's cousin then set up a tent over the site and charged the curious two bits to look at it; the entrance fee quickly doubled.

Eventually, Hull sold the Giant to a syndicate for a tidy $37,000, about $589,000 today. The Giant went off to Syracuse, where he drew more crowds. P. T. Barnum tried to buy him, and when the owners wouldn't sell, he hired a sculptor to make one of his own, which he displayed as the *real* Giant, claiming the first one was a fraud. The Giant's owners sued Barnum, but the judge found that no one can sue somebody else for calling his fake a fake.

The Giant was then displayed in New York, in the Farmers' Museum in Cooperstown. Another Giant, said to be Barnum's copy, adorned Marvin's Marvelous Mechanical Museum in Farmington, Michigan. The Giant just won't go away, reappearing in at least one novel, several films, and even a broadcast séance as late as 2009; how one speaks to a piece of rock remains unclear.[3]

Some imitations of the Giant appeared—one was "found" in Beulah, Colorado, and dubbed the Solid Muldoon. One tale about Muldoon says he was also Hull's creation. Muldoon was a disgusting mix of rock dust, clay, plaster, ground bones, and real meat. Another fake showed up—in New York again—the creation of a hotel owner, and in 1899 a "petrified man" appeared in Fort Benton, Montana, said to be the remains of Civil War general Thomas Francis Meagher, who had already fallen from a steamboat during an 1867 drinking bout and drowned in the Missouri River.

The most successful petrified man in the West belonged to Soapy Smith, a master swindler who operated in Denver and Creede, Colorado, before moving his operation to Skagway, Alaska. McGinty, or Colonel Stone, as this fake was called, was a real corpse, loaded with embalming fluid—mostly arsenic. This noxious mixture had the effect of ossifying the body, precisely the

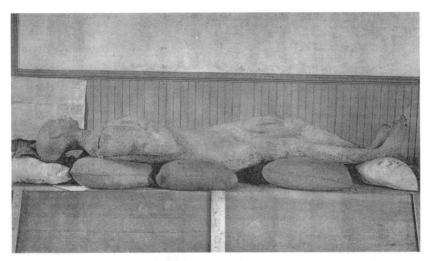

Solid Muldoon (History Colorado)

means later used to preserve Oklahoma's most inept bandit, Elmer McCurdy, for a long and successful second career in various museums.

Although the swindlers are still with us, their golden era was the nineteenth century, heyday of Doc Baggs, Soapy Smith, the Blonger boys, and Canada Bill Jones. "There's a sucker born every minute" supposedly quipped P. T. Barnum, who skinned a few himself. He was right—more right than he knew, for eventually, he too was skinned.

So Many Con Games

The swindlers ran confidence games ranging from the simple to the complex. Soapy Smith was named for his favorite swindle, as we shall see later. Three-card Monte was another perennial fraud. Monte, like most of the other ploys used to harvest suckers' money, was simple enough, and like many others involved use of accomplices, known in the swindling trade as "shills." British con men added another convincing wrinkle: often a shill was dressed as a clergyman; who could doubt a man of the cloth? One British version sometimes used a small group of con men. They would help trick the mark into a Monte game, and take turns losing or "winning" to lull the pigeon into a sense of confidence.[4]

Monte mostly depended on the agile hands of the dealer. One refinement required the dealer's partner—often called a "roper" or "steerer"—to watch the mark win a couple of games, then whisper confidentially that the target card had a slight crease in it. At which the mark would bet heavily, point to the creased card, and only then discover he had chosen the wrong card. The dealer had quickly uncreased the card and creased one of the others. Monte survived well into the next century since it was simple to play and generally successful.

Another old-time con was the Gold Brick. The idea was to sell a brick of solid gold to a credulous buyer for a large chunk of money. The object was in fact a real brick or a brick shaped of base metal gilded to resemble the real thing. Naturally people with an IQ greater than eleven tended to doubt whether the golden lump was really gold, so the swindler and his mark would repair to an assayer's office, generally a phony storefront run by an accomplice. The clincher was a piece of "gold" pried from the brick and pronounced the real thing. If a real assayer were used, the piece submitted was a chunk of real gold, thoughtfully planted in the brick.

The Gold Brick would not have fooled a real miner or mining engineer—unless the brick were lead. Yet the scam often took in sophisticated businessmen who should have known better. In 1939, a couple of Texas bankers were taken for a reputed $300,000, about $4.6 million today, for a gilded brick.[5]

On the other hand, the Green Goods swindle unashamedly appealed to obvious dishonesty. "I'll sell you lots of the world's finest counterfeit bills," said the con man, "for just a trifling amount. The bills are undetectable," the swindler said, "and here's a photo." The photo, of course, was a snapshot of real money. "Give me your money"—sometimes required to be in a plain brown parcel—"and I'll hand over this carpetbag full of my counterfeit bills." There was a bag, of course, but the contents were cut paper or something else worthless.

The two men parted in a hurry, since what they were doing was plainly illegal; later, presumably in private, the sucker would open the bag and find he had been sold a carefully cut ream or so of paper, and was thus "left holding the bag." If he wanted to report the swindle, the mark had to admit to the police he was trying to commit a crime; few did.

Banco came to the United States from England before our Civil War, and is said to be the genesis of the words "bunkum," or "buncombe" and finally plain old "bunco," the generic name for all swindles. It required a little more complex set-up, a cloth betting surface and either dice or a deck of cards. When the sucker played with dice, there were fourteen spaces on the cloth on which he could bet; if the game was played with cards, there were forty-three, one blank, the rest numbered. The mark had no chance at all, for the cards were marked and dice loaded: both were as crooked as the dealer.

Today the term "shell game" is also synonymous with the word "swindle," often used to describe a confidence game or even a political ploy. The shell game originally was played with three real walnut shells and a pea. The sucker was supposed to guess where the shell concealing the pea ended up as the dealer rapidly moved the shells face downward, changing their order on some simple flat surface.

Old Swindles

There were other frauds, almost beyond counting—grifters have succeeded through the years in part because variations of old swindles have constantly been reinvented. Some were simple, others quite complicated, but they all had some things in common.

A successful swindle requires more than a smooth line of patter and the greed or gullibility of the mark. There must be something unique about the scheme, something believable, something to make the sucker go deeper and deeper into the plan, whatever doubts he begins with. The Western con man understood this well, and the sheer variety and ingenuity of his swindles is amazing. Here are a few.

Thirty-One was a seemingly simple game played with—or even without—dice, simply by alternately counting numbers with the swindler, adding the numbers together until one of the two players reached thirty-one. Neither player could call a number greater than those appearing on the dice—one through six.

The game was only marginally crooked, since it really did not matter who started counting first, nor were the dice always loaded. The swindler always knew something the sucker did not; if he counted so that his call, added to the others, reached three, ten, seventeen, or twenty-four, he was a sure winner, and there was no way the sucker could beat him.

The "scientific breakthrough" swindles were more complex. "Gaston Bulmar" sold an energy pill, which could become gasoline after adding water. Almost as a joke, General Electric sent a young executive to visit Bulmar at his hotel. The grifter admitted his claim sounded like moonshine, but invited a test: the young man could choose any pill from ten lying on the table and drop it in a bucket. Then Bulmar walked into the neighboring bathroom and added water to the bucket. A stench of gasoline filled the room.[6]

The young man reported back to the company. "I don't know how it happens," he said, "but here's the test bucket." On analysis, its contents did indeed turn out to be gasoline. A more senior man visited Bulmar, and was treated to the same spiel and demonstration. "Here's what I want," said Bulmar. "Once word of this gets out, my life is in terrible danger from the oil companies. I'll send all these pills with you and you can analyze them, but my price is $100,000 up front. I intend to disappear, and I need a week to do it; I'll leave my formula in a safety-deposit box, which you can open within a week."

It almost worked. General Electric sent a Nobel Prize researcher who uncovered the swindle by simply walking into the bathroom and turning on the tap himself, only to be greeted by the unmistakable smell of pure gasoline, fed into the faucet by the grifter's own small pump. Sadly, no one knows who Bulmar really was; by the time the police called for him, he had vanished.

Enricht's "Green Gas" additive was also guaranteed to turn water into gasoline. Similarly, Keely's "Energy Machine" introduced in

1872 supposedly would produce enough energy to move a train for long distances when water was added. Keely astounded witnesses with energy that drove bullets through thick planks and distorted iron. The witnesses' astonishment sold lots of stock in Keely's firm. The demonstrations of the marvelous machine were rare, and always held in Keely's "gas plant." This was so because the "energy" did not come from his secret formula and a little water, but from a supply of compressed air hidden in the basement below. Keely worked this swindle throughout his life; nobody found out the truth until after his death.

The "Gold Accumulator" was the brainchild of Prescott Jernegan, a sometime minister turned to sin, who worked the East Coast. The Accumulator was coated with mercury and the "secret formula" then lowered into the sea to attract and capture all that gold supposed to be floating about in seawater. The next morning, behold! The device was crusted with real gold. A blind man could see that the gold must have gotten there the night before.

Indeed it had, but not by some magic accumulation. Jernegan, apparently an accomplished swimmer, replaced the original during the night with the gold-coated replica. Jernegan and an accomplice fleeced credulous stock-buyers of more than $300,000— about $5.3 million today—then intelligently decamped to Europe with their booty, there to live the high life.

A more rudimentary swindle carried out by cattle dealers involved denying the stock water for days on their way to market, then letting them drink their fill just before sale. Since the thirsty beasts drank long and deep, their weight escalated abruptly, and the buyer could not know he had bought a lot of water until a day or two later. By then, the seller was gone. Daniel Drew was one of the early practitioners of this grift. Drew went on to greater things, swindling Commodore Vanderbilt not once, but twice. First, Drew ran a steamboat in competition with Vanderbilt's own vessel at a substantial and intentional losing rate, undercutting Vanderbilt so drastically that the Commodore bought Drew out.

Years later, Drew took the Commodore again, this time feeding on Vanderbilt's ambition to control the stock of the Erie Railroad, in which Drew also owned stock. As Vanderbilt bought more and more stock, Drew sold it short, until Vanderbilt had cornered the market and the price per share had plummeted.

Once Vanderbilt had his corner, he could ruin Drew, who had to buy back the stock he had sold short. But Erie stock kept appearing on the market, until the day when a broker picked up a stock certificate and the ink smudged his finger. Drew had been using Erie convertible bonds to create more stock, and the bottom fell out of the market. Vanderbilt is said to have "lost $7,000,000, about $95,000,000 today, in fifteen minutes."[7]

Crooked Games

The venerable crap game—when played by professionals—was also a sure loser for the sucker. Some of the swindlers who specialized in crooked games could roll any number they wanted, generally using loaded dice or shills who played for the house.

The classic game of chuck-a-luck—sometimes and inexplicably called "hyronemus"—involved three dice, either rolled into a wooden bowl or cup, or contained in an hourglass-shaped sort of birdcage on a swivel. Simply turning the cage dropped the dice into the other end, its bottom lined with leather. This game was also a winner for the crooked dealer, who used loaded dice or an electric current from a concealed battery to induce the dice to beat the innocent players. Chuck-a-luck was unsophisticated, and generally did not appeal to high rollers; but it drew suckers by the dozens at county fairs and the like. A full day of small bets could make the dealer a very good return.

Roulette played in honest houses has an honorable history offering a reasonable chance of winning. The rules are different today, but in the nineteenth century, it was simple enough: On the roulette wheel were thirty-six numbers, plus zero and double zero. These two were the house's numbers; if the ball dropped in either one, the house won. If the number the player chose was, say, black, and the ball dropped into a red slot, or if the player bet even and the ball stopped on odd, the house also collected. People bet on various numbers, red or black, odd or even, and their odds remained about the same. One con man wrote that the honest house—he was referring to Monte Carlo—had an edge of a respectable 5 percent.[8]

The crooked gambler created an even better edge for himself: it was easy enough to rig the wheel so that the croupier or a shill could control the wheel, either by electricity or a simple brake. A less elaborate version was called the Arrow Spindle, the Squeeze Wheel, or Spinning Arrow, but the result was exactly the same. The same fix used a simple circle with pegs around the circumference, the spaces between labeled red or black. In the center was a metal arrow on a pivot, which the dealer spun. This one was also absolutely controlled, either with a foot or stomach brake, or, in its original, British version, by simply tilting the table a little.

Roulette games in some houses were pure swindles. At first the croupier controlled the play with a lever under the table or one he could press his stomach against; press it at the right moment and, presto, the house won. Later this was done with electricity. Wires led beneath the table to the red numbers and the black, the odd and the even, and the first, middle, and last group of twelve numbers. The croupier had a series of buttons beneath his feet, and the little hollow ball was magnetized iron. If betting was heaviest on odd, he pressed the button for even; if most of the money was down on red, he pressed the control for black. This was chastely called an "advantage wheel," and that it surely was. There was no 5 percent margin for the house; the house's bulge was exactly what the house wanted it to be.

Draw poker, common everywhere in the American West, could be honest, particularly a game among friends or at least close acquaintants. The occasional professional even played a straight game, relying on his skill. Or, like Doc Baggs, just used his big diamond ring as a mirror. That was fair in his eyes, and his cheating was nothing like the raw thievery common in crooked games, where the "cold deck" was common.

Like most consistently successful swindles, cold-decking was basically quite simple. The dealer, starting with an honest deck, honestly cut, would substitute an identical deck of appropriately marked cards. This required practice, since the dealer not only had to work his marked deck, but get rid of the other one. He watched his chance, and helped himself by looking his quarry in the eye, deflecting the dupe's attention from the dealer's hands.

The marking of the cold deck was an art unto itself. Sometimes the con man used a knife, inscribing faint grooves in the intricate scrollwork that covered the back of most cards in those days. The dealer could tilt a card just slightly and pick up the otherwise invisible mark; trouble was, so could a player, especially if he knew what he was looking for. The most sophisticated fix, however, was to use a dye of the general color of the card backs. Only a minute part of the scroll work was left un-dyed, and only the dealer knew what to look for. Such carefully dyed decks were available for sale: one proficient producer, said to have been a college professor, sold his marked decks at the bargain rate of thirty-six dollars a dozen.[9]

Draw poker could be fraudulent enough. Much easier to fake was a five-card stud game. This scam generally involved a shill sitting in on the game. This man knew the marks on the cards, and could instantly tell what down-cards the other players were holding—so could the dealer. The shill would stay in the game with a good hand: his winnings would be later split with the house, or he was paid a set fee per hour. If he lost, that only reassured the other players. The marked cards helped the dealer too. He knew what he was up against, and therefore whether to bet high or not.

Ancient Cons

Much more complex were ancient cons like the Spanish Prisoner, which had been around since at least our Civil War. The beauty of this one is that it started with a letter; if the addressee did not answer, there was nothing lost but the stamp; if the con man got a reply, the con was begun. There were a number of variations, but the basic fraud went like this: It started when the sucker got a letter from somebody behind bars in Spain or Mexico, or someplace else far away. It succeeded in part because it appealed not only to greed, but to the basic chivalry of old-fashioned Americans. The writer said he had received the mark's name from a fellow prisoner, who of course had to remain anonymous to protect his family name. The simplest form of the con involved an appeal for money to pay the prisoner's fine and get him back his freedom. The fine—maybe $1,000 in 1865, or about $14,000 today—was a small price for a wealthy man to pay, but for this prisoner it meant life itself; and so on.

In a more complicated version, the prisoner had a large cache of money, or jewels, or one or more certified checks—he desperately wanted to provide for his young daughter at home in America, but he couldn't get at his stash. That was in a trunk or suitcase stored in the United States, but the claim check that would recover the luggage was in a false-bottomed suitcase impounded by the country that had imprisoned him. If the mark would come up with the amount of the fine the prisoner owed and recover the luggage, he would also retrieve the claim check that would make him rich.

The come-on was a sizable chunk of money, usually in the form of a certified check secreted in the luggage along with the claim check. The mark would have the check just for redeeming the luggage, and if he would also engage to help the writer's beloved daughter, he would share in another fabulous sum—the hoard stored in the stateside trunk. Sometimes a fetching picture of the "daughter" would be enclosed.

If the mark fell for this line, he sometimes ended up traveling to wherever-it-was—in later days, Mexico—where he was further duped by a contact man and a phony prison guard, both of whom behaved in an appropriately conspiratorial way. Then the sucker was told that the government had discovered the plot and was searching for him. "But," said the guard, "I have broken into the prisoner's luggage: here is the claim check for the luggage in the United States, and the promised certified check."

The guard promised that he would get the fine paid so the sucker could leave the country quickly and unmolested. Usually, the dupe was only too willing to give the guard the required "fine" —perhaps $10,000—and then pocket the claim check and the certified check and get quickly out of wherever-it-was before he was arrested.

Predictably, when he got back home, the certified check turned out to be worthless, and both trunk and "daughter" pure fantasy. In a variation of the basic tale, the sucker was told that the suitcases would be sold at auction unless the fine was paid by a certain date. Still another variation made the prize the location of a sunken ship carrying treasure.

Nearly as easy as this scheme was making fraudulent claims against a dead man's estate. After the estate was settled, the swindler or swindlers filed a series of small claims under different names, small enough individually that the estate paid them without any real investigation.[10] Worse still was a small-time scam in which the con man visited the local cemetery, made some notes on memorials grown shabby with the years. He then called on the next of kin, offering to "renovate" the departed's headstone for a trifling amount. He didn't make much per stone, but then, he didn't do any work either.

Among the other more elaborate cons was one in Britain called The Mushroom Farm, although the swindle could be worked with nearly any sort of "business." In this one, the grifter advertised for men to supervise at the farm, and when dupes came to see him they were told they would be paid a reasonable salary—he named the figure—but they would be required to post a larger sum as a "deposit." If the farm prospered—as it always had—they would share in the profits.

A surprising number of men bought into this fraud, and the swindler notified them that at a certain date and time, he would have their "share certificates" ready for them. But on that glorious day, when the victims appeared at the grifter's hotel, they found that nobody there had ever heard of the entrepreneur. It was small comfort that they could share their disappointment with a small army of other investors, as luckless as they.[11]

The Big Store

One consistently fruitful con was the Big Store, and it had a dozen variations. Most common were the fight and footrace stores, the rag and payoff stores, and the wire stores. All of them involved renting or borrowing a storefront room or rooms, and equipping them with whatever paraphernalia was needed to work the scam. The rag, for example, was basically a phony stock exchange or trading operation, where the sucker could invest and profit hugely in a very short time.

The wire store was probably the most elaborate, and one is faithfully reproduced in the all-time best film about swindlers, *The Sting*. Like most good cons, the thesis for the wire store was simple. The store presented itself as an illegal, underground betting parlor, complete with furniture, a big board where odds were regularly posted, lots of customers—whom the sucker saw winning and collecting on their bets—and even a ticker receiving race results. It was busy when the sucker saw it, full of people betting and winning. The usual targets were businessmen, roped in by a plausible business prospect, a prospect who in fact was an expert roper for the con. It goes like this:

The roper—usually seconded by a "friend" or "relative" —reveals his secret to the mark: he has a means of getting race results early, through his contact at Western Union. That way, he can put down a bet on the winner if he is quick enough to get to the bookie's shop before the real results arrive.

As the roper distracts the mark with professional-sounding talk about some glittering and non-existent business opportunity, the roper takes the dupe to a bogus telegraph office complete with Western Union sign. This plant—in a rented storefront—will disappear the moment the two leave. Here the shill introduces the mark to his friend, presented as the telegrapher who will pass the results to the shill and the mark at some spot near the book. The dupe is then introduced to the betting parlor itself. Everybody there is a shill, including the staff and the "customers," and the money flying back and forth all belongs to the con man running the swindle, but it sure looks real.

The introduction to the betting parlor sets the stage for the next move. The plan is to go to such-and-such a place near the book, maybe a bar or drugstore, and wait for the crucial call from the telegrapher. "Then," says the shill, "we go immediately to the bookie and get our bet down before they get the race results."

And so it goes; both men place a small bet and win. The process is then repeated, until the mark is convinced he's on to a world-beating system. Then comes the kill. A bet is decided upon, a big one, and the mark agrees to put up the money, sometimes converting assets to realize the cash. The shill and the mark discuss and agree on a split, and the stage is set. The mark goes home to raise the money, and when he returns the bet is placed. To ensure that the dupe doesn't get cold feet, or go to an honest cop, the bookie sometimes sends a man to tail him, to report if anything suspicious happens. If not, when the mark returns with the cash, the con goes into high gear.

The advance results are called into the phone in the bar or other waiting spot, and the mark and the grifter hurry to get the bet down with the phony bookie. Generally, the odds are good, to whet the dupe's appetite. The race starts. He stands transfixed, and is appalled when the horse he bet on does not win, but places second. After the race is over, there is a confrontation with the "contact," at which the "Western Union" man angrily asserts he told them to bet on the horse not to win but to place.

Generally, that explains the disaster to the mark, or at least keeps him pacified for the time being. Meanwhile, the betting parlor disappears as if by magic—telegraph, board, customers, employees, and all—unless the mark can be induced to recoup his loss by repeating the process. In that happy event, the betting parlor stays in existence long enough to fleece him again.

Faro

Faro began life as a legitimate gambling game. The odds were in favor of the house, of course, the common denominator of all games of chance. But at least the player, if he had a little luck, stood some measurable chance of winning. The rig is simple: a little box, generally nickel-plated, spring-loaded to hold a deck of cards. On the table are painted thirteen cards, ace first, then the rest of the suit, ending in the king. The players bet on one or more of the cards. The procedure, greatly simplified, is this: the dealer pulls two cards, one at a time; the card pulled second loses, the next one wins.

Once three cards of the same denomination have been pulled, the remaining matching card pays off at even money. Especially on this card, the player has a fifty-fifty chance of winning. If the game is fairly played, that is. The favorite prey of the crooked dealer is a neophyte, or an unvigilant drunk, for the cards can be marked by nicking the edges to the point that the dealer knows what card comes next. If that card would be a winner for the player, the dealer's practiced hand pulls two cards, and shows the next one.

There is a second conspirator, called the "case keeper." He presides over the "case," an abacus-like device on which he is supposed to record each card as it appears. If he cheats on his job, the odds for the house get even better, since the player cannot accurately tell what cards have already appeared. In any case, the house wins; the mark loses.

The faro game produced a more elaborate swindle, in which the crooked dealer makes the acquaintance of a likely victim, who always has money and greed in abundance. The dealer complains bitterly about some wrong he has suffered at the hands of his employer, and offers to cheat the house of big money if the mark helps out. They will split the booty. The dealer will even bring a faro deck and box with him, and shows his victim how he can manipulate the deck so the mark will win.

Suitably impressed, the victim agrees. "Bring lots of money," says the dealer. "We want the house to believe you're a high roller." The mark does, and bets the table limit several times in succession, losing each time. Then, when he has his last bet down where the dealer told him to put it, just when he expects the big killing, the "proprietor" of the gambling hall comes to the table, tells the dealer to take a rest, and deals himself. Away goes the mark's last dollar, and he leaves empty of all but regrets and bitter experience.

Oscar's Drake Con

The most ambitious con, however, was probably the least complicated. It was bossed by a single man based in Des Moines, and worked without elaborate props or shills. The con had been

Oscar Hartzell's mug shot (Author's Collection)

around since the 1830s, and the premier practitioner was a country boy called Oscar Hartzell.[12] The swindle went like this:

The primary targets were credulous people called Drake, although the con men even roped in people of other names. The story was that the rube was one of the heirs to a gigantic fortune left behind by Sir Francis Drake. It was being pursued for the heirs even then by British solicitors—unscrupulous, of course, busily engaged in unraveling complicated family trees and bribing officials when it was necessary—and Oscar recruited a corps of assistants, including the pair who had fleeced his mother. People by the thousands gave money to cover the very large "expenses" involved, including the entire population of an Illinois town and a good many more from a settlement in North Dakota.

Oscar spent some time in England too, posing as a Texas cattleman, spending money like water, and oozing charm. Along the way he managed to impregnate a barmaid; when her father visited Oscar to complain, Oscar promptly sold him on the notion that the father himself was one of the Drake heirs. Oscar kept the transatlantic cable hot, firing off news of his progress, and steadily inflating the amount of money involved, until finally his glittering account of gold at the end of the Drake rainbow reached the apex at five billion dollars. Meanwhile, his followers kept the money coming in.

Oscar himself got swindled by a clever English woman who convinced him she was an efficient medium. Full of firewater, Oscar spilled his con to her, and she took full advantage. Apparently he did not remember what he had said in his cups, but she did. She could predict the future, she said, and told him all her psychic revelations about the progress of his scam. Oscar paid her to keep quiet, but he could afford it, for the take in America continued to be huge. Oscar spent nine years in England, sending wire after wire trumpeting amazing progress, closer and closer to the promised billions.

There were obstacles, of course, he said, and Oscar spun endless conspiracy stories designed to show just how difficult his task in England was. He talked about the Spanish Inquisition and a "secret ecclesiastical court" in Britain. There were powerful forces in the way, he said, including Woodrow Wilson. And there was a sort of ranking among the heirs, too, for some of them, according to Oscar, were descended from a mating between Drake and Queen Elizabeth I. That anybody bought this nonsense was a commentary on the willingness to believe so common among Americans, particularly those from rural towns.

But in time suspicion inevitably raised its head, and diverse American officials began to smell a rat. When American authorities requested an investigation, Scotland Yard called on Oscar, and a legitimate Drake heir ridiculed his whole scheme. Oscar was deported by the British government after a hearing in which one inspector testified that he had searched ancient court records and found a record of the probate of Sir Francis's estate.

Oscar was then charged with violation of U.S. postal regulations. Out on bail, he continued recruiting Drake heirs, but he was only delaying the inevitable. He got ten years in Leavenworth, and finally ended his days in a mental institution with "delusions of grandeur." Oscar had come to believe his own lies.

Some Famous Con Artists

There were dozens of elaborate big cons, but most of the scam artists operated much smaller swindles, again and again, often repeatedly in the same town. The story of likeable Soapy Smith is a good example. Others—for example smooth veteran Doc Baggs—spent a long and lucrative lifetime defrauding people and then moving quickly off to greener pastures.

Perversely, a lot of the con men were inveterate gamblers themselves, bucking the odds in games they knew were stacked against them. When Canada Bill Jones was warned that a game in which he was playing was crooked, Canada Bill clearly explained the reason why so many con men ended up broke: "Sure," he said, "but it was the only game in town."

The same statement is also attributed to a con man called the "Narrow-gauge Kid," and maybe he said it too (his name, legend says, stemmed from his height, precisely the same as the width between narrow-gauge rails). A lot of the fraternity might well have made that same plaintive statement, considering the common practice in the trade of gambling away—often at faro—the money they had fleeced from others.

Many of the swindlers who survived often did so by greasing the right palms—the city fathers were often corrupt and so were the police—and they usually at least turned a blind eye on the swindler if he left residents alone and preyed only on tourists and other innocents just passing through town. And generally a lot of the populace turned a blind eye too; so long as only outsiders were fleeced, the result was new money in town, and that ended up in the pockets of the locals.

And after all, most members of the con fraternity were generous and public-spirited: who can be angry with a man who doesn't try to fleece locals but gives lots of money to charity, takes care of widows and orphans, and even, like Soapy Smith, gives the city money for more night watchmen? It's easy to be charitable with other people's money, and it pays off.

For most of the confidence men it was easy come, easy go. After all, there was always another sucker with money in his pockets, just around the corner. Besides gambling, there were other vices available. Some grifters became narcotics users, even addicts, although all tried to hide it. It was as shameful then as it is today.

Other cheats were more careful with their loot. Take Elmer Mead, sometimes called the "Christ Kid," or the "Christian Kid," for his pious appearance and regular church attendance. Apparently his piety did not extend much past Sunday, for over the years he swindled dozens of people, maybe hundreds. But Mead saved his money, buying land and stashing money and securities in safety-deposit boxes all over the country.[13]

As noted later, the con fraternity had its own language, an argot undecipherable by anybody but grifters and cops. And colorful and descriptive names were common in the swindling profession. Besides the Christ Kid, the Harmony Kid, and the Narrow-gauge Kid, there were Farmer Brown, the High Ass Kid (he was very tall), Slobbering Bob, Brickyard Jimmy, and Big Alabama (there was a Little Alabama too). Bow-legged Lip had both a harelip and noticeable bowlegs; Crooked Arm was named for an injury suffered when he jumped through a window during his thieving days.

And then there was the Yenshee Kid (he smoked yen-shee, an opium gum), the Mormon Kid, and Pretty Billy, the Seldom Seen Kid, Proud of His Tail, Slewfoot, Cockroach Gary, and a character intriguingly called Devil's Island Eddie, about whom we have discovered absolutely nothing.

That people were credulous enough to fall for the con man's line so often and so readily, may have something to do with the times. Those were days of greater trust, in which a man's word was supposed to be his bond and generally was. Everybody knew there were liars and thieves about, but still people tended to believe what they were told by a straight-talking, respectable-looking stranger.

If an individual really did judge a man in part by his appearance, as most people did in those far-off days, the con men were winners, normally careful with their dress and cultivated in their manners. Even those who during a con dressed like a farmer and talked like one seemed entirely authentic. Most swindlers were genial sorts as well, and people tended to like them; that helped too.

And customs and mores were different. Kids didn't smoke in those days, or if they did they got a sore fanny if their parents found out. The same taboo went for booze; kids were strictly warned away from John Barleycorn. Although at the same time any drugstore would sell an adult a matchbox-sized container of morphine or cocaine for a dime, nobody knew what marijuana was, and hashish was something that the assassins smoked someplace in the Near East in preparation for murdering somebody. Generally speaking, people were far more likely to take a stranger at face value, to come to the aid of somebody in trouble, to leave their doors unlocked, and to deal honestly with strangers.

All kinds of hoaxes were used to strike up the acquaintance of a likely victim. Often it was just a friendly smile and a phony story. Sometimes it was a little more complex, like the ploy of a con man who worked the trains. In those days men wore hats, and it was common for a traveler to stick his ticket stub in the outside band of his hat. Deep in the night, when he and others in the car were sleeping in their seats, a roper might steal up, snaffle the stub from the victim's hat, and then wake the mark to inquire whether this was his stub, "found on the floor."

Generally, a friendly conversation followed with the grateful mark, and in time the grifter came along and joined them, posing as a rustic farmer or cattleman with a broad accent and a fat roll of bills. He told a story about getting taken in a game of three-card Monte, and later buying the dealer's marked deck. In time he began to show off, clumsily dealing, and inevitably a game followed—the mark lost, of course, after the usual hands thrown to the roper.

Mining Scams

So the spirit of the times played a large part in the success of the confidence fraternity. The gold rushes of California, the wild enthusiasm of the Yukon, the fortunes made in the Comstock lode, the money pouring in from a variety of mineral mining ventures all over the West, the opportunities for riches in a booming economy expanding at the speed of light—all of these phenomena together produced a sort of contagion, a fever to get on the bandwagon and get rich. The enthusiasm touched the cupidity of all sorts of people, rich and otherwise.

It was a con man's heaven.

The mining boom produced all sorts of cons, the most common being the salting of gold mines and even diamond deposits. Almost anybody could work that one if they found the right sucker and could invest in a little gold to make their hole look like a real mine. Some of the others simply salted an empty shaft or drift; some used flakes of gold; if they were good at switching envelopes, they could sometimes use the flakes to swindle several dupes, one after the other.

Even newspaper writers plugged some of the mines—solid or not—in return for shares in the venture, sometimes in the form of so many "feet" of ore. One of these was none other than one Sam Clemens, better known in later years as Mark Twain, the name he created for his mining articles and carried on to later fame as a writer. He appeared in Virginia City, Nevada, as a reporter for the *Territorial Enterprise* in 1861, and described the reporters' work there.

> We generally said something to the effect that "indications were good" . . . or that the rock "resembled the Comstock." . . . If the mine was a "developed" one and had no ore to show (and of course it hadn't) we praised the tunnel; said it was one of the most infatuating tunnels in the land . . . we would squander half a column of adulation on a shaft, or a new wire rope, or a dressed-pine windlass, or a fascinating force-pump . . . but never a word about the rock.[14]

Clemens wrote about the North Ophir mine, so named to borrow some fame from the Ophir, a real rich strike indeed; sadly, if the Ophir was a bonanza, the North Ophir wasn't. This made the developers unhappy, so they remedied the situation by pouring melted silver dollars into strategic spots in the shaft. Before some attentive soul noted the traces of eagle heads in the "ore," shares in the mine jumped from thirteen to forty-five dollars a foot in just one day. The developers of this and other phony strikes could then sell for huge profits.

There was also the friendly telegraph, which abounded with coded messages about new strikes or the lack of them. People like San Francisco's powerful William Sharon of the Bank of California got insider information that way, as did others, and enterprising outsiders tried to—and sometimes did—break their codes and profit with them.

Other mine operators even went so far as to confine one or more shifts of miners in the area of the digging, and on at least one occasion a shift was held at the bottom of a shaft. Generally, the miners didn't mind: there was extra pay for hanging around, plus the whiskey and cigars the company furnished gratis to help while away the time. This modified form of kidnapping served to delay any word of a major strike making its way to the public. That gave the operators time to buy stock at a lower price, knowing it would jump once the news got out.

The mining passion also produced a rich array of talented amateur swindlers. One such was "Chicken Bill" Lovell, so called from driving a wagon-load of chickens through a blizzard. In Leadville, Colorado, he conned mining magnate Horace Tabor—who should have known better—into buying his mining claim near Tabor's hugely successful Little Pittsburgh. The idea was that Chicken Bill could tap into an offshoot of Tabor's high-grade vein.

Chicken Bill got some high-grade silver ore from Tabor's own mine, then dumped some of the ore in his own shaft and left the rest at the top. Tabor bought into the con, assessing the ore as the equivalent of the rich ore being harvested in his own mine, which of course it was, because that's where it came from. Chicken Bill made no secret of his fraud, bragging that he had rooked the great Tabor. Tabor, hearing this, is said to have stopped Chicken Bill on a street in Leadville; this conversation allegedly followed:

Tabor: "I thought you said there was good ore on that property."

Bill: "I know that there was, because I put it there myself."[15]

But sometimes what goes around really does come around, and so it was with Chicken Bill's swindle of Tabor. Tabor, then the owner of a worthless hole in the ground, nevertheless persevered, and drove the shaft a little farther down. And behold! What he found was indeed an extension of Tabor's rich find, and Tabor prospered further.

The Infamous Doc Fowler and Others

Probably the most able of all the con men of all time was Richard C. Flower, called "Doc." He had studied medicine all right, likewise law and, paradoxically, theology, all of which disciplines he used to defraud the innocent. Flower was a triple-threat con man, swindling in medicine, mining, irrigation, stock sales, and religion, among other fraudulent endeavors.

At one point in his infamous career, he operated as a faith healer, and claimed to have healed, among others, more than 4,000 cancer patients. These and other illnesses he could diagnose simply by holding the patient's hand. He was assisted by a corps of equally phony assistants, variously and mysteriously called "magnetizers" and "electricians." Tragically, an untold number of desperate people fell for his malarkey. And not only did thousands of patients flock in for his miraculous cures, but newspapers actually wrote reams of paeans praising the doctor's wondrous powers. He could not have asked for better publicity.

Doc was also well known for his psychic ability to predict the stock market's inscrutable fluctuations. This ability was described as "his intuitional powers in detecting the actual conditions of the markets [which] seem almost infallible." "Incredible" would have been a more accurate word. It was natural, then, for Doc to turn his considerable fraudulent talents to new and lucrative fields of dishonesty. Given the passion of the day for mining adventures and allied get-rich-quick schemes, it was his natural milieu.

There are many, many more, lesser-known swindles like Tin Sin Kuk, an oriental gambling scam, the Treasury Agent fraud, and the Paddy Hustle—also called Miss Murphy or the Carpet Game—in which the bunco man poses as a hotel manager, hooking a mark looking for a woman by switching the dupe's money-filled envelope for an identical one filled with paper. Timing was especially important for this one: if the victim was impatient, as he was likely to be, it behooved the grifter to disappear with all dispatch. It was not good to be nearby when the mark realized the state of things—no woman, no money, no manager, no carnal delights.

Every con had its risks, of course. The law was not always

friendly, and at times others in the confidence business could be downright hostile. For example, Lou Blonger, the longtime criminal king of Denver, waxed righteous when a colleague conned him out of a thousand dollars, and actually lodged a criminal complaint against the sinner.

And con man Reed Waddell, black sheep of a good family back East, came to grief at the hands of a colleague in the swindler's trade. Waddell, a practitioner of the gold brick scam not only in the United States but also in Europe, was an artist, making sure that a core of real gold was buried in the brick: if the mark was dubious and wanted a separate assay, part of the core could be pried out and handed over to a chemist, legitimate or otherwise.

But Waddell finally argued with the wrong confederate and came out on the short end. He discovered the hard way that it is best never to bring only a loud mouth to a gunfight. His opponent pulled a pistol and plugged him in the heart—it was the place, as one writer astutely put it, in which people thought him least vulnerable.[16]

Pros and Cons

A lot of Western hustlers appear in this book. Some pass by as mere shadows, minor characters on the big screen of crime. Others deserve more space, like Soapy Smith, who gets a whole chapter, or Doc Baggs, who gets most of one, or Doc Flower or the egregious Lou Blonger of Denver, who also get a full chapter. But all of them share a couple of characteristics. They were clever, of course, especially the quick-fingered thimbleriggers and cardsharps; they were persuasive, able to sell their marks on tales that no ordinary person could put over; some were masterful planners and organizers. And they were amoral, at least to some degree.

No doubt some of them loved their mothers and dogs and children—even the Dalton boys revered dear old mom. A lot of them gave liberal handouts to folks down on their luck; some, like the Christ Kid, regularly gave to the church; some helped buy city improvements, although lots of their charity was cynically designed to curry favor not only with the public, but down at city hall and the police department.

But in the end, they were simply thieves.

Old West Swindlers

CHAPTER 1

Doc Baggs and Some Kindred Spirits

Over all the years, even during the nineteenth-century heyday of flamboyant scam and fraud, no confidence man worked more smoothly and survived more ably than Charles Baggs. He was called "Doc" in the trade, a long-faced, dark-bearded, dignified sort who simply oozed respectability, courtesy, and reliability. Like many other con men, he started out as a steerer for other people, then graduated to running operations himself.

Doc did not waste his time with multiple-victim, small-time cons. He looked for the big money and milked it, one victim at a time. Baggs professed to be disappointed in Soapy Smith, successful as Soapy was, because he had swindled for what to Doc were nickels and dimes. According to one history of Soapy's Denver days, Doc put it this way:

> It's as easy to make big money as little money . . . In my profession, a hundred dollars is just chicken feed. We think in thousands, not tens . . . It is as easy to separate a sucker—the right sucker—from five thousand dollars as from fifty.[1]

Nobody could even take a look at Doc without trusting him. In addition to the dignified face and beard, Doc was given to wearing the best of clothing under his stovepipe hat; who could distrust a man in a cutaway coat and striped trousers, a man who carried a silk umbrella?

He was well known in Denver, and his appearance was so impressive that the *Denver News* published a neat bit of doggerel about him. It appeared on the occasion of the Denver visit of famed Irish poet Oscar Wilde. It seems that Wilde's favorite expression of delight was, "too, too, divine." A long, anonymous poem in the *News* responded thus:

> If thou dost boast of being too, we will/Produce Doc Baggs, M.D., who is as too/As thou are, and a durned sight tooer.[2]

Doc was proud of his profession, especially his well-known reluctance to swindle the ordinary man. "I defy the newspapers," he said,

> to put their hands on a single man I ever beat that was not financially able to stand it. I am emotionally insane. When I see anyone looking in a jewelry store window thinking about how they would like to get away with the diamonds, an irresistible impulse comes over me to skin them. I don't drink, smoke, chew, or cheat poor people. I pay my debts.[3]

All of which was probably true, although it did not keep the law from dogging Doc's footsteps from time to time. At one point—in about 1892—Doc told a reporter in Denver that he had been arrested "about a thousand times" —presumably a pardonable exaggeration—but said he was never convicted, which may also have been true. If so, it was quite a record, since Doc had worked all over the West, including a time in Omaha working with John Bull, another legendary con man.

There is a tale that Doc once defended himself and won a dismissal of the charge, arguing that there was no such statutory crime as "bunco-steering," the charge on which he had been arrested. There was not even such a phrase in the dictionary, he said, and according to legend, that ended the case. Well, maybe.

Doc Invents the Gold Brick Con

Legend credits Doc with inventing the Gold Brick con, which had the potential to turn a very large profit with a single sucker. And that was Doc's philosophy. What point was there in swindling little guys out of their little stashes of money, when there were folks around with pockets full of dollars, and even whole banks crammed with legal tender? The Gold Brick was just the sort of scam he liked best, and with it he trimmed Tom Fitch and L. B. Howard, powers in something called the Cedros Island Mining Company. The outfit was based on the West Coast, and whether Fitch and Howard had a real mine or not, they surely had money. They fell victim to a variation of the Gold Brick fraud, this time the "Mexican" variation, talked about below.

The Gold Brick con was basically quite simple. All the grifter had to do was sell this wonderfully valuable thing to somebody for lots of money. Trouble was, of course, that the brick wasn't gold at all, but instead some base metal or even a real brick, coated with a film of gilt or some other facsimile of the real thing. Nobody with enough money to buy such a thing lacked the sense to make sure what they were buying was the real McCoy. What better way to satisfy the buyer than an assay by a reputable assay office? "Sure," the grifter said, as he took customer and brick to a phony assay office, which pronounced this chunk of metal genuine gold.

Or, if the mark insisted on an appraisal, the con man readily agreed. "Tell you what we'll do," he said. "Here, I'll dig a chunk out of the brick, and we'll take it to be assayed." And they did. What could be fairer than that? Surely that should satisfy any buyer, and it usually did. Trouble was, the con man knew precisely where to dig out his sample. After all, it came from a plug of real gold carefully incorporated in the brick for just such a contingency.

Doc got some $15,000 out of Howard and Fitch, and he did even better with Leadville, Colorado, entrepreneur H. M. Smith, whom he took for some $20,000. The con had the "Mexican" wrinkle both times: the owner of the brick was a Mexican, Baggs said, living in a shack and anxious to sell a gold brick stolen in a robbery. A confederate played the "Mexican," and Doc was the "interpreter."

Doc Employs the Policy Shop Con

Along the way, using still another con, in about 1882 he bilked Miguel Otero (1829-82), a Las Vegas, New Mexico, businessman, earlier the governor of his state, who had come to Denver to attend a lecture by the Irish poet Oscar Wilde. Otero was taken in a sort of "policy shop" racket. Denver in those days had a number of policy shops for access to the state-run lottery. This one was a phony.

Baggs sent a bunco steerer to "accidentally" meet Otero. The steerer asked Otero to go to the policy shop with him to see if he held a winning ticket. Otero did so, and the scam was on. The shop operator was Doc Baggs, of course, and the party was joined by still another steerer, a "friend" of the first. The first man did not win, but the friend did, and revealed that he had a surefire system. When he won again and ran his stake up to $2,400, he asked Otero to bankroll him on still another bet, fifty-fifty, and Otero agreed.

The next step was easy. When the steerer bet the whole stake, Baggs said he could not deliver that much cash without evidence of the bettors' ability to pay if they lost. Otero ponied up his note for $2,400, about $53,000 today—according to another account it was a check—which was promptly discounted, completing the scam. The man who tried to negotiate the note was arrested and the note confiscated, but he promptly sued for the value of the lost property.

The deception would have produced an even better haul had not Otero in the nick of time stopped collection on a $5,000 check he had also put up as part of the scam. Doc was entirely unrepentant over swindling Otero. "I am a poor man," he said to a local newspaper, "and Otero is rich . . . Has served several terms in Congress and is afraid of publicity. I need the money and he can afford to lose it. He dares not complain."[4]

But Otero did complain, and the Denver police searched for Doc, according to the *Denver News*, even staking out the offices of Baggs' lawyer, "industriously examining the water closets, hanging around the back stairs and patrolling all parts of the building."[5] Doc apparently was arrested for this one, but he had read his quarry aright. Otero did not appear to testify against him, perhaps because his son ultimately managed to recover the note. At least, that is how the *Denver Republican* told the tale.[6]

Doc Operates Mostly in Denver

Doc shared the Denver stage with the Blonger boys, sometime rivals of Soapy Smith and longtime scam kingpins of the city. Sam and Lou Blonger had been around. In earlier days, around Council Bluffs, Iowa, the Blongers had been in "business," as had Baggs, Canada Bill Jones, George Devol, John Bull, and Frank Tarbeaux—as thoroughly crooked a collection as ever fleeced a mark.

Doc did, however, have his good side. He apparently was a dutiful family man, and he had a certain loyalty to the steerers and cappers who worked for him. And he professed to be astonished and angry when any con man turned to violence. As he delivered himself of that pious sentiment, a Denver newspaper described Doc as "this distinguished . . . disciple of Aesculapius." the ancient god of medicine.[7] It was a neat phrase, and perfectly accurate.

Like a good many of his colleagues, Doc was given to moving around a lot. When a con man swindled important folks out of large amounts of money, it paid to depart as quickly as possible thereafter. Sometimes, however, the victims of the con were too embarrassed to complain to the police or anybody else, and in such cases the con man could remain in town and carry on. Some grifters even became well-known celebrities, regarded as a species of local hero, especially those who limited their dirty work to visitors from out of town.

Much of Doc's best work was done in Denver, where he fleeced Otero, Smith, Howard and Fitch, and no doubt a host of others. Doc knew that the more imposing the façade of the scam, the more likely it was to succeed. And so, said a *Denver Times* story in 1915, he created an "office," complete with adjoining doors bearing glass panels marked "manager," "attorney," and so on. Clerks (shills, of course) labored diligently at nearby desks, apparently working on ledgers that befitted a master of finance.

The furniture was high-quality, but better yet, the huge safe was exactly what the dupes would expect to see in the office of a grand financier. The thing was fully seven feet square, very imposing, and full of the usual pigeonholes and documents, its door labeled with the maker's name and red-and-blue lines by way of decoration.

Only the safe—pigeonholes and all—was silk, painted carefully

in perspective; or, according to others, it was made of wood, carefully painted to show its interior, its pigeonholes, and so on.

Whatever it was made of, the "safe" sat behind Baggs' desk,
away from any minute scrutiny by the visitor. If trouble threatened and it was high time to disappear, Baggs simply tore the
"safe" from the wall, rolled it up, and walked off with it; or, if the
tales about it being wood were correct, he folded the thing up so
that it disappeared with him, disguised as a sort of suitcase.

Meanwhile, his "clerks" got rid of the phony ledgers and pushed
the marked connecting doors into the false partitions that had
doubled as office walls. Although that sounds like too much work
to do quickly, remember that practice makes perfect, and preparation for flight was accelerated by the certain knowledge that an
angry, disgruntled dupe might soon appear at the "office" door,
brandishing a revolver or, more often, bringing a couple of policemen with him. Some of them did.

By the time the coppers and the vengeful mark arrived, of
course, the "office" was gone—lock, stock, and barrel. The room
was, instead, a lady's bedroom, complete with an agitated Chinese
servant to say "Missy was out." In Denver, at least, the constabu-
lary may well have known they would find nothing, and a pretty accurate notion of who had turned something into that nothing and
departed. However, many of the police were on the payroll—like
many city officials—and all of the officers could at least honestly
say later under oath, "Your Honor, we responded promptly, but we
just couldn't find a thing."

Despite the gambling temptations rampant in the towns of the
booming West, Doc seems to have held on to at least some of his
spoil. His fellow swindler Frank Tarbeaux claimed that at ninety-
three, Doc Baggs was still living happily "on an estate" in New
York.[8] Perhaps.

Dick Clark: An "Honest Gambler"

In Doc's time Denver was full of con men, and many of them
worked for Soapy Smith. These included disbarred attorney and

champion jury-fixer "Judge" Van Horn, and "Reverend" Charley Bowers, who, in a time when fraternal societies such as the Freemasons were highly popular, knew all the lodge grips and passwords. So much the better for Bowers, since lodge brothers often tended to trust even a stranger in those innocent days.

Some of the swindlers were members of the gambling fraternity, in their own way as crooked as the men who ran the great confidence games. Take Dick Clark, for example, who was as famous as Soapy Smith, Doc Baggs, or the Blonger boys in his time. Clark spent years in Tombstone, Arizona. He considered himself an honest gambler since he did not use marked decks; still, he saw nothing wrong with reversing a cut or stacking a deck while he was shuffling it. He never stooped to hiding an ace in his sleeve, since he considered that sort of pedestrian trick dishonorable.

Nor did Clark see anything wrong with using his big diamond ring to read the cards as he was dealing; he would hide the thing among his stacks of chips, to reflect the faces of the cards as they flashed past. He is said to have actually been able to read and remember the lay of the cards around a table. To Clark, that wasn't cheating, but only using his manual dexterity and his prodigious memory to help his game along. It was a curious distinction.

Clark moved to Tombstone after the heyday of the railhead towns was past, and there he and his partners opened the Alhambra. It was quite a place, according to the *Epitaph:*

> Last night the portals were thrown open and the public permitted to gaze on the most elegantly furnished saloon this side of the favored city at the Golden Gate.[9]

The article waxed poetic about the furnishings of the new gambling palace, even describing the lighting. The paper's enthusiasm may have minor overstatement, perhaps, but at least the much-touted—and expensive—grandeur of the place gave evidence that Clark and his partners had come to town to stay.

Like so many other gamblers and con men, he was generous to charities and scrupulously honored his debts. On one occasion—with other businessmen—he stood as a bondsman for the county treasurer. And when that bureaucrat defaulted, Clark was the only one to pay his share of the bond—$5,000, about $110,000 today—with the same good grace he displayed when he had a bad night at the tables.

Clark was popular in Tombstone and the other towns he occasionally visited. He was courteous, urbane, and a fine figure of a man. Clark carried himself erect, perhaps a legacy from his days of soldiering during the Civil War. He had served his gambling apprenticeship in the Kansas cow towns—Newton, Abilene, Dodge City, Ellsworth, and the rest—moving with the "hell on wheels" collection of brothels, saloons, and rude gambling houses that followed the railhead west. He gambled with such luminaries as Wild Bill Hickok (who was also the city marshal of Abilene), and deadly Texas gunman Ben Thompson.

Business was good for Clark and other professional gamblers who flocked to collect those cowboy wages. In 1871 and the next year, Newton had as many as eight gambling houses and twenty-seven saloons, hunting grounds for an estimated eighty professionals, not counting the eager amateurs.[10] Nobody closed, night or day. Any trouble was either ignored or summarily dealt with by the town police, who in Newton were paid by the local gamblers.

Clark was a peaceful sort, unlike some other cardsharps and con men. He did not get drunk and throw his weight around, like Soapy Smith, nor did he ever fire a shot in anger, like dapper Luke Short, so far as is known. In his only recorded incident of violence, a man tried to hold up Clark's Alhambra gambling hall at 4:00 a.m., as Clark and an assistant were closing up. The assistant grabbed the man's gun hand, and Clark drew his own weapon and creased the malefactor's head with it. And this was a time when nobody would have thought twice about ridding the world of another criminal.

Clark and his partners—including Wyatt Earp—also leased the gambling hall at the Oriental. When their lease ran out, the owner, a friend of crooked sheriff and Earp rival John Behan, would not renew. After learning somehow that Behan was undercapitalized, Clark and Earp "bucked the tiger" one night at Behan's faro bank, long enough to win some $6,000; they demanded payment, and that broke Behan's bank. Behan managed to stay in business, but his enterprise never flourished.

Among other veterans of Clark's standing was Lucky Bill Thornton, one of the premier thimbleriggers the West ever saw. He headquartered in Sacramento, California, and gambled in several places, including The Stinking Tent. Thornton worked hard at his trade, carefully keeping his fingernails well-trimmed and long, for they were his tools in scooping up the "pea" —generally a little cork ball—and like most professionals he cut a suave, elegant figure. He was a master of patter, the sort of gambler lingo that pulled men into the game and incidentally tended to distract the players from what Thornton was doing with the shells and pea.

The Stinking Tent was dirt-floored and tiny. While customers passed to and away from the gambling tables inside, Thornton ran his swindle near the door of the tent. His operating costs were minimal, since the table on which he performed his legerdemain was just a wooden tray that hung from a strap around his neck. His only other gear was the "pea" and the three shells, generally three tiny cups shaped like walnut shells. It was all Thornton needed, and he prospered: at one point he had made $20,000 or so in just a couple of months, real money in those days.

Life as a grifter had its own hazards though. Once Thornton shared a coach with several passengers, and one turned out to be the brother of a man Thornton had fleeced. The other man pulled a wicked-looking Bowie knife and swore he would use it to dissect Thornton. The coach stopped to let the two men fight it out, and both ended up needing a doctor: Thornton with a knife wound in his side, his opponent with a slug in the shoulder. It had been a long day for Thornton, for he was on the coach to escape angry miners from Hangtown, tough, hard-working men Thornton and a partner had taken for some $2,000.

George Devol: Hard Head, Soft Heart

Not all the swindlers were shy, retiring, and dignified. One of the pioneers of dirty tricks was tough, grizzled George Devol. He started out as a riverboat cabin boy and bootblack, learned the swindler's trade a little at a time, and graduated to full-time

George Devol (Library of Congress)

gambler, working the Mississippi steamboats. Devol survived a whole series of brawls and gunfights and several wrecks.

He claimed to be present during the ghastly explosion and sinking of the *Princess*, which killed some "one hundred souls . . . and among them were fourteen preachers."[11] Most of the gamblers survived in the barbershop. He also wrote about an endless series of confrontations with angry marks and jealous rivals. Devol was a smooth, able, and joyful fighter.

He was a strong man, with a big reputation, hard fists, and an extraordinarily thick head, perhaps the product of some abnormality. His famous head-butts could knock the biggest man unconscious. Devol also carried a pistol, and he was not shy about pulling it.

Devol was proud of his hard head and reputation, and wrote in his memoirs of a good many riverboat fights. After one of them his opponent died, and Devol hastily left town until he learned that the dead man had been found to have the "d.t.s [the shakes from alcoholism], and could only have lived a short time." Devol claimed that he later gave money and property to the dead man's wife,[12] an act of gallantry like the one in which he returned jewelry to a woman whose husband had lost it to Devol gambling.

And in at least one instance, his charitable disposition was Devol's undoing. He spotted a likely mark closely watching him play cards, and then walked over to talk to the bartender. He asked who Devol was, and then commented that one of the cards had a "little spot" on it. As usual, when he finally sat down to play, Devol milked him of his money. And then the dupe went into his act:

Mr. DeVol, I am a poor man, with a wife and four little children. That money I lost was all I had in the world, and it was given to me by friends to start me a little business . . . If I don't get that money my wife and little children will starve to death for I will never see them again.[13]

And much more of the same. Devol wrote later that he took pity and gave the man $500, only to hear the mark laugh as Devol turned away. He looked back to see his dupe grinning at him, brandishing a hand full of $100 bills. "I haven't got no wife nor no four children," said the dupe, at which Devol started after him. The man fled, and Devol bought himself a whip, "but I never had the nerve to use it."

Well, maybe, and maybe it never happened at all, for Devol was a great self-inflater. He even went so far as to include a final chapter in his memoirs purporting to quote someone saying wonderful things about Devol to the *Cincinnati Inquirer.* The quote begins, "There goes the most remarkable man in the country . . ." and is followed by much more of the same. Maybe it did come from the *Inquirer,* but it sure sounds like vintage Devol.

He knew the conventional gambling trade well, but as a youngster he dabbled in keno and something called "rondo." He also gambled ashore, and used some of the booty to buy real estate and build houses. Before the Civil War he also won several slaves gambling.

Frank Tarbeaux: The Rube Act

Frank Tarbeaux was another tall-tale egoist, and also an accomplished three-card Monte shark; he too worked the railroads. Doc Baggs, George Devol, and John Bull were steerers for Tarbeaux the Monte master. Bull shot and killed a couple of gunfighters along the way. Tarbeaux's system depended on another passenger, his steerer, to rope in a victim. His success was due in part to his hick appearance. Tarbeaux dressed and talked like a farmer— a "rube" in his words—flashing a fat roll and boasting about the big deal he had just pulled off; selling a herd of cattle, for instance.

The steerer raised his hat to signal Tarbeaux that they had a live one. Tarbeaux, speaking like a country boy, would drawl a tale about his time in the big city. He would genially tell the mark he had been fleeced at Monte once, but had paid his fleecer for the deck he was using. He had been practicing, he said, so that he could now choose the winning card himself. His clumsy dealing led the victim to believe Tarbeaux was a farm boy who did not know what he was doing.

The steerer won a bet or two from Tarbeaux, who promptly started to fold his game and depart. The next step closed the trap: the steerer urged the "rube" dealer to try it just one more time, and he agreed, but the steerer told Tarbeaux he would only play for all the money Tarbeaux had. Tarbeaux would produce a fat roll of bills, and when the sucker matched it, in the best old Monte fashion the confederate winked and told the victim about the tiny crease in the winning card. Of course, the victim took the bait and chose the wrong card. Tarbeaux and his boys had won another small jackpot. Sometimes they could swindle a couple of marks in the same night.

When he wasn't using his "rube act," Tarbeaux pretended to be the same sort of genial, cultured, well-dressed gentleman as Doc Baggs. Tarbeaux was dignified, and had just the sense of humor to lure the unwary into a sense of security. He was, as one writer put it, a "striking, clean shaven, good looking man . . . I never met a man with greater social gifts."[14] He was also a consummate inventor and creator of his own mythology.

Canada Bill Jones: An Idiot Savant

William "Canada Bill" Jones was English by birth, coming to the United States by way of Canada. He won a fortune at his specialty, three-card Monte, but like many of the other professionals, he could not resist other games. Like Soapy Smith and a good many other masters of the con, he loved faro, and gambled away most of his suckers' money "bucking the tiger."

Jones turned passenger trains into gold mines, from which he and others extracted millions until the railroads shut them down. One tale says that riverboat gambler George Devol triggered the closing of the mines by choosing the wrong mark. George won more than $1,000 from a fellow traveler, who turned out to be a director of the Union Pacific and who promptly banned gambling and threatened to fire any conductor who permitted it. Supposedly, Canada Bill wrote the Union Pacific, offering to pay $10,000 for the exclusive right to run a Monte game on their trains, "promising to limit his victims to commercial travelers from Chicago and Methodist preachers," and was refused.

Much of Canada Bill's success depended on his appearance. He was a slight man, given to a shuffling gait and scruffy clothing several sizes too large, who, as his longtime colleague George Devol later wrote, "when his countenance was in repose, resembled an idiot . . . he had a squeaking, girlish voice and gawky manners, and a way of asking fool questions and putting on a good-natured sort of grin."[15] No wonder he drew potential marks like flies to honey.

Canada Bill has been portrayed as a sort of villain, a swindler without conscience, an evil man. One "converted gambler," as

Devol called him, described Bill as a big man, with a "nose highly illuminated by whiskey and heat . . . he drank himself to death."[16] This disparaging portrait was written by one Mason Long, a less-than-successful gambler by his own admission. He did catch the essence of Canada Bill's appearance and manner:

> A rustic looking creature munching a huge piece of pie, which he ate with palpable relish. He was . . . dressed in coarse clothes, with sunburned countenance . . . and an expression of indescribable greenness and "freshness" about him.[17]

George Devol had a different view of Canada Bill's appearance and character, writing that his longtime friend and partner was a small man, and never touched whiskey at all. His tipple was, said Devol, "Christian cider." Devol added this to Canada Bill in his own memoirs of life on the shady side:

> There never lived a better hearted man. He was liberal to a fault. I have known him to turn back when we were on the street and give to some poor object we had passed. Many a time I have seen him walk up to a Sister of Charity and make her a present of as much as $50.[18]

The good sister could make better use of it to help the poor, said Canada Bill—at least according to Devol. No doubt. Still, charity is easiest with somebody else's money. Bill died broke, like so many of his colleagues, and his old friends raised enough money to pay the cost of his burial and erect a stone to his memory.

Con Men Long Gone

And so passed a few of the more successful of the con men. Some actually survived the years of dealing with angry victims and retired in comfort; some of them bragged a little and produced a volume of memoirs, like Devol and Tarbeaux; some of them never made it past the booze and the faro banks. But all of them shared a common quality.

They made life interesting.

CHAPTER 2

Elmer Mead: Master of the Magic Wallet

William Elmer Mead wouldn't have made a good movie con man; nobody would have thought of casting him in *The Sting*. He was quiet, thin and balding, and wore pince-nez glasses perched on the end of his beak-like nose. From his description and his photograph, he resembled an insignificant clerk out of a Dickens novel. He was wholly unprepossessing, which is one very good reason why, over forty years or so, he successfully fleeced countless dupes out of more than two million dollars.

Mug shot of Elmer Mead, the Christ Kid.(Van Cise Fighting the Underworld)

His origins were hardly what one would expect in a master criminal. Mead grew up in a fundamentalist Iowa family. He ran away while he was still in his teens, but some of that strict upbringing stuck, for he was never known to swear, smoke, chew, or drink, which made him a notable exception among the swindling fraternity, indeed, a notable exception on the American frontier. Elmer was known for his virtuous habits, serious, mild-mannered demeanor, and regular appearance in church on Sundays. These shining attributes, together with a lifelong habit of contributing to all sorts of religious causes, won him the trade nickname of the "Christian Kid," or the "Christ Kid."

Fixing Footraces and Warning Marks

In those simpler times, a sporting event—a race of any kind or even a boxing match—was indeed an entertainment. There were lots of suckers who would lay down a bet on nearly anything, especially if the swindle was worked by a crooked genius like Elmer Mead.

Whatever Elmer's inner feelings may have been, his obvious devotion did not extend to all of the Ten Commandments, especially the one that commands, "Thou shalt not steal." Elmer worked several cons, notably including such simple schemes as fixed footraces. These sells required a good deal of help. First, Elmer found the right local lawman, somebody who didn't mind making a buck by skirting the law he had sworn to uphold. Once the fix was made, Elmer's shills would find a likely prospect—a wealthy man who liked to gamble—and trick him into placing a bet on the race. The racers were also shills, of course, including the man Elmer "knew" would win.

Elmer's skill and appearance successfully convinced the dupe that Elmer knew what he was talking about, and the mark put down a fat bet, helped along by seeing phony "bets" by others of Elmer's pack. The race went as scheduled, with the favorite pulling far in front. As Elmer's shills voiced their pretended disappointment, the front-runner suddenly collapsed: thrashing, drooling, and pawing at his chest. He lost, of course, and about the time somebody else finished first, Elmer would cry the alarm that the law was coming to arrest everybody. Sure enough, right on cue, here came the local lawman—by prearrangement, of course—and all the spectators took to their heels. Elmer hustled the sucker to the train depot and got him out of town, arranging a future meeting someplace else. Elmer carried the money, of course, and all that remained was paying off the law and the shills and making tracks to other climes.

Ever the artist, Elmer even added a bit of drama to this con. As a neat finishing touch, he sent the mark a telegram wherever they were supposed to meet, warning him that the racer had died and advising him to keep moving. Since the sucker was concentrating on staying out of trouble with the law, his lost money became a lot less important.

Buying the Farm and Finding the Magic Wallet

He also worked an improvement on the old three-card Monte scam. This was the "country send," in which Elmer pretended to be shopping for a farm for his spinster sister. The wealthy farmer chosen as the victim showed Elmer around, and in the process the two just happened to meet a Monte dealer obviously carrying a lot of money—Elmer's man. Elmer and the farmer beat the dealer badly, but he refused to pay them unless they could show they would have been able to pay him had he won. "Why, sure," said Elmer, and whipped out perhaps $5,000 in real money.

The farmer, by then well taken-in, had to go to the bank for his matching $5,000, worth about $114,000 today, while Elmer waited with the dealer. Then, as arranged, the dupe would meet Elmer and the "dealer" —usually at a hotel—and there the swindle was completed. The mark's $5,000 was apparently tucked into the dealer's bagful of money, and the whole bag was handed over to the farmer. Reminding the dupe that the game was illegal and everybody should be careful, Elmer and the "dealer" vanished. The bag held nothing but paper, of course, and the farmer never saw his prospective customer again.

Elmer was a larceny innovator as well. He originated the "magic wallet," which was basically an entree to the confidence of the target. Success depended on finding a wealthy, honest man willing to gamble. Texas rancher J. Frank Norfleet, as we shall see in chapter 3, was just such a man. Norfleet or someone like him was set up to "find" a lost wallet full of money and other valuable papers, usually forged. With help from a shill, the target was able to find the wallet and return it to a grateful owner. The rest of the con went from there.

Capturing Halley's Comet

In the late 1890s, Elmer ended up in prison in California. After a few years there, he seemed destined for the paths of righteousness, at least for a while. He married and worked at some honest jobs, but then Old Scratch got him by the heel again, and Elmer never looked back. He abandoned his wife and returned to the crooked life, carefully enough that he was only imprisoned once more. He acquired a girlfriend—maybe she was a wife, although her status isn't clear—variously called Frisco Kate or Klondike Kate. The couple lived high on the hog between cons.

Kate and Elmer spent a lot of time hunting, fishing, and traveling the national parks. Elmer is said to have actually bought a ranch someplace in Oregon, all the while investing illicit profits in land and buildings across several states and stuffing several safety-deposit boxes with cash and securities.

Eventually, Elmer headquartered in Denver, a safe haven for con men working or resting, under the protective wing of Lou Blonger, uncrowned king of the city. Perhaps it was during a rest stop there that he thought up a most original con, capitalizing on the appearance of Halley's Comet in 1910. Many were terrified by this celestial marvel, and some thought it heralded the End of Days, but for Elmer, it was a bonanza.

The Halley's Comet swindle began when he met a wealthy contractor who was shopping for a palatial home. Elmer was posing as a judge for this con, and sure enough, the two found the Magic Wallet. The owner then appeared on cue, the wallet was returned, and the grateful owner joined them for lunch. The wallet's "owner" turned out to be a big-time promoter of sporting facilities, and in time he was discussing the construction of a large ball park; he wanted an estimate, he said, and the contractor began to see visions of dollars, lots of them.

Then it occurred to the sports promoter that the project would require considerable money and time. "Tell you what," he said, "it's the off-season, and my ball parks are empty. I'll lease them all to you," and he named an amount. "What in the world would I do with empty ball parks?" said the mark. "Why," the "ballpark mogul" replied, "Halley's Comet, that's what; it's the greatest spectacle of the age. People will flock to the parks to see the comet come, especially the people who think the world will end, and you'll make millions."

Elmer enthusiastically supported his shill. "Of course you will," he said. "What a wonderful idea!" Either he or his confederate would have with him a newspaper full of appropriate "the sky is falling" reports. With all those religious folks ready to congregate for the Great Day, there should be thousands of takers.

Of course the dupe should have asked, "Well, why don't you fill up your own ball parks?" But he didn't. Perhaps his doubts were eclipsed by the gratitude of the owner of the wallet and the practiced credibility of the two con men. Anyhow, the contractor wrote out a check for several thousand dollars, and the three parted company. Elmer and his confederate immediately cashed the check and vanished. The contractor only discovered he had been had when he thought to check out the ownership of one of the ball parks.

Elmer worked the swindle repeatedly until Halley's Comet proved to be a spectacular, harmless event rather than the end of the world that many feared.

Elmer then turned to a swindle so old it had gray whiskers. Once again he began with the Magic Wallet, crammed with important papers, the surefire entree to friendship and trust. The mark was a wealthy rancher or farmer. This time, however, the lure was the shill's offer to sell the sucker an interest in an existing viaduct or bridge. Elmer expertly touted the fees that might be charged each car and wagon crossing the structure. The sucker only realized he had been had when the police removed his homemade toll gates and motioned the angry drivers on through.

Buying Horses for the War

When World War I was in full swing and America was drifting toward involvement in 1917, Elmer created an extremely ambitious scam tailored to the Allies' demand for horses to replace equine combat casualties. Elmer and a corps of confederates fanned out across horse country in Wyoming, ready for action.

The shills, carrying fat wads of cash, sought out wealthy ranchers. They wanted to buy horses for the war effort, they said, and used the Magic Wallet to convince the unwary of Elmer's identity. This time he was a professor named Graystone, and his lost wallet contained a gold mine of money, big checks, and best of all, a cordial letter from the secretary of the treasury—forged of course. The letter passed along the president's warm regards, and asked on his behalf how their "deal" was progressing. The scheme was pure dynamite, especially considering Elmer's skinny, unprepossessing manner, enhanced by the pince-nez glasses perched on his nose.

Two of Elmer's boys conned one wealthy widow, offering to buy all her horses. Then entered shy "Professor Graystone," looking for his lost wallet; sure enough, it was the one the widow had just found. Overflowing with thanks, Elmer claimed that the president and the secretary of the treasury were short of money for their enormous expenses in bustling Washington, and so had ordered the treasury to print more money, like the thick wad of one-hundred-dollar bills Elmer flashed.

His mission, he said, as one of the president's trusted few, was to quietly sell these bills for half their worth, and send the proceeds to the impoverished leaders of the nation. This was good for everybody, he said, financing the two politicians in their crucial official duties in the service of the country, and at the same time making loyal citizens wealthy. After all, the same thing had been done by every president since Abraham Lincoln.

The widow took the bait. "I'll tell you what I'll do," said the professor. "I'll sell each of you $100,000 of the new money for the bargain price of just $35,000 apiece." "Fine," said the widow, "I'll go to my Denver bank and withdraw my share." As it happened, of course, Elmer and his two stooges were also going to Denver. The end was classic con: Elmer produced three sealed packages, the gold at the end of the rainbow. "Remember, this is a service to the nation, and *nobody must know about it*," said Elmer, "so wait until you get home to open it in private." The packages held nothing more than plain paper, and before the widow opened the box, the con men were long gone.

Settling Down—in Prison!

Such happy times were not to last. Elmer went down with the fall of the Blonger criminal empire in Denver. When Blonger refused to bail poor Elmer out of jail, Klondike Kate berated him and threatened to go to the prosecutor. When Blonger brushed her off again, she grabbed him by the nose, crying, "You dirty [SOB] . . . now I got you." She would not let go, and threatened to chew off his ear until Blonger capitulated.

But Elmer's troubles were not over yet. The feds were after him for huge amounts of delinquent income tax, and the postal authorities wanted him for mail fraud. When he was sixty-three the postal bulldogs caught him, and Elmer went back to prison for two years. His sentence served, Elmer headed for free air again, only to find federal agents waiting for him at the prison gates. This time it was the old federal charge filed in Florida. It might have led only to a minimal sentence or even acquittal, but Elmer wasn't taking any chances. He jumped bail again, and fled to England, where he cheated the public until the British police hauled him off to the jail on Bow Street and eventual deportation.

Frank Tarbeaux and His Life of Crime

The swindler Frank Tarbeaux, whom we met earlier, became famous writing about "my life in crime." His autobiography positively drips pomposity. He was a Colorado-born early devotee of the swindling profession who specialized in three-card Monte, working the trains, and playing the "rube," with the broadest possible rural accent and manners.

Frank claimed he created "the foot race gyp," another variation on the basic running or prizefighting cons. And he also turned his

hand, he said, to what he called the "horse gyp," peddling horses using invented tales of the animals' breeding and capabilities. Tarbeaux
boasted that he sold a magnificent Clydesdale named George, about
once a day. George looked good, but he wouldn't pull a thing; the new
owner was glad, said Tarbeaux, to sell the critter back for a fraction of
what he had paid. He peddled "reconstructed" rubies as the real thing
across England and Scotland; he needed the money; he supposedly
spent "two or three hundred pounds" each night. Some of his peddling
was done to "my friend, the Khedive [Viceroy] of Egypt."

He and his father "opened the Chisholm trail," he wrote, and
counted popular Western novelist Ned Buntline, Wild Bill Hickok,
Buffalo Bill Cody, Wild West impresario "Texas Jack" Omo-
hundro, Calamity Jane, Oscar Wilde, the Marquis of Queensbury,
and even the king of Hawaii among his friends.

Buffalo Bill Cody, Tarbeaux wrote, "was just a butcher, plain
simple . . . when I had occasion to slap his face in a hotel in Vien-
na" Cody simply cringed. In addition to slapping Cody, Tarbeaux
boasted a good deal about all the other fights he had—some with
guns and knives. And of course, he won them all.

After one such killing, he was "kidnapped" from the Transvaal
and taken to London for trial, where he was defended by two of
the leading barristers of the age, and did twenty-seven months
before parole. Along the way, he lived in England "in grand style,
both in town and country." He had a butler and a footman, of
course, except when he was hanging around "the dives of London," including a flophouse in "Jack the Ripper Alley."[1]

In short, Tarbeaux was an active but unremarkable swindler
and gambler who really excelled at reinventing himself by writing pure mythology. He was not a memorable con man, as were
Elmer Mead and Doc Baggs, but was the classic "I bin everwhar"
braggart who seemed to know everybody. Frank never ran out of
tall tales. He also became a wealthy stockman, he said, and for a
while ran with a gang of robbers. In his spare time he "shot Bob
Ford," the man who killed Jesse James, and did extensive scout-
ing for the frontier Army, thus winning permission to recruit real
and actual Sioux warriors for Buffalo Bill's Wild West Show.

It also got him "unofficially" attached to George Armstrong Custer's command, he said, and he survived the Little Big Horn debacle because he was taking a message from Custer to General Alfred Terry. That was odd, since the history books reveal that Terry assigned scout George Herendeen to accompany Custer, to return with a message from Custer. Had a message been sent, Herendeen would logically have carried it; Herendeen fought through the battle and survived. Tarbeaux later admitted that well, yes he had been there, but he was with another command, like at least twenty other "sole survivors" or "witnesses" to Custer's end.

Tarbeaux was not shy about chronicling his sexual exploits either. At one point he "was having affairs with a half-dozen girls at one time."[2] One was a "beautiful senorita," daughter of "one of the wealthy mining and cattle kings of Chihuahua."[3] And he bragged about one affair with a woman then being kept by another man, from whom Tarbeaux won $50,000. That doesn't even count Indian maidens, a variety of foreign princesses, or time spent with Princess X in a "big house" in Paris. Nor does it include visits to the brothel of Madame Jesus in Madeira, an establishment of young, inventive girls on which Tarbeaux called "every time" he visited Madeira. It's a wonder he had time to swindle anybody.

J. Frank Dobie's monumental *Guide to Life and Literature of the Southwest* condemns a book by Frank Harris as a "blatant farrago of lies," and then adds that *The Autobiography of Frank Tarbeaux* written by Donald Henderson Clarke is "as equally worthless." Dobie knew his West, and it's hard to disagree with him. So all in all, if Tarbeaux wasn't the greatest con man of all time, he surely was the most inventive creator of mythical adventures since Baron Munchausen. His tales are vastly entertaining though, and the reader almost wishes it had all fallen out as he said it did. It didn't.

"Lady" Grifters

The masters of the grift were not all men. Many fewer women

than men took to the scam as a profession, but those practitioners were superb.

The classic example was probably Kitty Leroy, who plied her trade in the Black Hills. Kitty ran a gambling hall, and married for profit on the side. She died young, of a bullet, but she was quite a lady—a beautiful woman, at least by frontier standards in the Black Hills:

> She had five husbands, a dozen bowie knives and always went armed to the teeth . . . the magnetism about her marvelous beauty was such as to drive her lovers crazy . . . more men had been killed around her than all the other women in the hills combined.[4]

Kitty only married money. She wed one newly rich prospector, but when she had run through $8,000 worth of gold and the claim petered out, she bashed him in the head with a bottle and departed. Kitty married and defrauded her way through husband number five, who got to his gun quicker than she got to hers. He shot her quite dead before she was thirty and then committed suicide, leaving the West less colorful.

In a day when "respectable" women were automatically held in high regard, a "dame with class" could sell iceboxes at the North Pole. Philadelphia swindler Sophie Beck, one of the most accomplished con women in the business, was just such an artist. She had her counterparts in the West and elsewhere.

Sophie operated a classic Ponzi scheme selling stock in the Story Cotton Company, on a cash only basis, promising to return 50 percent on investment, and quickly. Gullible investors flocked to invest, and when she had enough—maybe as much as $2,000,000—she caught a boat for Europe and retired in comfort.[5]

Cassie Chadwick wasn't as lucky. She did fine for a time, convincing many who should have known better that she was the illegitimate daughter of steel magnate Andrew Carnegie. She borrowed enormous sums on the strength of that dubious relationship, asserting that her father had given her a sizeable chunk of his wealth and even waved phony promissory notes from Carnegie around occasionally. She didn't have the sense to run as Sophie had, and at last a potential investor got access to her safety-deposit box and discovered the notes were forged. When police went to her apartment, she was in bed, and wearing a money belt stuffed with an alleged $100,000. All that money didn't do her a bit of good; she got ten years, and never breathed free air again.

A badger game specialist would climb into bed with any moneyed man, and then, when the mark was fully compromised, was shocked, shocked as her angry "husband burst in." There wouldn't be a scandal, the accessory said, but it would cost the seduced sucker plenty to keep things quiet and avoid trouble at home. The queen of badgers was Chicago May Churchill, who worked all over the world, and caused at least five suicides. Among her lovers was Eddie Guerin, the king of French thieves. When love bloomed no more, she hired an assassin to kill poor Eddie. May went off to Devil's Island for that one, and finally died alone in poverty back in the United States, a photograph of Guerin close by.

Probably the most interesting of the female con artists was Edith Salomen, also known as the Swami, who worked not only in America, but on at least two other continents.[6] Early in her career she developed a particular skill for hoaxes: while awaiting trial for a $200,000 swindle, she got herself hospitalized for an opium habit, and promptly began running down the halls screaming. She even stabbed an orderly, prompting the doctors to send her off to an asylum for a year.

Later, Edith posed as the illegitimate child of King Ludwig of Bavaria—aka "crazy Ludwig" —and his lover, the then famous vamp and singer Lola Montez. Edith could envision things, she said; not only that, but she held séances at which she could—and did—summon up spirits of the dead to order. Among other luminaries of the dead-and-famous, she summoned Charlemagne and Frederick the Great, who appeared wearing his crown for a few dollars more. Cicero and Shakespeare were also on call. On one occasion the Bard even produced an ode for one of Edith's suckers.

Edith married several men whom she dropped when they were broke or no longer useful. At various times and places Edith also called herself, among other things, Countess Landsveldt, Madame

Ava, and Sister Mary, in which avatar she raised money for a nonexistent orphanage.

She lectured on all manner of psychic subjects, and ran the Theosophical University, which handed out fraudulent degrees until the South African police closed it down. Edith simply moved to England, where she pitched her imaginary religion, something called "Theocratic Unity." Lots of money flowed in from converts, but in the end the British police were stronger than the spirits.

Edith got seven well-deserved years, but she emerged from prison and sailed back to America unabashed and undaunted, leaving reporters to ponder this gem: "I am a principle for the Unecclesiastical Court. The foundation for that principle is the Lord."[7] Whatever that meant. Any court today would consider placing Edith back in an asylum, but in those times she was simply an odd duck who dropped from history after her return to the United States.

There were others, like Ellen Peck, a sexual athlete of legendary ability.[8] Ellen was superb at getting dupes into bed in quantity, men who surrendered all manner of jewels, land titles, money, and stock. She even managed to seduce Jay Gould—as unscrupulous as she was, but on the larger scale—and she was in her fifties then. She wore out one elderly man to the point he had to take to a bed in her home; Ellen retained a nurse to care for her dupe. And then, discovering the nurse had some savings, she climbed into bed with the nurse, whom she fleeced of whatever small amount she had saved.

Ellen and her sisters in the trade rank right down there with the medical fakers who gave hope to ill people who—or whose children—might have been saved had they stuck with conventional medical treatment. But the world would have been less interesting without the ladies.

But What about Elmer?

And what happened to Elmer Mead? When he was deported from England, he still faced the Florida charge that prompted him to jump bond. Some say he was arrested years later on some minor charge, but was identified and charged for prior crimes because he had thoughtfully dipped his fingertips in acid.[9] Eventually, it seems, Elmer retired to enjoy his carefully stashed fortune.

CHAPTER 3

Relentless: The Odyssey of J. Frank Norfleet

Usually a con victim had to be content with retreating in shame and disappointment. Sometimes he went to the police, usually without result, particularly in towns like Denver, where the police department and city hall were largely bought and paid for. Sometimes the victim was mad and courageous enough to raise hell and follow the swindler like an avenging fury. Such a man was J. Frank Norfleet.

His autobiography reads like pure melodrama, since he helped capture several swindlers, yet his story is corroborated at least in part by others. These notably include Colonel Philip S. Van Cise (1884-1969), the incorruptible district attorney in Denver, who used Norfleet to help finish Lou Blonger's long run as king of Denver crime.

Frank Norfleet was a cattleman from Texas, a substantial rancher, and a county deputy sheriff who was far too intelligent to fall for the age-old investment con sometimes called the Rag. Norfleet had money, an illustrious background, and a trusting nature. His father had been a Texas Ranger, and his wife's family was distantly related to the Lees of Virginia. Norfleet neither drank nor used tobacco, and was never heard to swear. He was *honest,* and that made him the ideal mark.

In the Rag, the victim is lured into buying "stock," and with the aid of huge, unlikely short-term returns is convinced to invest still more and more. Eventually the entire investment, as well as "earnest money" allegedly required to assure the "exchange," simply disappears, leaving the investor with nothing. Norfleet fell for the Rag in Fort Worth, and he fell hard.

Hell Hath No Fury Like Joe Furey

Joe Furey was the culprit. Furey was a veteran full-time con man, who ran a ring of similar hoodlums under the overall direction of Lou Blonger, the swindler boss of Denver whom we will meet in chapter 5. And it was Furey's gang who took in Norfleet, the substantial, trusting citizen with a big cowboy hat and a Wyatt Earp mustache. The cattleman was initially roped in by the ancient "Lost Wallet" scam, valuable property which he was intended to find and return to its owner.

The con began simply. Norfleet was alone in Dallas, waiting to see the possible buyer of more than 2,000 acres, the money from which he intended to use to purchase a larger piece of land. He met a stranger who called himself Miller—in fact one of Furey's boys, Reno Hamlin. "Perhaps I can help," said Hamlin, "for a man I know is negotiating for land out in that part of Texas. He has a potential seller already, but if that deal falls through he might be interested in your land."

On cue, enter the "friend," who called himself Spencer. Conversation followed and, amazingly, Spencer was indeed interested in Norfleet's land. "The man who was to share my hotel room could not do so," Spencer said, "so why not share it with me; I'll show you my credentials, and we can get acquainted."

And so it was. And in due course Spencer received a wire from Oklahoma City, saying that the land sounded promising, and telling Spencer to visit it, take soil samples, and report. The sender was called Thompson, another shill, of course. In a second telegram Thompson announced that he would stop over in Dallas on a trip west. He would stay at the Adolphus Hotel, still a very fine hotel today, and he wanted to meet Norfleet. The choice of the Adolphus was no accident, for the swindlers who ran high-class scams like this one preferred respectable, high-class surroundings. Such surroundings assured the mark and added to the phony stature of the con men. No whispers in alleys for this gang.

While Norfleet and Spencer waited in the sumptuous Adolphus lobby, the Magic Wallet ended up in the very chair in which

J. Frank Norfleet (left) (Western History Collection, University of Oklahoma)

Norfleet was sitting. They examined the Magic Wallet and found it full of money and documents indicating the owner to be one Stetson, a stockbroker who was a Mason. The wallet also contained a bond guaranteeing his performance, and what seemed to be a code key.

Stetson was staying at the Adolphus, of course, and was effusive in his thanks when Norfleet and Spencer returned his wallet.

Not only were the other papers very valuable, but he could not decode messages from his powerful employer without the code key. "Let me give you $100 apiece," he said. Honest Norfleet refused the money; Miller took his reward. "Mr. Norfleet, I'll invest it for you instead," said Stetson, and by the next day—*voilà!*—Norfleet had made $800.

Along the way, Norfleet contracted elsewhere to sell his land, but the con went on. Norfleet's winnings, when reinvested, quickly grew to monumental proportions and were reinvested again. "No money required up front," said the con man. "You can reinvest on my account as a broker." Spencer agreed at once.

"I'll even show you around the stock exchange," said Stetson, and he did, giving a long and convincing tour of the building. During the tour, another man approached, identified himself as the exchange secretary, and told Norfleet apologetically that since he was not a member, he had to leave.

"No more involvement for me," said Norfleet, but Spencer said he knew a good deal about the market and would do the actual investing. Norfleet agreed.

With Norfleet comfortable, the scam went forward. The wallet owner spun a credible yarn about his influence in the exchange and his connection with powerful commercial interests, and made a great show of decoding secret messages about huge transactions. His room at the Adolphus was filled with trunks full of expensive clothing, and he exuded wealth and power. More reinvestment followed; Stetson even appeared with a monstrous wad of bills, and counted out $28,000 as Norfleet's share alone.

From that moment the con went into high gear. There were more and bigger stock bids to follow, and then re-entered the "secretary" of the exchange. "To confirm bids like these," he said, "we have to have some earnest money up front."

And so Stetson, Spencer, and Norfleet concurred. Spencer would provide $35,000 and Norfleet $20,000, about $246,000 today; the rest would come from Stetson.

Norfleet and Spencer then traveled to Norfleet's home ranch, and Spencer made a great show of investigating the land as a possible purchase by the huge, powerful—and mythical—land company he represented. He even visited nearby farms to assess the wheat crops, and he took the promised soil samples. "Yes," he said, "I think we can get you the price you require to complete your land deal."

The finale was simple. The three met again in Fort Worth, where Spencer "mistakenly" bid to buy a stock, instead of to sell it as the three had agreed, and to correct the error, Stetson hurried to buy on margin. Then reappeared the "secretary" of the exchange (in fact Furey's accomplice Charles Gerber). He announced that they had chosen right again: this time their take was $160,000, but because they were not exchange members, they would have to post $80,000 as earnest money. Home again went Norfleet to raise his share—$25,000. Spencer would go home to Kansas to mortgage the family farm, and Stetson would make up the balance.

Norfleet managed to borrow his share, but Spencer returned $10,000 short. When Stetson insisted on putting up what they had as partial payment to the exchange, Norfleet smelled a rat, and stopped him in the act of calling the elevator, stuck a revolver in his side, and pushed him back to the room. A stormy scene followed, including Spencer on his knees brandishing a Bible and swearing on his "angel mother" that all was well. Finally, as Norfleet called them both crooks (how right he was) and turned his pistol on Stetson as well, Stetson made the "grand hailing sign of distress of a Master Mason" and things quieted down.

Stetson made soothing noises about trust and such, and then Spencer providentially received word that his non-existent employer—something called the Green Immigration Land Company—had agreed to buy Norfleet's land. "I'll go home and cash some war bonds for my last $10,000," he said, "and I'll credit it to Norfleet as part of the down payment on his land. The company is wiring me another $30,000, and I'll put the ten with it."

Sure enough, the $30,000 arrived. After Norfleet saw the money, Spencer put it in a bag with the purchase contract for Norfleet's land and said he would put it in a safety-deposit box to be held pending title verification. Stetson would take the $70,000 in cash to Dallas, confirm the bid with the Dallas exchange, and take care of business for his company. Both swindlers left, and that was the last Norfleet was to see of them . . . until much later. Norfleet talked to the Pinkerton detective agency, and the Fort Worth police, who could not help him; the swindlers were long gone. The safety-deposit box was empty, of course, and Norfleet realized he had been taken for $45,000, about $553,000 today. He still owed $90,000 to the man from whom he had agreed to buy land in Texas, but Norfleet did not give up.

There are several versions, of course, but this is the way Norfleet himself told it in his published account, and as it is preferred here.[1]

Norfleet Vows Revenge

The normal dupe would have swallowed his loss and his embarrassment and gone home to nurse his wounds, but not Norfleet. Furey and his little helpers, by then scattered in all directions, had awakened the proverbial sleeping giant, and this ogre would never go away. Norfleet's dogged pursuit became his life work, and the whole swindler fraternity in Denver would have no peace afterward.

Norfleet vowed to run the grifters down, no matter how long it took. He had some money left, and so, over the next five years he dedicated most of his days to a long and deliberate manhunt. He financed it all himself, save for a few hundred dollars contributed by Texas and Colorado authorities. Norfleet had started out as a placid, trusting man. He finished his hunt as an avenging angel, and along the way managed to land dozens of con men in jail.

Norfleet had a couple of weapons himself. The first was his deputy sheriff's identification, which won him help that otherwise would not have been available. The other was his wife's memory and good sense. She remembered Spencer's bragging when he visited them. "It seemed to me," she said, "that he talked about every state in the union—except California. Strike you at all funny?" The more Norfleet thought about it, the more he wondered whether a professional con artist would not carefully omit from

J. Frank Norfleet (right) vowed to find the men who swindled him (Western
History Collection, University of Oklahoma)

his boasting his special place of refuge. And then he remembered
a small red address book he had found in the hotel room after the
con men disappeared. The book he had given back to Stetson, but
he remembered one name: Cathey.

He started his long search in San Bernardino, California, having
no logical place to begin, moving on from town to town, talking
to police officers, looking for any clue that might get his search
off on the right foot. And by the purest good luck, he hit pay dirt
early. The San Bernardino County sheriff listened carefully, and
then reflected that just maybe he could help. He led the way into

the jail, and there, in the same cell, sat E. J. Ward and Charles Gerber, the secretaries of the "stock exchanges" in Dallas and Fort Worth. Both men would go to trial, and Ward would kill himself rather than face long years in prison.

"I found these two through a newspaper clipping," the sheriff said. "A man brought me the clipping telling about your loss and describing some of the gang. This man said he'd started dealing with a couple of men on a stock deal and wondered if they could be the same ones."

"Who gave you the clipping?" asked Norfleet. "A man named Cathey," said the lawman.

Cathey told Norfleet that he too had been fooled by the "Magic Wallet," but had smelled a rat when he read about Norfleet's disaster. In addition to Ward and Gerber, Stetson and Spencer had been part of the crew too, but had disappeared down a fire escape before the law could lay hands on them.

Norfleet kept on the road, with a side trip to Fort Worth to watch Gerber and Ward tried, and then went back to the hunt. His next help came from a United States Secret Service agent who identified the two captured swindlers as part of Joe Furey's band of crooks. Norfleet had not heard of Furey before, but from then on the veteran con leader was writ large in Norfleet's book of wanted men.

And the agent was even more help. "Stetson's" papers were quite real, he said, for Furey had stolen the lot, including the owner's Masonic card.

Gone Huntin'—in Florida

Norfleet's next hunting ground was Florida, and he had chosen well. He began in Jacksonville and worked his way through the state, city by city, helped by understanding policemen and "prominent men" whose names he had gotten from a helpful Jacksonville lawman. Norfleet haunted bars, beaches, and "cabarets." He looked at thousands of faces, but drew a blank until, one afternoon in St. Petersburg, he came upon an elderly couple who had bought a house and orange grove, spending their life savings on the dream home.

The rest of their story Norfleet knew only too well. The couple had tried to be careful with their purchase, which was for hard cash, as the property's "owner" and his "agent" insisted. They even employed a lawyer—another shill—represented to them as a combination attorney and bank official. They met with him as he carefully reviewed the "deed," in which he noted a small typo. "That should be retyped," he said, and a "third man," part of the scam, volunteered to retype it on his portable typewriter, which he just happened to have with him.

And so the couple waited, holding a bag full of cash, while the volunteer typed and retyped, always making some small error that required him to start over. Their attorney disappeared during the process. Then, as the closing hour for the bank approached, they decided to put their savings in a safety-deposit box for the night, closing the deal the following day. At this sudden turn of events, all three con men jumped up, snatched the satchel, ran out the door, and jumped into a car.

Norfleet volunteered to help the devastated pair, and began his search of St. Augustine. He found a young streetwise mechanic who told him that a building calling itself a "country club" in fact "was headquarters for an internationally known gang of confidence men and wire tappers." And so Norfleet followed the tip and hit pay dirt. After spending much of one night watching the "club" and the procession of people going to it, he went to a nearby café. And there he noticed three men, two of whom matched the old couple's description of the con men.

The police were no help, and so he approached the sheriff, who looked at Norfleet's deputy sheriff identification and endorsed the warrants Norfleet was carrying for Furey, Hamlin, and Spencer. Norfleet found no clues and set off for Tampa, where, he heard, "three confidence men" had been arrested. This time he was wise enough not to reveal himself to the local law, but did learn that some of the swindler fraternity frequented a hotel in Sanford, Florida.

Norfleet promptly went there, and saw several men whom he identified as confidence man types. He sat in the lobby advertising himself as a celery farmer from Blackwell, Oklahoma, ready to spend as much as $50,000 on a celery farm. Norfleet had learned how to talk about celery, and even had the mud on his shoes to prove his agricultural history. Next day, as he expected, he was approached, and in time the shill introduced him to one "Johnson," said to be a stock market expert and magnate. Norfleet could see the con coming.

The stock market man "invested" a small sum for the shill, which of course immediately paid a fine return. Norfleet was apprehensive, but drove with the shill and stock expert to a "country club." In fact, Norfleet had been inveigled into a full-scale "Big Store" wire con, and he knew it. The place was full of activity, piles of money in the open, complete with armed guards, somebody busily chalking numbers on a board, and a teletype clattering away. The telegrapher wore a reassuring green eye shade.

Norfleet sensed danger quickly when a third man handed his new companions a note. Norfleet said he had to leave, and when they tried to stop him, pulled his revolver. Since neither one was armed, Norfleet backed them out to a car and forced the hired driver to take all three away. Finally, he ordered both to run for it, but not before he read the crumpled note given them in the clubhouse. It told him a great deal:

> That is Norfleet himself. Don't let him get started. If you do, he'll kill every dam one of you. Don't let him get away, boys. Don't let him get away! Joe.[2]

Joe. That could be Joe Furey himself. Norfleet knew he was getting closer to his quarry. He got closer still in Miami, where he ran across a Canadian who said he had been swindled by "three men." Norfleet showed the victim a couple of photographs, and the Canadian pointed to Furey, saying, "That's him!" But Furey was still a jump ahead; he had left Miami, and Norfleet guessed that Spencer had gone with him. The next source of information was a farmer from Key West, who was able to show Norfleet the site of the "stock exchange."

Norfleet watched it for a while without result. In fact, Furey had escaped out the back door and to a boat on the river. Frustrated again, Norfleet returned to San Antonio, trying to pick up the cold trail. He remembered that Furey had stolen a woman's fur coat from a hotel there. Reasoning that Furey might have shipped it to a safe address he knew elsewhere—maybe California—he asked for help from the post office, and was allowed to go through their shipping records. After going over page after dusty page, Norfleet found a package shipped from nobody to nobody. There was no return address, no name, only an address in San Francisco, apartment 506 in San Francisco's Stanford Court.

"California, Here I Come!"

The package had been shipped close to the time of Furey's stay, and having nothing else to go on, Norfleet left for California. He stopped over in San Bernardino, where his search began, and again talked to the county sheriff, and then did something he should have done during his last visit. He checked the files of the hotel where Furey had stayed, and discovered a call to Glendale had been charged to Furey's room. Norfleet took a long chance and called the number. A woman answered, and when Norfleet asked to whom he was talking, the voice replied, "Mrs. Furey."

Norfleet headed for Glendale, which in that far-off day was "a lovely little town about an hour out of Los Angeles."[3] Furey's address appeared in the telephone book, and Norfleet found a large home in an apparently wealthy neighborhood. Across the street a large hospital was under construction, and for several days Norfleet hung around the job site, trying to act like a landscape gardener or one of the building crew, making a great show of pacing off distances and driving stakes (which he had whittled himself) at appropriate places in what would eventually be the garden. Finally, he got lucky, when a small boy chased a ball across the street almost directly toward Norfleet.

The Texan tossed the ball to the boy, and engaged the friendly child in conversation. "You should have a puppy," said Norfleet, and the boy broke into a smile. "I'm going to get one," he said, "when my papa comes home." That, said the boy, would be in just a few days, and his father would then give him the money for the dog.

Norfleet returned to Los Angeles and found the undersheriff he had met on his last visit. The lawman listened and agreed to help, assigning two deputies to the job. The plan, wrote Norfleet, was for the two to masquerade as telephone company employees. That done, Norfleet headed for San Francisco, to take a personal look at the Stanford Court Apartments, to which the anonymous parcel had been sent from San Antonio. First he and local law officers looked over the Oakland Hotel across the bay, a sort of headquarters, the lawmen said, for con men of all descriptions. That proved to be, as the oilmen said, a "dry hole," and so Norfleet went back across the bay and took the Powell Street cable car to the intersection of California Street, where stood the apartment building.

And there he hit another obstacle. The high-rent building was secured by a pair of house guards. "Nobody comes in who doesn't live here," they told him. Norfleet was thrown out when he persisted in coming back; he only escaped the guards' grip by drawing a pistol. Norfleet had not dared to ask who lived in apartment 506.

Finally Norfleet had the young daughter of an acquaintance knock on the door of apartment 506 and tell whoever answered that the puppy they ordered was ready to be delivered. She was given a slip of paper with 506 written on it, with the final digit carefully blurred to resemble a "one," to provide her a facile excuse if she were somehow suspected. She got an answer at 506, but the woman who answered the door was brusque, and there was no sign of Furey, either in person or in a photo.

The girl was an inventive sort who would have made an excellent con woman. She went back downstairs and flirted a bit with the kid who ran the elevator, talking about her failure to sell her dog. Maybe, she said, maybe when the man of the house came home, she would have better luck. "Here," she said, "is my telephone number." Would he call her when that man returned home? If she made the sale after that, she would split the price with the elevator boy. He agreed. During her modest flirt, the girl also learned a couple of very useful things: first, the man who lived in 506 was heavy—so was Furey—and only came home every six months or so; second, he was due home soon.

Norfleet returned to Los Angeles, only to find that the police officers who had agreed to watch Furey's lair said that nothing had happened. Norfleet did not believe it, and kept on asking questions.

He became convinced that the officers had seen or heard something, but wouldn't tell him.

Success in the Sunshine State

Norfleet then learned with a little snooping that Furey had wired money to his wife. The wire came from Jacksonville, Florida. Norfleet went there and managed to see the governor. "Yes," said the governor, "if you can find Furey, you can have him." He authorized Norfleet in writing to arrest and extradite Furey. Working with his son Pete, Norfleet covered the city's major hotels, and at last he found his quarry, sitting at a café table. Norfleet wasted no time, but drew his gun and told Furey he was under arrest.

Furey immediately yelled that he was being robbed, and made such a fuss that the dining room emptied in panic; friends of Furey attacked Norfleet, but he grimly held on to Furey until son Pete fought his way through the wave of fleeing diners and appeared, pistol in hand. The police arrived, and, not knowing who to arrest, took Furey, Norfleet, and Pete to the station, where a long argument with the desk sergeant ensued. Norfleet showed him his warrant, but did not back the sergeant off until he played his trump, the endorsement from the governor himself.

That did it. Norfleet handcuffed Furey, and he and his son hired a car to take them across the Georgia line. Norfleet had the driver stop the car at a remote spot near a minor railroad station where a lawman had told Norfleet he could flag a train. "Not so," said a local man. "The train doesn't stop here." Norfleet realized he had been set up by the lawman, the only person who could have known that he and his prisoner were headed there.

Furey bid for his freedom; he offered Norfleet $20,000, and said he would come up the rest of Norfleet's swindled money later. The Texan wasn't having any, but he got more interested when Furey ratted on his comrades and told Norfleet where they were staying in Jacksonville. He even wrote out an "order" for his colleagues on a scrap of paper. He told Pete he could take it to Spencer at that address, and Spencer would provide money.

Norfleet debated, fearing he was sending his son into a trap, but Pete was ready and eager to go. While he was away, Norfleet was confronted by two carloads of armed men, but held them off with Furey's help. "Don't do anything," shouted the con man frantically, no doubt influenced by the steady cold muzzle of Norfleet's .45 behind his ear and his knowledge that Norfleet was remorseless and meant exactly what he said: any attempt to free the con man would leave Furey dead. Norfleet held his ground until his son arrived, and the two drove away with their prisoner, in what Norfleet described as a speed that "didn't seem possible," the then dizzying pace of seventy-eight miles per hour.

At one point Furey tried to wrest control of the car from its driver, forcing the vehicle off the road into a forested area. But Norfleet creased Furey's skull with his gun barrel, and the driver kept the vehicle upright, tearing through trees until he regained the road. They finally shook off their pursuers, reached Jacksonville, and caught a train west. It had been quite a night, but it still wasn't over; Furey broke a car window and dove through it into the night. Pete was right behind him, chasing Furey down the tracks, until the swindler swung onto a switch engine and disappeared toward Jacksonville.

Norfleet managed to get a wire sent to Jacksonville from a railroad signal tower, alerting a reliable Jacksonville policeman that Furey was loose and headed in his direction. He and Pete then talked to another engineer, explained that they were lawmen chasing a fugitive, and the railroad man agreed to help. A monumental chase followed, until the switch engine halted and the police officer arrested Furey. The troubled night was still not over, until Norfleet and his son got Furey out of the station just ahead of Furey's lawyer, on the way to file a writ of *habeas corpus.*

An honest officer drove Furey and his captors to a safe house, where they spent what was left of the night with Furey chained to a bed. Early next day they were on a train west. During a stopover in New Orleans, another attempt to free Furey was made by two men who called themselves railroad police, but Norfleet's pair of revolvers discouraged the attempt. Furey spent that night in jail, but managed to feign illness well enough to get himself collected by the sympathetic ladies of something Norfleet called the "humane society." This time, Pete's pistol was the key to recovering Furey, and the three again made a train west. This time the next stop was a safe one: the Tarrant County Jail in Fort Worth. It had been five long days since the governor of Florida had signed the extradition warrant.

End of the Line in Texas and Oklahoma

The arrival in Tarrant County marked the end of the line for Joe Furey. In spite of his predictable pleas for clemency, he got twenty years in Huntsville Prison. Furey did not survive prison, even though he was a model prisoner and conned his way into the job of Sunday school superintendent.

His one glimmer of hope was a jailbreak, and a bloody one did take place. Some forty-two convicts escaped, but Furey wasn't one of them. Someone had tipped Norfleet, and the warden had moved Furey into isolation. His wife may have helped smuggle pistols into the prison, but Furey would not meet her, nor take the private plane waiting for him in a nearby field.

Spencer was the only man who cheated Norfleet and remained free. Until, that is, Spencer's buddy Hamlin jumped bail and vanished. Norfleet put him back on his personal wanted list, but there was one consolation: Norfleet reasoned that wherever Spencer was, Hamlin would be there also. The tough Texan went back to the hunt.

It didn't take long. Norfleet received a tip, then called a lawman in Oklahoma City, and told him that Hamlin was supposed to be in town; his wife was there, at least. Almost immediately, the Oklahoman spotted Hamlin, and wired the good news to Norfleet that Hamlin was safely in jail. At last, the string had run out for Hamlin. One version of this story relates that Norfleet found Hamlin in a "Montana whorehouse," roped him, and dragged him through the streets to jail.[4]

O Canada!

Norfleet's next stop was Wichita, where Spencer's father-in-law lived. While there, Norfleet learned that Spencer's wife lived "in luxury" in Montreal, but spent her winters in Florida. And so Norfleet and his son headed for Canada.

Pete found three con men and played the part of the hick looking for easy money, and the trio told him that a real financial wizard—one "Spencewood" —would arrive in town shortly. The wizard might consider helping Pete with his investments. And so the Norfleets went to the train depot at the appointed time.

They spotted Spencer and gave chase, but were blocked by Spencer confederates and a huge crowd gathered to watch a famous building climber billed as the "human spider." Norfleet laid hands on his quarry once, but somebody slugged the Texan, and Spencer pulled free. The chase went through the streets into a theater, where Spencer ran upstairs to the third floor, with Norfleet close behind.

Once Norfleet caught his quarry, Spencer predictably yelled, "He's robbing me, help, help!" Public-spirited citizens—and the theater manager—understandably sided with the swindler. Not until Norfleet was on his way to jail did he have the chance to show his warrant; once they saw it, the officers tried to help, but it was too late.

Norfleet then turned to the Burns detective agency, which had offices in several cities, and agreed to assist, but there was a problem. Although Norfleet and his son knew Spencer by sight, they had not yet found a photograph. Finally, Pete found one in Omaha, where Spencer had been arrested as "Harris" alias "Schultz." Another photograph was discovered in Kansas City, giving the Norfleets an important tool. Norfleet sent copies across the nation, asking for help.

Grand Sweep in Denver

The search then led to Denver, where District Attorney Van Cise was planning to break the Blonger gang. When Norfleet contacted the DA's office, he was asked not to let his personal crusade interfere with the DA's efforts. Norfleet had changed his appearance. He had dyed his hair and changed his mustache from a Wyatt Earp droop to a fancy turned-up imitation of matinee idol Adolphe Menjou. A change from his usual Western clothing to a pinch-waisted fancy suit completed the transformation.

Norfleet then experienced more of his phenomenal luck. His long, weary hours and days and months of learning about the confidence man fraternity and studying their photographs paid off. Almost immediately he recognized a "blind man" tapping his way along the pavement, following Norfleet. Immediately he visited Van Cise, and gave the DA a photo of Spencer. "I'd like to help," said Norfleet, and Van Cise agreed, although he clearly feared that acting on his own, Norfleet might threaten the DA's own long, hard undercover operation. "Don't talk to anybody in the police department," the colonel warned, "and don't come to my office again." He gave the Texan a private number in case he found anything useful, and Norfleet agreed to report anything he found to Van Cise.

Once Norfleet had some hard information, he again called Van Cise's office. The DA's chief investigator invited him to a private home, where he met Van Cise and some of his close operatives. Norfleet reported that he had spotted a grifter he recognized, and had agreed to meet him the next morning. Van Cise gave Norfleet a free hand to act as he saw fit. The Texan did not keep the appointment with the con man, but instead followed the swindler at a distance until the man entered a hotel.

Norfleet hoped that the grifter might lead him to Spencer, so once again he played the moneyed rube. Soon the swindlers tried to rope him in for a stock market swindle, and he duly reported their names to Van Cise. The Texan also played along, until his "winnings" numbered in the thousands of dollars. He knew the game; this was the time for the swindlers' trap to close. And when it did, they asked for $100,000. Norfleet boasted about his oil interests at home, and actually sent a wire to his wife— "Mrs. Mullican" —in Ferris, Texas, directing her to "Sign the oil lease" and send the money on to him.

There was one complication. The con men wanted Norfleet to stay with them until the money arrived, and the Texan had little choice. He knew he had to get out before the "money" failed to arrive, so he contracted a toothache, which got worse and worse until, he said, he had to find treatment. He was running out of energy too, spending his nights sitting up with his hand on his gun.

As Norfleet expected, the con men went with him to a dentist's office. Once they were alone, Norfleet asked if the doctor knew Colonel Van Cise. "He's a friend," the dentist said. Norfleet, much relieved, asked the dentist to notify the DA, and to say in the presence of the two con men that he couldn't finish the job on Norfleet's tortured tooth until after hours. The doctor obliged, and when Norfleet returned to the dentist's office he found Van Cise waiting on the phone.

Norfleet scored his last, long-delayed point as a result of the Van Cise sweep of Denver's grifters. Once Kid Duffy, Blonger's chief of staff, began to talk, Norfleet confronted him, backed by a pair of Texas friends. "Where's Spencer?" he asked. Duffy told Norfleet he didn't know for sure, but Spencer's suitcase was still at the Empire Hotel. Norfleet and his friends followed up, but Duffy had warned Spencer to disappear, threatening to turn him over to Norfleet if he tarried in Denver. Spencer took the hint.

"Don't Mess with Texas!"

As we shall see later, after all the years of riding the crest of the wave, Blonger's empire was about to come crashing into ruin, and

dozens of his grifters would go down with him, in no small measure due to the efforts of J. Frank Norfleet. The relentless Texan
was largely responsible for their fall.

The *New York Times* put it pretty well:

> Just because a man is born a sucker, is no sign that he may not
> turn into a tiger before his earthly course is run. J. Frank Norfleet
> made the evolutionary jump almost overnight.[5]

That stated the case exactly, although the *Times* might have
added, "Never try to swindle a Texas lawman."

CHAPTER 4

Soapy Smith: The Soap Man Cometh

He was genial, likeable, humorous, and accommodating. Only of medium height, in time he would cast a very long shadow in the West. He hailed from Georgia, born there about 1860, and had the manners of the Southern gentlemen. When he was about sixteen, his family moved west to Round Rock, Texas, where only two years later Texas Rangers exterminated fabled robber Sam Bass. Jeff Smith, as he called himself, came of good stock, but turned out to be the black sheep of his family. His father was a lawyer, and so were two of his brothers; three more became doctors, one more a farmer, and still another was a minister. And Jeff? A con man, a gang leader, a downright criminal.

About the time Sam Bass shuffled off to his dubious reward, Smith began hawking cheap trinkets and running simple con games. People tended to like and trust him. And those engaging qualities were his stock in trade, for despite his apparent cultivation, Jeff Smith was a swindler of the first order.

Thimblerigging: The Oldest Con in the Old West

Smith started small, with a thimblerig, one of the most common confidence games in the Old West. The fraud was simple enough. Any flat surface served as a platform for a thimblerigger, who challenged anybody around to bet that he could follow a pea closely enough to tell beneath which of three walnut shells or thimbles the object came to rest. The thimblerigger put the pea under one thimble, and then shifted them rapidly, changing the order in which they sat on the table. The professional often operated from a tripod on which sat his "keister," a satchel that not only provided a surface on which to operate, but also served to transport his small store of equipment.

Winning a bet like that should have been simple enough for the sucker, if only the pea really remained under the thimble beneath which it seemed to start. The gimmick was that the thimblerigger's agile fingers could palm the pea before the mark's very eyes. And sometimes the rigger squished the pea and smeared the remains under the rim of the walnut shell. This took a good deal of practice, but for the consummate swindler, it worked.

One version of Soapy's life says he began honestly enough, and even studied for the ministry. He worked as a cowboy for a while too, at least until he ran into a swindler probably called Old Man Taylor. Taylor took him for half a month's pay, and Soapy immediately saw the possibilities. Instead of attacking Taylor, he learned the con from him, and in time struck out on his own.

Smith was good at the thimblerigging game—he may have learned it first from "Clubfoot Hall." Soon he graduated to other shady dealings. Though then and always he called himself Jeff, one of his first scams won him his nickname, simply "Soapy."

The Old Soap Scam

In Leadville, Colorado, Soapy would set up shop in the street, with only his tripod, keister, and a supply of small soap bars. Soapy then wrapped a number of bars, including inside some of the wrappers a bill of anything from $20 to $100. He ended up with a tableful of wrapped soap bars, and then invited all comers to step right up and buy some soap, guessing which wrapper contained both soap and money. The price began low enough, maybe a dollar, but increased as more and more bars were sold and the remainder of the pile on the table dwindled.

A man would step out of the crowd, pay his money, and choose a bar. Behold, when he unwrapped it, it did indeed contain a sizable bill. The lucky winner rejoiced aloud, piquing intense interest among the rest of the burgeoning crowd. Trouble was, the lucky winner was Soapy's shill, and Soapy's educated fingers had palmed the other bills that seemed to have been wrapped with the rest of the soap bars. The crowd of eager bettors happily parted with their money, but somehow they had little or no luck. Soapy did reasonably well with this scheme, but he had his eyes on greater things.

Soapy was good at his soap shenanigans, but there was more money to be made elsewhere. And so he moved to booming Denver. An engaging tale says he was arrested there for running his soap scam, and the arresting officer, unable to remember anything but Smith's last name, simply wrote down "Soapy."[1] Well, maybe.

Soapy's Gang

Denver was heaven for Soapy, a city of unlimited opportunity that abounded in saloons and dance halls. Gambling was available everywhere. The leading place for a man to enjoy himself and lose his money was the Palace Theater, where the owner sat by the hour with his shotgun across his knees. If behavior was passable at the Palace, it often got ugly at a joint run by one Murphy, commonly known as the Slaughter House, from the frequent homicides committed there.[2] Those interested in such entertainment could also visit the Bucket of Blood, The Morgue, or maybe the Chicken Coop.

Soapy recruited a gang of similarly dishonest folk, known in time as the "soap gang." They included Doc Baggs, whose specialty then was land swindles, and Canada Bill Jones, who masqueraded as a hayseed stock man with a full wallet. Jones usually operated on trains, where his quick hands and fast patter earned him a lot of other people's money.

At the height of his career, Soapy is said to have employed as many as a hundred steerers, the foot soldiers who recruited gullible suckers. Among them was "Reverend" John Bowers, a

Canada Bill, a member of Soapy Smith's "soap gang" (American Heritage Center, University of Wyoming)

part-time minister who piously warned newcomers of the dangers of the city and then took them to a place where they could find an "honest" game. He was a champion steerer—in the trade called a "grip man"—for he was equipped with all manner of lodge emblems, grips, and passwords and such. For that was the heyday of the Masons, the Odd Fellows, and other lodges, and nothing won a stranger's confidence more easily than meeting a "brother."

Soapy also employed "Professor" Jackson, who held himself out as an expert in mining and often got legal advice from a pair of disbarred lawyers, who were apparently competent enough if their clients didn't let them handle their money. Among the multitude of longtime steerers were "Yank Fewclothes," "Eat-em-up Jake Cohen," the "Great Gobblefish," and "Dolly" Brooks.[3] The Gobblefish was a moneylender, among other things, charging a mere 10 percent per week. He was a fence too, and so acquisitive that he was given to falling to the ground in the street, crying out, "Whiskey! Whiskey!" until some passerby took pity on him and handed over a bottle.[4]

Soapy enforcers dealt with anyone who objected to being cheated. These included Fatty Gray, also known as "Shoot-your-eyes-out," and 300-pound Banjo Parker, perhaps even Texas Jack Vermillion, who made his reputation as a shooter down in Tombstone, Arizona. Another Smith goon was "Ice Box" Murphy, so called because in his safecracking days Murphy had invaded a darkened meat market and in the gloom mistook the cooler for the safe and blew steaks and chops everywhere.[5]

The fleecing of Bob Fitzsimmons, later to become heavyweight boxing champion of the world, was typical. While visiting in Denver with his wife Ruby, Bob met a man who introduced himself as none other than Collis P. Huntington, president of the Southern Pacific railroad. "Huntington" introduced him to Soapy and "Judge" Van Horn. During the inevitable crooked card game that followed, Fitzsimmons lost his shirt. "Never mind," said Huntington. "Come to my private railroad car tonight, and I'll repay your losses. Then I'll take you and your wife to dinner."

There was no car, of course, no Huntington, no money, no dinner, no nothing, and Soapy was a good deal richer.[6]

Soapy Cleans Out Denver

Soapy could not operate so freely without the help of the city fathers, who were easily bought. Generally, Soapy and his gang also avoided fleecing local folks, since they voted and the local politicians, however crooked, wanted to be re-elected.

Soapy had his good side: he sincerely detested any sort of cruelty to animals, and he was generous, giving freely to local charities and other good causes. After all, it's not hard to be open-handed with somebody else's money. He had a genial Southern temperament and charm that served him well, except when he was drunk. His charity and general good nature—not to mention the money he and his followers spread around town—kept him popular and generally insulated from the law. His steerers often worked around the train depot, collecting likely-looking visitors from elsewhere; in the eyes of many citizens, the lambs from other pastures were fair game, and besides, the money fleeced from them stayed in town.

His Tivoli Club offered all kinds of gambling, roulette and faro being the local favorites. Soapy himself was a faro addict, and spent a lot of time "bucking the tiger," as the saying went. He added one quaint extra touch to the Tivoli, posting a warning at the front door that told the visitor "*caveat emptor.*" The few victims who spoke Latin knew that meant "let the buyer beware," but didn't care. For the rest, ignorance was bliss.

One inspired Smith swindle was the "up and down" stock exchange, set up in a saloon. On a big blackboard were recorded the values of certain stocks, supposedly taken from a ticker tape busily clacking away—it was a real ticker, but the quotes came from a telegraph only a few doors away. Aided by "tips" from Soapy's cappers, men bet on whether the stocks would rise or fall in value. It was generally fall.[7]

Even Soapy's seemingly legitimate enterprises were fronts for shady or downright criminal activities. His brother Bascomb ran a cigar store, where a rigged card game was always available to the sucker. And then there were Soapy's phony lotteries, and the storefronts that peddled overpriced jewelry. For those who wanted to get rich quick, Soapy also offered stock in mining enterprises—phony, of course. As Mark Twain supposedly commented, "A mine is a hole in the ground with a fool on the outside."

Still, the swindling lifestyle was not carefree in Denver or anyplace else the gang operated. They were regularly stalked by bands of reformers and civic crusaders, but their biggest problems were with competing criminal organizations. Twice Soapy stayed alive by a hair. Soapy survived a murder attempt in a rail car at the Pocatello, Idaho, depot, but had half his mustache shot away.

Late in the nineteenth century, Denver criminal underworld competition became fierce, with the emergence of brothers Sam and Lou Blonger. Soapy's business declined, due in part to the competition of the Blonger boys and other swindlers, but Soapy hurt himself by being a mean drunk. "He is," said the *Rocky Mountain News*, "no calla lily."[8] He became so dangerous that the city fathers could no longer pretend he wasn't there, even though they had been dancing with Soapy and his money for years.

Soapy was not a professional shooter, but he was good with a gun, habitually carried one, and was not afraid to use it. That reputation helped him when the Rincon Kid tried to intrude on Soapy's turf. Soapy lectured him about the hazards of staying in Denver and convinced the Kid to depart.

This reputation did not concern Texas Kid Barnett. A year later in Creede, Soapy left him a brief note politely inviting him to leave town. Instead, Barnett strode into Soapy's place with his gun drawn. The Kid had come, he said, to ventilate whoever left the note telling him to leave Creede before sundown. He meant business, and when Soapy's man Joe Palmer slid his hand down toward his own gun, the Kid somehow blew both of Palmer's thumbs off. Everybody else went for their revolvers, and the Kid departed at the high lope, never to return.

Probably Soapy's worst mistake was attacking Colonel John Arkins, who owned and managed the *Rocky Mountain News,* after it ran a story that revealed Soapy for what he was. The report was circulated in Idaho Springs, where Soapy had gone with his family. Polite society there then turned its back on the family, and Soapy was furious. So he and monstrous Banjo Parker accosted Arkins in the street, and Soapy nearly killed the publisher with a cane, fracturing his skull. The headline predictably described him as "SOAPY THE ASSASSIN," who "lurked in shadows as black as his soul," and so on.[9]

Soapy further aggravated Denver by getting into a couple of gunfights, and found it best to leave town for a while. Some communities had heard all about Soapy and wanted no part of his scams. Cheyenne, Wyoming, was one of them. Hearing that Denver's passion for law and order had somewhat abated, Soapy returned to operate there for a while and even helped to fix an election and get out the "vote." One Smith partisan voted 299 times, one critic carped.

Soapy's Creede

Eventually, Soapy and his crew tired of the sporadic "reform" efforts and increasing pressure from the Blongers. In 1892 they moved to the silver mining camp at Creede, Colorado, one of the most wide-open towns on earth. A miner named Nicholas Creede started it all by stumbling upon a ledge packed with silver and supposedly exclaiming, "Holy Moses!" And so was born the rich Holy Moses mine.[10] Other big strikes followed.

The settlement grew to some 10,000 souls in a matter of weeks. This was no metropolis. Much of the building was done during the first winter, the workers driving pilings through the ice to support the flimsy buildings; when spring blossomed, the town discovered that Willow Creek ran right down Main Street.[11]

Creede was called simply "Jimtown" when Soapy moved in and began buying a series of buildings along the main street for his gambling and saloon operations. That March, the *Silverton Standard* quipped that the "land board" in Creede sold some seven hundred parcels of land "which in the spring can only be reached by boat" to affluent fools.

This was Soapy's kind of town. "I consider," he once wrote, "bunco steering more honorable than the life led by the average politician." Considering his experiences with city officials in Denver and Creede and even Deadwood, he may well have been right. He made friends easily as usual, and became known for his charity and good nature. One of his friends was Bat Masterson, then manager of the Denver Exchange in Creede. Bat averted a shooting war between Soapy and a dealer at the exchange. Soapy was backed up by Peg Leg Charlie Adams, reputed to carry not only two revolvers, but a pair of derringers as well.[12]

Smith brought along most of his Denver gang of con men and enforcers. Legend says that his crew included Dirty Dave Rudabaugh, later to be killed near Cripple Creek in a miners' riot, except that it's reasonably certain that Dirty Dave was actually killed in Parral, Chihuahua, Mexico, after he killed a couple of residents and the rest cut off his ugly head.

He imported a bevy of women, then called Cypriots, soiled doves, fallen women, ladies of the evening, and so on. They must have been most welcome—and profitable—since Creede ran wide-open twenty-four hours a day, seven days a week. At least one of the girls who once rejoiced in the name Slanting Annie is buried in the Creede cemetery. There may well be an explanation of the name, but that is perhaps better not written about here.

Bob Ford was prominent among the local hoodlums—loud, arrogant, and notorious for back-shooting Jesse James in Missouri. Ford ran a saloon tent until Ed Kelly (sometimes O'Kelly) exterminated him there, blowing a load of buckshot through Ford's throat, gold collar button and all. Kelly spent some years in prison and upon his release went off to Oklahoma City, where he picked a fight with a very tough cop and got himself killed. It is not recorded that anybody mourned.

There is another story in the *Creede Candle* that Soapy and his people pressured gamblers into $500 "contributions" and conspired to "pack the boarding houses with fraudulent voters, consider the falsification of returns . . . hire thugs and repeaters for use at the polls," and this was just for starters.

The Ford brothers were living proof that booze and arrogance don't mix. The *Rocky Mountain News* reported that a man Charlie and Robert Ford attacked in one brawl was badly cut up around the head by blows with pistol barrels. The victim alleged that the chief of police was present during the brawl and did nothing, and the injured man—presumably no angel himself—swore to kill Soapy on sight. According to the report, he sarcastically said if anybody questioned his injuries, they "were caused by a cable car accident." It was just another ordinary day in Creede.

Soapy soon produced a fantasy worthy of P. T. Barnum. He claimed that "McGinty," or "Colonel Stone," was a real petrified man, whom he had bought from some miners. The crowds flocked to pay a dime just to see this relic of some vanished age.

McGinty was a noxious sort of ossified corpse, but apparently this didn't occur to any of the curious. And of course, as they eagerly stood in line to view this wonder of the ancient world, there were rigged games available to pass the time. Soapy made a killing with McGinty, leasing him to sideshows and selling a half-interest in him to speculators, several times. As late as 1897 Soapy was still selling shares in McGinty to the gullible.[13]

Chances are, as inventive as Soapy was, McGinty was probably not his original idea. The Solid Muldoon appeared in Beulah, Colorado, in 1876. Muldoon was made of an ugly mixture of ground bone, rock dust, and even meat, but people paid four bits apiece to look at him. Both Muldoon and McGinty were preceded by the Cardiff Giant, a nine-foot "petrified man" made of stone. His "discovery" seemed to fulfill the passage from Genesis proclaiming that "there were giants in the earth in those days."

Only in Denver

The Denver city leaders decided in 1892 that the reform movement had been bad for business—a lot of the more lucrative operations had moved to booming Creede. And so Soapy and his crew were welcomed back to Denver. The move was lucky; in June of 1892 a fire consumed everything in the Creede business district, including Soapy's Orleans Club.

So it was Denver again, just like the good old days, with Soapy's Tivoli Club running wide open, but the halcyon times wouldn't last. The new state governor, David Waite, was a pillar of the Populist Party, the same movement that elected Sockless Jerry Simpson as governor back in Kansas. Waite was determined to clean up Denver, and he started big, removing members of the fire and police board, doubtless part of the casual corruption that had so long characterized the town. The rest of the city government, also threatened with having to get a real job, corporately refused to obey any order the governor gave, and the governor declared war. Literally.

City officials fortified the city hall and enlisted all the help they could find. That included Soapy and the rest of the Denver underworld. Soapy even became a special deputy of sorts, despite being the king of con men. His crew took up defensive positions in the upper part of the building, while firemen and lawmen of all sorts held the fort below. Everybody was equipped with various firearms and a collection of dynamite bombs. And for a while, at least, the city hall defenders must have felt they had the upper hand.

But the governor meant business. He sent in the state militia as promised; worse, his troops brought artillery pieces and a pair of Gatling guns.

The militia and the minions of the city government confronted each other for a day or so. At least one account relates that the militia was several times ordered to open fire, and just as often was told to stand down. The whole affair eventually evaporated. Gambling went back into full swing, though somewhat more tastefully hidden away behind closed doors to spare the feelings of the innocent. Soapy kept his deputy's badge and made good use of it.

Soapy then started raiding his own gambling houses, trying to strike at the precise moment that one or more of his customers had just won a large pot. He usually picked on men who were strangers in town. Once they arrived at the city jail, the victims were treated with sympathy by an officer who agreed to drop charges if they left town immediately—without their money.

Still, Soapy became his worst enemy again. Smith and his brother Bascomb were constantly involved in saloon brawls, some of which came to shooting. In 1895 Bascomb got a year in jail for the attempted murder of a rival saloon owner, and Soapy intelligently skipped town. Since he could no longer run his businesses save by the occasional nocturnal visit, Soapy steadily lost ground to the equally crooked Blonger Brothers, and so at last Soapy called it quits.

But only in Denver.

North to Alaska!

Soapy turned his attention to Alaska in 1896. By the next year, tons of gold had been shipped south, and the great Klondike gold rush was in full swing, attracting gold-seekers and the usual army of hangers-on. Some were legitimate businessmen—store owners and such—cheek to jowl with the usual army of promoters, thieves, confidence men, gamblers, and whores. Among the soiled doves were such colorful ladies as the aptly titled Mollie Fewclothes, the ever formidable Ethel the Moose, the Virgin, and Sitting Maude. There was lots of business, and one writer accurately called the ladies "of a more robust class than usual among their kind."[14]

Not everybody got rich in the goldfields, but most of those who were on their way to try had money to spend—at least for a while—and those who really did find their own bonanza had plenty of gold to spread around. Soapy was ready to help them "share the wealth."

The settlement called Skagway (Skaguay) was the gateway to the riches of the Klondike. The road to prosperity led from there over the White Pass and into the land everybody was sure would be their El Dorado. In Skagway, Soapy followed his old pattern, dipping a finger into whatever crooked scheme promised appropriate reward.

He had his detractors, and not just among the law-abiding. One fellow con man said that

> as a grafter . . . [he was] nothing more than a poor fool . . . he couldn't manipulate, he couldn't steer, he couldn't do anything.

But he had a lot of nerve and fight, and was just conceited enough to pose as a bad man. That made him valuable whenever the grafters needed a head and protector.[15]

Skagway was not all that different from Denver and Creede, since the local law—a deputy United States marshal—was quite willing to turn a blind eye to whatever nasty doings Soapy and company perpetrated. Also, those bilked by Soapy and his boys were generally either too eager to get on to the goldfields or out of Alaska to complain much. The only place Soapy did not operate was across the line in Canada, for that meant bucking the Northwest Mounted Police. No one, and certainly not Soapy, was eager to challenge the Mounties. Soapy tried it once, when some of his boys set up a shell game there. "Take a hike," said the Mounties, "and don't come back." And Soapy got the message.

He only tried once more to buck the Mounties, this time trying to intercept a very large shipment of gold, customs duties being sent out through Skagway under the stern command of Inspector Zachary Taylor Wood. Again the Mounties were alert and ready to shoot. They proved too formidable for Soapy's hoodlums, and Woods' troopers were reinforced at the port by armed sailors from the steamer *Tartar,* who took the gold on to Canada.

Still, there was lots of money to be made in Skagway. New marks poured into Alaska on every ship, jammed on board in thousands. It was, of course, only a courtesy to let the folks back home know their wandering adventurers had arrived safely in the realms of gold. One tale—apparently true—is that Soapy recognized that need by creating the Skagway telegraph office, which offered bargain rates to gold-seekers. A newcomer could send a wire anyplace on earth for just five bucks. Trouble was, there weren't any telegraph wires out of Skagway during 1897 and 1898. The line to Juneau was completed only in 1901.

Later in the day the newcomer was approached by the same friendly clerk who had "sent" his message. "There was a reply," the clerk said. "The office is closed, but for an extra fiver I'll get you in, and you can read the message." When they arrived at the office, sure enough, there was a poker game going on, and an empty chair provided for the eager customer. He played—and lost, of course, while the clerk went off to retrieve the message. One account tells that the victim always got a reply within a couple of hours—collect, of course.[16]

Or maybe the telegraph operator did not return, and the victim, eager to get on into the goldfields, was unlikely to stick around to complain to the law the next day. Suckers the world over are loath to admit they've been had, and that reluctance played into Soapy's hands as well.

He also operated the Reliable Packers who, his shills told newcomers, would get them over White Pass and into the goldfields at a reasonable rate. But inside Reliable Packers waited Soapy's men. When the greenhorn pulled out his wallet, somebody grabbed it, the owner ended up on the floor, and Soapy's crew vanished out the door. The same dirty tricks were played in Soapy's Merchant's Exchange and the Cut-rate Ticket Office.

Soapy was generous as ever in his donations to Skagway charities and public works; he even gave enough money to local government to fund not one, but two night watchmen. The gesture was appreciated by the law-abiding. After all, Soapy and his boys weren't out breaking into buildings in the middle of the night. Generosity in this case didn't hurt business at all. Neither did Soapy's open-handed support of the humane society and the volunteer fire department. He even helped build the town's first church and school.

The Handwriting on the Wall

Soapy acquired several saloons—heavily patronized in the new boomtown—the most well-known of which was "Jeff Smith's Parlor." This was Soapy's headquarters as well, from which he ran his various operations at a profit and in safety, at least for a while. It would not last, for as civilization advanced in Skagway, so did a natural yen for real law and order. Supposedly the citizens became discontent with the open competition between Soapy and

Soapy Smith at the bar in "Jeff Smith's Parlor" (Skagway Museum)

his boys—generally called the "bunco men"—and a band of un-scrupulous real estate promoters. City sentiment tended to ig-nore the real estate promoters in favor of chasing the bunco men, and in time a vigilante organization began to emerge.

In March of 1898 Soapy and his crew were notified by a vigilante group known only as "101" that all grifters had to leave Skagway forthwith, and threatening "prompt action" if their warning went unheeded. Soapy's response was quick and to the point, warning that a mysterious group of 317 citizens would retaliate against "blackmailers and vigilantes." If not artistic, the vigilantes' notice was certainly explicit. Soapy didn't pay any attention though, re-lying on his glowing reputation and good local connections. He even had the raw nerve to convene his own law and order meet-ing, and had enough support to justify another poster, this one addressed to "the body of men styling themselves 101."

The law and order society consisting of 317 citizens will see that Justice is dealt out to its full extent as no Blackmailers or Vigilan-tes will be tolerated.

This edict was signed "The Law and Order Committee of 317." For the moment, stalemate and peace prevailed, and it must have seemed to Soapy and the rest of the bunco men that the bluff had worked famously. For the moment it had, due in part to Soapy's popularity with a large part of the population and the efficiency of his goons, who numbered among them Yeah Mow Hopkins, a veteran of the San Francisco tong wars.

The distant sinking of an American warship helped keep the peace. When the battleship *Maine* blew up and sank in Havana harbor in 1898 and war loomed with Spain, Skagway erupted with patriotic fervor. Soapy was in the forefront as usual, and organized an amateur unit that he grandly called the Skagway Military Company. Soapy was elected captain, of course—or maybe he appointed himself—and promptly wrote the War Department seeking official recognition. He got it, at least conditionally.

According to one version of the tale, the departmental letter said his offer would be "considered." Another version says Soapy's request was politely denied, and another states that he got his unit recognized, but with the inconvenient permission to drill the unit at Fort St. Michael, which unfortunately happened to be something like a thousand miles away. Still, the letter looked good, being official and all, and so Soapy hung it up in Jeff Smith's Parlor.

There wouldn't be any migration to the fort, of course. But what Soapy *had* gained was more favorable recognition, which gave him a sort of semi-official private army, a good thing to have if he was going to remain the criminal boss of the town. This action added some real luster to his name, and even led to what must have been his proudest moment, leading his company through town on July 4, 1898, Skagway's first parade on the Glorious Fourth. Soapy was followed by a red-white-and-blue wagon in which rode a bald eagle, called Fitzhugh Lee, in a cage.

The whole thing was all very festive, and Soapy basked in the sunlight of his self-generated fame. Yet on that proud July day, Soapy had almost run out of reputation, connections, smooth talk, and plausible excuses, all at once. He seemed to be at the pinnacle of his dubious career, for he had just been feted as the grand marshal of Skagway's first Independence Day parade, and shared the spotlight with the governor of Alaska Territory.

This glory was not to last, for the vigilantes were still out there, still determined, still unforgiving. And they had a potent ally.

The White Pass and Yukon Railway Company was laying track into Skagway, and that connection to the goldfields was a major threat, both to Soapy and to legitimate businessmen. If gold-hungry visitors could go straight from ship to train, how could Skagway business extract money from them? Even worse was the thought that men returning with pokes full of gold might leave the train in Skagway and embark on ships without leaving any treasure behind.

That state of affairs was perfect for the railway: nice fares in and out of town, and no hoodlums to give the line to Skagway a bad name. So the railroad wanted to see the end of Soapy as soon as possible. The road's investors guessed, no doubt quite accurately, that Soapy and his henchmen would oppose the railroad in any way possible. Local businessmen were also becoming tired of Soapy and his crew. Skagway had progressed to the point that widespread criminal activity was proving bad for legitimate business.

Soapy had to go.

Soapy's Last Stand

Soapy himself provided the opportunity, when his minions robbed a man called John Stewart of some $3,000 in gold, about $76,000 today, in the usual crooked three-card Monte game. When Stewart complained about his losses, Soapy's boys simply snatched the whole poke and ran away. Stewart complained to the United States commissioner (modern term U.S. magistrate), who ordered Soapy to return Stewart's gold. Soapy refused. Word of this blatant crime quickly spread, and the vigilantes listened. So did the rival gangs of real estate grifters, equally eager to be rid of Soapy and his crew.

Soapy tried to stonewall the town, claiming that Stewart lost his poke fair and square, but almost nobody bought the story, and the vigilantes met on the night of July 8 to chart their future course. Word somehow leaked to a newspaperman, who warned Soapy. Full of booze, carrying two pistols, and never a shrinking violet in any case, Soapy picked up his rifle and headed for the wharf where stood the warehouse in which the vigilantes met; he was followed at a distance by some of his gang.

When he reached the warehouse, Soapy discovered four armed vigilante guards barring his way. Soapy demanded entry to the meeting, the guards said no, and all his long history of cheating and scamming caught up with him. Soapy chose to confront surveyor Frank Reid, a longtime opponent, who told him, "You can't go down there, Smith." "Damn you, Reid," said Soapy, "you have been at the bottom of this."[17] Those may have been his last words, or maybe it was, "My God, don't shoot!"[18]

As the two men argued, Soapy tried to hit Reid with his rifle barrel. Reid blocked the blow, then grabbed the barrel with his left hand. The two men struggled for the rifle, and Reid settled the dispute by pulling a pistol and opening fire. Soapy jerked his rifle loose and shot Reid, who fell, mortally wounded. But Soapy had run his last bit of luck and went down dying. The *Skaguay News* headline trumpeted:

Soapy Smith's Last Bluff Called by Frank Reid

And the same paper quickly added that the "Jail Quickly Filled with Members of 'Soapy's' gang." Some of them successfully escaped Alaska to greener pastures, and in no time Soapy's mob was scattered to the winds. Some went to federal prison, including the helpful deputy marshal. Others were simply escorted to the dock and told to disappear.

There are many stories about Soapy's demise. One says that somebody else shot Soapy, maybe another guard called Jesse Murphy. Another one of the guards did name Murphy as the shooter, and there is also a theory that after Soapy and Reid both fell, Murphy picked up Soapy's own rifle and finished the job. Other witnesses claimed they heard as many as eight shots, and Soapy's brother predictably alleged that Soapy had been shot in the back.

"Soapy Smith's" Skull - Skagway, Alaska

Dedman

A rock above the graveyard in Skagway painted after Smith's death (Skagway Museum)

Even so, Skagway's newspapers gave Reid the credit, maybe because he died from his wounds. In any case, a grateful public saw to it that Reid's rest was commemorated by a granite memorial.

Soapy got only a simple wooden marker, but later his time in Skagway was commemorated by what was either a parting blessing or a lingering curse. On a rock above the graveyard, somebody carved a thirty-foot skull and the legend "Soapy Smith."[19]

Soapy Smith, the veteran gambler, had chosen to "buck the tiger," and this time the tiger won.

CHAPTER 5

Lou Blonger: The King of Denver

Early Denver had more than its share of charlatans, con men, and grifters. Most of the accomplished swindlers of the nineteenth and twentieth centuries operated there at one time or another. This unsavory group included notable scam artists such as Soapy Smith, Doc Baggs, and Canada Bill Jones—with good reason. Denver was a very young town reaching for the sky, brimming with energy, with abundant opportunities to fleece the gullible.

Grifters did well in Denver. Some stayed for a while; most moved on. But for almost forty years, the king of the city was Lou Blonger, crooked as a dog's hind leg and a consummate organizer. He commanded a disreputable army that once included about five hundred confidence men and had a finger in every crooked deal in the city. Many were independent operators, whom Lou allowed to run their own cons so long as they split their take with him, fifty-fifty. This was not a bad arrangement for the independents, since they were largely protected from the law.

Like Soapy Smith, Blonger and his associates operated virtually with impunity, since Lou never neglected to grease the eager palms of the city fathers and the police. There was enough corruption in both places to ensure that Blonger and his crew could harvest other people's hard-earned money without much consequence. Some say that for many years he had a private telephone line that ran directly into the office of the chief of police.[1] Lou is said to have been so powerful that he could order the arrest or release of anybody in Denver. Over a span of twenty years, nobody in Lou's network went to prison.

Blonger was fat and red-faced, as short as his older brother Sam was huge and burly. Sam had lost an eye in a fight along the way, which did not mellow his ugly temper. Lou, unlike a good many successful grifters like Doc Baggs, was an unattractive figure on his best days.

But Lou was smart and patient; he believed in organization, and he was very good at it. He even had a chief of staff, whose job was to oversee the other swindlers and collect and account for the flood of money from the rackets. One source claims that one Loftis, called the Sleepy Kid, was the chief of staff.[2] Other accounts name Adolph W. Duff, called Kid Duffy, as the day-to-day operations boss, overseeing not only Blonger's own con men, but the independents Lou permitted to operate. He arranged protection, and collected Blonger's substantial cut of the independents' swindle for a couple of decades.

Duffy was a thoroughgoing scoundrel in his own right. He had been a member of several highly efficient gangs before he joined Blonger, working fixed footraces, and picking pockets. He was apparently good at what he did, save for the occasional bout with opium, but his real genius was organization.

As Blonger's gang grew from its modest beginnings, his winter operations spread from Denver to warmer climes; under Duffy's direction, contingents of Blonger's men defrauded suckers in Texas, Louisiana, and Florida. Summers were spent in Denver, rooking the out-of-town visitors. And for a long time Blonger's crooked empire rolled merrily along.

For many years Blonger was untouchable, at least until the appearance of Philip Van Cise and Frank Norfleet, whom we have already met.

A Good Reputation—at First

Blonger arrived in Denver about 1880. Born in Vermont, he left home early for the American mining towns. The Blonger brothers worked at a variety of jobs, even as "detectives" and lawmen. Sam, at least, was well thought of, as the *Albuquerque Evening Review* said in the spring of 1892. After Sam merely arrested a man who took a shot at him, the paper called him "a good one . . . Marshal Blonger's conduct Saturday night proved that he was a brave man and no wanton killer. Had he shot him, he would have been promptly acquitted."

While so engaged in Albuquerque, the Blongers are said to have sheltered Wyatt Earp and some of his close followers who had left Tombstone for their health and safety. But Albuquerque wasn't big enough for the Blonger boys. They tried Denver and found it a fertile ground for the ancient swindling profession. Lou started out in a small way, opening a saloon, Sam tending bar, with a full-scale gambling operation inside. The games were uniformly crooked, of course, and Lou hired a bevy of "hostesses" who rented by the night.

He owned a series of saloons, mostly along notorious Larimer Street, until at last he opened the Elite Saloon at the corner of Seventeenth and Stout, a joint considered the very pinnacle of booze parlors. On October 6, 1896, the *Denver Evening Post* waxed positively poetic.

> It is a veritable palace of luxury—mahogany fixtures and frescoed ceilings at a cost of $8,000, marble floors and an elegant café . . . The interior of the new saloon is without doubt one that will be a feast for the eyes for anyone who loves the beautiful.

And so on, *ad nauseam*. But in those days everybody talked that way, especially journalists. Some two weeks later the *Rocky Mountain News* chimed in with another blissful paean:

> They have constructed a temple—a palace . . . for the accommodation of gentlemen who, for infirmities and for good fellowship, now and then indulge a cup that braces up and cheers.

Things Get Tough, and So Does Lou

Lou owned saloon after saloon, and he turned a good profit on at least some of them, until he opened the Elite, which was, for a while, Denver's plushest watering hole. Things got tough for a time, during one of Denver's periodic spasms of law and order, but Blonger persevered, and when the good old days returned he was open for business again . . . wide open.

Lou was temporarily closed up in April of 1892, for, as the *Denver Times* plainly put it, "running a systematic bunco game." That didn't last, of course. Blonger survived still another setback in February of 1897, when his flossy Elite was foreclosed and sold—a temporary inconvenience.

Blonger had his share of other bad moments. One of them came when one of Blonger's men—recently recruited—tried to con a deputy sheriff, a Colorado officer in town on official business. The deputy was approached in the lobby of the hotel where he was staying. He immediately recognized a swindle when he saw it. He found a fellow officer, and the two promptly apprehended the crook. Lou himself showed up, asked what the problem was, and got a full explanation. Blonger had his own rules, including the long-established fiat against choosing suckers from among local folks, particularly visiting cops. His directive to his sinning minion is worth quoting.

> "You were recommended to me as a first-class bunco artist, and the first thing you do, you damned bastard, is pick up a deputy sheriff. What the hell are you tackling the law for, anyway? Don't you have sense enough to let Colorado people alone in Denver? I paid your transportation to Denver and put you to work. Now you walk back, and start now."[3]

Blonger and the two officers then hailed a taxi, took the disgraced swindler to the city limits, and bade him farewell. Blonger insisted on discipline, and this sinning grifter got off lightly; on occasion a Denver con man who didn't follow Lou's rules was rewarded with a savage beating.

Lou Dabbles in Politics

The Blonger boys also ran a prosperous sideline in election fixing. In an election held just after the turn of the century, a minion called Jack Hall is said to have voted for four men no fewer than fourteen times each. Hirelings collected the names of all sorts of men and saw to it that they voted for the right candidate, whether the voter was actually present—or alive—or not. And some voters were herded to the polls by police officers.

The March 20, 1890, edition of the *Rocky Mountain News* reported that various Blongerites brought in names wholesale: somebody called Sheeny Sam had delivered cigar boxes of paper slips, a total of almost two hundred names and addresses. The *Rocky Mountain News* was appropriately angry, writing that the con man combine had plotted to:

> blackmail the gamblers, to bulldoze the saloon keepers . . . to pack the boarding houses with fraudulent voters, to consider the falsification of returns . . . to crowd the court house with heelers and boosters for the prevention of honest registration, to hire thugs and repeaters for use at polls, to supply slanders and falsehoods.[4]

The newspaper named equally crooked Soapy Smith as one of the leaders of this band of fixers. This was before Soapy lost ground to the Blonger boys and moved his operations to bustling Creede, but it was the sort of fraud in which the Blongers routinely indulged. They expected a return on their investment, of course, in the form of favors from city hall, but what they got wasn't always what they wanted. The Blongers' candidates, as the *Elbert County Banner* wryly commented, suffered badly from the law-abiding electorate's long-delayed anger at the brothers' blatant violation of the democratic process.

> But when we saw the ignorance displayed by the Democratic leaders in winking at the dirty work of the Blongers . . . and other criminals . . . we felt such decent Democrats would revolt, and they did with a vengeance.[5]

Fate Steps In

Still, for those first twenty years or so, all went well in the dirty world of Lou Blonger's Denver graft, whether his minions practiced at home or away, especially after Soapy Smith moved the heart of his own swindles to booming Creede, Colorado. There were rough spots, of course, like the day somebody tried to dynamite a police "patrol wagon" near the Silver Moon restaurant, at a moment when Lou was standing casually nearby. The dynamite incident was blamed on "reckless friends" of some "40 hobos" arrested that very day, but with Lou standing by, of course seeing nothing, one wonders.

And then there was the occasional craving for law and order, which Lou and his boys always survived. Inevitably, however, the gang made a fatal mistake. Down in Fort Worth, a sub-unit commanded by Joe Furey swindled the wrong man. The con was swindler Elmer Mead's old Magic Wallet fraud, and the target was Texas rancher and one-time lawman J. Frank Norfleet. The result of that unwise con was the unleashing of a determined Texas lawman who dedicated the rest of his life to tracking down and bringing to justice the whole swindler fraternity in Denver.

Although no one understood it yet, fate itself was about to step in and destroy the Blonger organization. Their back trail was littered with victims, rich and poor. They included substantial men like Norfleet and Greek immigrant George Kanavuts, of Sapulpa, Oklahoma. Kanavuts had been skinned for some $25,000, about $589,000 today, on the Rag, the phony stock market swindle. Kanavuts, who spoke only broken English, went to the police, and of course Blonger's pet cops told him there was nothing they could do. He could not find the "stock market" room again, but he was determined, and he talked to the DA, staunchly honest Colonel Philip Van Cise. The DA promptly recruited him to provide intelligence directly to the prosecutor's office.

Fleecing intelligent, sophisticated men of means was bad enough, but many of the victims were citizens who didn't have much money; some of them lost every penny they had. As the Emporia, Kansas, *Gazette* commented in some anger:

> The motive for the suicide of Harry B. Waldorf of Newton, Kansas who killed himself in Denver last June, has been revealed . . . he was beaten out of $400 in cash and a revolver and forced to sign checks for money he did not possess.[6]

According to the paper, the young man grew morose over the possibility that he would bring disgrace on his family when his "checks" proved to be phony, and so he took his own life. The newspaper article named Lou Blonger specifically, and added that Lou calmly denied he ever heard of Waldorf. One may assume that neither he nor anybody else in the Blonger organization cared. A sucker was a sucker, and there was another one coming along tomorrow. *Caveat emptor:* let the buyer beware.

No one was immune. America swarmed with new immigrants in those days, and many of them spoke very rudimentary English, if any at all. A Swedish-English-language newspaper indignantly reported that a Swede had been swindled in Denver; an English sugar broker was conned out of almost half a million dollars by Louis Mushnik, known in the trade as "Thick Lips."

The profits were enormous. District Attorney Van Cise, Blonger's nemesis, roughly estimated that the Blonger combine had swindled an unknown number of men out of somewhere between one and three million dollars a year, and that was just for the years 1919-22, in a day when a buck was far more formidable than it is today. And that leaves out a great many unreported big scams and a multitude of small cons that rooked ordinary people—like the innocent Swede—out of hard-earned money, sometimes all they had.

Lou Creates Enemies

At various times in the Blonger days, Denver hosted most of the swindling luminaries of the time. Some didn't last. Some broke Lou's rules in Denver, and either were beaten or run out of town. And there was no mercy for other swindlers who conned Blonger. Charley Fegenbush (or Fegen-Bush), called "The Baron," even rooked Lou out of $1,000, money that Lou had loaned Charley at usurious interest, believing it was to be used as bait in the Baron's own scam. To the amazement of many who knew his wicked ways, Lou went to the police and protested mightily that he had been wronged. The Baron ended up in the slammer. Other lesser lights who incurred Lou's wrath included the Painter Kid, who ratted on Lou's operation to the Denver district attorney.

Besides the relentless Norfleet and able, honest Van Cise, another nemesis of the Blongers was Davis H. "Bloody Bridles" Waite, governor of Colorado, who was so named for proclaiming to an 1893 Populist convention, "It is better . . . that blood should flow to the horses' bridles rather than our liberties be destroyed." Waite rode the same Populist wave that swept "Sockless Jerry" Simpson to power in Kansas. He was a relentless law-and-order man, who went so far as to mobilize the state National Guard to clean Denver of rascals. His chief target was the notorious Soapy Smith, rival to the Blongers, but the governor's attempt failed without casualties in the face of determined armed resistance by the criminal element of the city.

After a decent, but short, period of more-or-less orderly recovery from a spasm of righteousness, Denver slid straight back into its usual morass of sin. Since the swindlers generally only victimized visitors from other places, the locals were untouched and unconcerned.

Even so, Van Cise was determined to cleanse the streets of Denver of these perpetual predators. He planned carefully for more than a year, relying on some reliable assistants, a few trustworthy lawmen, and the omnipresent J. Frank Norfleet as well as Postal Inspector H. M. Graham, who had a long career of chasing grifters all over the country. "Denver," he told Van Cise, "is the worst place in the country in the summer, but Florida is paradise for them in the winter."[7] Many of the Florida con men were Blonger's boys, of course, operating in the sunshine away from snowy Denver.

Graham added that Denver was the source of some of the finest phony stock certificates in the country, and handed one of them to Van Cise. The document was printed on high-grade paper purporting to come from the fictitious "Metropolitan Bonding and Security Company."

Van Cise started by meeting all the owners of gambling halls large and small. He told them that what was past was just history, but now he intended to enforce the gambling laws. Accustomed to the usual police blind eye, they ignored his warning; Andrew

Sorenson even told him to go to hell. Not surprisingly, he became the first target.

A number of other gamblers heeded Van Cise's warning; when nothing happened immediately, some of them reopened. Sorenson was one of those who kept on running, but when Van Cise was ready, he struck, and struck hard. Sorenson's joint, the Quincy Club, was at the top of a long set of stairs. There was an elevator too, but a lookout at a peephole in the door of the place had a clear view of anybody coming to that floor. The Quincy was rigged for quick dismantling, but it had an elaborate inside security system as well. The windows and the glass fronts to the doors were not only painted, but covered with sheet iron and backed up by boxes of sawdust. How to get past the lookout and the armored door?

The answer was an honest city cop, a big man named Ed Young. Young, who reputedly had the "largest foot" on the Denver police, got a friend—a member of this private club—to go in and distract the lookout. While the friend kept the man's attention, Young hid next to the door, out of sight. Then another club member, also a friend of Young's, knocked at the door and was duly admitted. Right behind him was Young, followed by the district attorney and a crew of honest cops.

The operation was in full swing, with money all over the place. Everybody got arrested, and Van Cise's men destroyed the sheet iron and sawdust boxes with axes, ripped out the alarm buttons, and chopped the peephole out of the door. Sorenson was present too, and the DA could not resist a bit of irony: "How about it, Sorenson," he said, "do I go to hell or do you plead guilty?"[8]

The DA's final gesture was to give the establishment's furniture away to fire stations and charity. The landlord was told that if the joint reopened, the place would be closed up. The word began to get around that the new prosecutor meant business.

Van Cise followed up with a raid on a bookie and gambling joint run by one Julius Epstein, who had cleared almost $50,000 in six months on craps alone. Julius got some jail time, but he was excused on Sunday for church attendance. Since Julius was Jewish, the judge ultimately annulled that part of the sentence after some complaints, but by that time Denver knew Epstein no more.

The closing of these two thriving joints alarmed the swindling community, even as Van Cise received more and more tips. Anonymous letters, some quite long, gave him many details about Blonger's organization and operations, both in Denver and in the Southeast.

The best of the letters—signed, "A Friend"—came anonymously from Colorado and Kansas. The writer claimed he had been a bunco steerer for Blonger for three years and was believed because he knew the details of the George Kanavuts swindle. Other tips came in by phone and whispered conversations from some of the many enemies the Blonger boys had made over the years.

Public-spirited citizens quietly helped fund Van Cise as he patiently built an effective intelligence organization that missed nothing. The contents of Blonger's office building wastebasket were regularly delivered to Van Cise. Lou's phone was tapped, his mail examined, and his telegrams read before they were delivered to him. A complex wiring system, masquerading as innocuous telegraph lines, fed Blonger's headquarters conversations straight to Van Cise's men through an office recording device called a Dictaphone. There was little about Blonger's and his chief of staff's activities that Van Cise did not know.

Lou the Fixer Gets Fixed—in the Bull's-eye

Lou the Fixer eventually realized that he was targeted, but neither he nor his men could unravel the complexities of Van Cise's undercover investigation until it was far too late. Blonger put too much faith in his crooked connections: "The district attorney is working for an indictment," he said, "but we have a man on that grand jury. He tells us everything."[9] Not everything; not even close to everything. The trusty Dictaphone even recorded Blonger's boast about fixing the jury.

Van Cise realized he could not rely on the Denver police, many of whom had been and still were in Blonger's pay. And so he recruited a group of honest lawmen, private citizens, and some carefully selected state troopers, present and past federal officers, including a Secret Service agent, and all the postal inspectors Van Cise could find. He included several hand-picked Denver police officers, and carefully avoided alerting city hall and its coterie of crooked cops.

Along with many others, Norfleet participated in the operation, as briefly described previously. He became one "Mullican," and acted as bait in a grift that he knew only too well from past experience. The Rag was a play for huge stakes in a phony stock swindle. The con men stuck to Norfleet like glue, finally demanding he take the train to Texas, where he would get his money from his wife, a variation on the old "Country Send." He avoided this scam by shamming a terrible toothache, supposedly to be treated by a dentist friendly to Van Cise. Norfleet called the DA from the dental office with a problem: if he went farther, especially taking the train, the whole plot might be suspected. Van Cise decided the time had come to strike.

Van Cise told the dentist: "Will, Norfleet must give all the appearance of a suffering patient. Dump everything in the shop on his tooth and mouth so you can smell it for a block and fix it up swell."[10] The dentist said he would, and did a thorough job of camouflaging Norfleet as a really sick man. The Texan reeked of chemicals and promptly threw up all over the grifters' Cadillac. Norfleet spent a bad night at his hotel, still accompanied by a vigilant grifter.

Meanwhile, Van Cise called his legion of honest men together; some traveled through the night to be at their jump-off positions by first light. At dawn, Lou Blonger and his chief of staff, Kid Duffy, were among the first to be picked up. The contents of their desks were summarily piled into suitcases and taken along; the documents were a gold mine for the DA. Once the kingpins were safely out of circulation the DA's men picked up thirty-two of Blonger's boys; more went into the bag the next day.

Since taking the prisoners to the city jail would only alert Blonger's hirelings, other lodgings were found. The First Universalist Church basement featured barred windows, inconspicuous access down an alley, and a back door through which to deliver those arrested. One of Blonger's men told his boss that he had a standing arrangement with his lawyer to call the city jail daily. "If I'm there," said the grifter, "he is to immediately appear with a writ of *habeas corpus.*" But his pet lawyer did not think of calling a church. Said one disgruntled prisoner, "I haven't been to church for twenty years, and by God, it will be another forty before I ever go again."[11]

The Trial of the Century

Blonger tried every trick in the book to avoid trial. He sent emissaries all over the nation, offering his victims money to stay away from Colorado; if the prosecution had no evidence, it could gain no conviction. A few turned out to be either fainthearted or simply content to get some of their lost money "restored."[12]

A grifter named Les Randle turned state's evidence and was threatened with death if he testified. Van Cise's men knew the threat might be made, having heard Blonger discuss the danger from Randle over their Dictaphone. "You will never live to testify, Les, so look out," said Blonger's emissary. To his everlasting credit, Randle's response was a classic, "Get out. I am going to bed now. I am tired."

There was also talk of shooting a con man witness right in the courtroom if he testified. A veteran, honest deputy sheriff stopped that plan by confronting the Blonger hood who would direct the assassination. He was unmistakably plain: "God---n you," said the officer, "if you or your men even show up, I'll be in the courtroom with my men and we'll shoot you down." That was simple enough, and that particular threat was ended. Those were simpler times.

Two victims from Oklahoma reported to Van Cise Blonger's attempts to buy them off. The tough Sapulpa theater owner and Greek immigrant George Kanavuts put it pretty well:

> Some [SOB] come in here and offered me $20,000 if I no go to Denver and testify against them. I ran them out of my movie. I tell them I cut their throats first.[13]

The DA then sent his men to contact his other witnesses and

ensure their presence at trial. And most of them remained loyal; one man came all the way from England, where Blonger's boys had swindled him.

At one point, Blonger imported from New York a fetching lady "built like a . . . Howard watch." The idea was to entrap Van Cise himself with the old badger game. Blonger men were ready to burst into the appointed hotel room, but the district attorney would not take the bait. The lady stuck around in an expensive hotel suite—paid for by one of Blonger's men—and got $2,000 out of the grifter by promising success, but she promptly hustled out of town on a midnight train, money and all, leaving the swindler swindled. Since the badger game did not pan out, the mob had no choice but to spend heavily on lawyers.

The trial was a sensation. Twenty defendants were represented by the best legal talent money could buy, there were weeks of legal fencing, and one major scandal erupted, providing fine copy for newspapers around the country. The prosecution team and defense counsel quarreled publicly, and not always with words alone. Colonel Van Cise was one of the combatants, and is said to have won his boxing match easily. He was barred from the courtroom after one such conflict with opposing counsel. That made no appreciable difference—the district attorney simply directed the prosecution from his office.

Faced with angry, incorruptible witnesses and fresh out of legal options, Blonger's grifters tried to buy off the jury. They only needed to corrupt one, for then, as now, a verdict of guilty required unanimity. Just to be sure, they hooked three. The other jurors weren't having any however. A tough Irishman named Herman Okuly was offered five hundred dollars for his vote; that was more money, he said, than he had ever seen at one time. He told the prosecution everything and turned the bribe over to the judge—and Van Cise went to work to counteract the bribery. If the case ended with a hung jury, with the witnesses scattered, there was little chance of a second trial. Blonger and his army of grifters would go free.

Weeks of bitter exchanges followed—disputes between counsel, a whole series of witnesses, and each other. The defense attacked the credibility of a very capable police officer, who testified one morning about the all-important microphones hidden away in Blonger's

Lou Blonger—a newspaper sketch printed during the trial
(Denver Times)

headquarters. "They're still there," he said, and the defense saw an opportunity. Blonger immediately sent people to remove them, hoping to impeach the witness and embarrass the prosecution. They found nothing.

Van Cise was a step ahead of them again. He had personally sent men to remove the equipment earlier. And then, when the defense confidently challenged the witness with the revelation that there were no such microphones where he had testified there were, they got the wrong answer. "Of course they're not there any more," said the cop. "Because we took them out."—"Here," he said, holding up two microphones, "here they are." The courtroom erupted in laughter—nothing hurts a case in the jury's eyes more than counsel looking like a fool.[14]

Of course not everything went the prosecution's way. George Kanavuts, the Sapulpa theater owner, testified well, but then picked a lawyer as the defendant instead of one of the men he said conned him. Since he identified one of the two correctly, his gaffe did not damage the overwhelming case against the Blongers.

Once the prosecution evidence was in, the defense attorneys announced they would call no witnesses. They also declared that if the prosecution agreed, they would submit the case to the jury without argument, based entirely on the judge's instruction. No doubt they expected the prosecution to insist on final argument, but Van Cise's men wisely agreed—an unprecedented move indeed, effectively cutting defense counsel off from any chance to rely on a powerful closing argument. This was an appallingly bad decision, no doubt prompted by the comfort of knowing that three jurors were bought and paid for.

The jury deliberated for days, as the three corrupt jurors held out for acquittal. An enterprising reporter went through the janitor's takings from the jury room wastebasket and advised that the jury stood nine to three for conviction at the end of the first day. No end was in sight.

In the jury room Okuly bluntly revealed the attempt to bribe him. Speaking directly to the false jurors, he minced no words: "The difference between me and you three [expletive] is that I got my five hundred dollars but turned it over to the judge, and you've still got yours."[15] The other honest jurors prodded and cajoled; they knew the three holdouts were crooked, and they kept pushing for a "guilty" verdict, based on the mass of very clear evidence.

The honest jurors refused to go back into the courtroom and announce that they were hung. They deliberated until first one of the corrupt jurors caved in, and then a second. At last, the third, one, Andrew Frank, agreed . . . very reluctantly.

When the jury announced its verdict of guilty, the defense naturally called for a poll of the jurors. Eleven of the jury stated plainly that was their verdict, and the whole long, exhausting case hinged on what the third bribed juror would say. He waffled, reluctant to agree with the guilty verdict, and finally the judge wisely stepped in. The judge asked three questions. The answers are worth recording:

> Judge: Is or is not this your verdict?
> Frank: Yes.
> Judge: Does the juror desire further time to deliberate?
> Frank: No. I want to get out of this.
> Judge: Do you, on your oath and on your honor as a juryman, say
>   that this is your verdict?
> Frank: Yes, this is my verdict and I stand by it.[16]

The Charges Stick, the Verdict Stands

And so, in the end, the prosecution made their charges stick. The jury verdict destroyed the Blongers and all their works. Lou Blonger and many of his gang members served time at Canon City prison. Joe Furey got a whopping twenty years.

Van Cise later wrote that Blonger personally appealed to him for a recommendation of early release due to his age and a long litany of afflictions, from kidney and heart problems to stomach and lung ailments. Van Cise would have none of it, and Blonger, the decades-long criminal boss of Denver, went off to prison on October 18, 1923. He left that place feet first.

Perhaps as children, Blonger, Furey, Duff, and all their ilk might have heard the quotations from Scripture that greeted them on signs in the church basement when they were brought to that impromptu jail: The Way of the Transgressor Is Hard, and The Way of the Ungodly Shall Perish. Maybe those lines had some special meaning for the Christian Kid, who was as knowledgeable about the Bible as he was the swindler's trade. He too went into the district attorney's bag.

Duff, who served as Blonger's chief of staff, went to Canon City as well. He left $200,000 in securities with his wife; on his release, she returned the loot and promptly divorced him. Duff blew the whole wad gambling, ended up broke, and committed suicide.

Lou Blonger, the ultimate Fixer, died in prison after only six months, bringing a close to a meteoric criminal career; it had been quite a run, but what goes up must come down.

For the onetime king of Denver, it came down hard.

CHAPTER 6

Dr. John Romulus Brinkley: The Rejuvenator

The young doctor was in a fix. John had struggled through three years of a four-year fly-by-night Chicago medical school before running out of money. He was stuck working as a "physician and clerk" in one of the most unpleasant places on earth—a meatpacking plant.

And yet, John had aspirations. He admired Dr. Albert Abrams of San Francisco above all other medical men, not knowing that he would someday rival his idol. Indeed, the medical world would soon be debating whether John Romulus Brinkley or Albert Abrams was America's most accomplished quack. While marking time near the blood and gore, Brinkley watched goats mating virtually minutes from slaughter and began thinking through a new business plan.

It was 1916, the year that Cole Younger of the James-Younger gang died quietly in Lee's Summit, Missouri.

Abrams was then a skilled surgeon with some strange ideas. Although he arguably became the most talented quack of an era that produced many notable competitors, he was hardly the first medical swindler who offered hope to the vulnerable for a quick profit.

A Short History of Quackery

The recorded modern history of medical quackery starts with patent medicines. Among the first in the late 1600s was an English patent issued for a laxative sold as Anderson's Scots Pills. One preposterous yet profitable patent medicine was sold as "Pillulae

Radiis Solis Extractae," which Lionel Lockyer (1600-1672) proclaimed to be an extract from captured sun rays. The tonic was popular enough to secure Lockyer an estate that would be worth about $2.5 million today and a marble monument in London's Southwark Cathedral that still stands. Andrew Daffy, whose name eventually became a word for silliness, created Daffy's Elixer, labeled Elixir Salutis, supposedly a cure for gout, kidney stones, melancholy, shortness of breath, and tuberculosis.[1]

The American Revolution disrupted the importation of such medicines into the colonies, forcing American pharmacists to fill empty bottles with their own vile concoctions. Dr. Thomas W. Dyott (1771-1861) made the first American patent medicine fortune in Philadelphia, posing as a physician named Robertson. He marketed such intriguing favorites as "Infallible Worm Destroying Lozenges" and "Vegetable Nervous Cordial" from about 1810 to 1837.

None of these recipes compare with old-fashioned Indian snake oil, a product first sold by the Kickapoo Indian Medicine Company of New York City. The scam was started by John E. Healy, Charles F. Bigelow, and N. T. Olivia. The last two characters passed themselves off as "Texas Charley" and "Nevada Ned."[2] Kickapoo ventured into southern Missouri, Arkansas, and Indian Territory as early as 1881 with pitchmen accompanied by Native Americans flogging such products as the "Chill and Ague Eliminator." Modern favorites such as Root Beer, Dr Pepper, and Coca-Cola were all originally sold as health drinks, first cousins to the Indian snake oils.

Much earlier, another scam created in Europe by Franz Joseph Gall (1758-1828) attracted Orson Squire Fowler and his college buddy Henry Ward Beecher, who became the famously philandering minister and abolitionist. When they graduated from Amherst in 1834, Fowler began lecturing on phrenology, a pseudo-science holding that a person's character was made up of thirty-seven "faculties," which could be analyzed through the shape of his head. Phrenology spread across America, but was eventually discarded by the public.[3] Before his death at age eighty, Fowler platted a town thirty miles east of Pueblo, Colorado, which still bears his name.

By 1850, hydrotherapy, later called hydropathy, had emerged

as the next big thing. An Austrian farmer had claimed about 1829 that he had healed his own broken ribs using cold water compacts. Vincent Preissnitz formulated three different treatments introduced to American patients by Dr. Joel Shew of New York about fifteen years later. Eventually, anyone could become a "water cure" doctor after some brief training and the payment of a fifty-dollar fee. The water cure spread across the American frontier, prompting one mother in Missouri to douse young Samuel Clemens (Mark Twain) every morning with cold buckets of water.

After the Civil War, those who described themselves as medical doctors were no more constrained by professional associations than lawyers. In fact, the first effort to organize a medical society in San Francisco was thwarted by unlicensed practitioners. Also, medical work on the frontier was so scarce in rural areas that most doctors had to also pursue other occupations, as was the experience of Dr. George L. Miller, who had a good medical education but was forced into politics in Omaha and, worse still, journalism in St. Joseph, Missouri, to supplement his income. Others simply retired from medicine, as did Berlin-trained Dr. S. Galland, who practiced in California, St. Louis, New Orleans, and Topeka, before opening a hotel in wild and woolly Dodge City, Kansas, during the era of Wyatt Earp and Bat Masterson.

Of course, quacks who offered cheap, quick, and fictitious fixes were not only tolerated, but sometimes praised on the American frontier.[4] The term itself originated as an abbreviation of the Dutch word for mercury—quacksalver—perhaps intended as an insult to Europeans who included valueless mercury salves in their treatments.[5]

Licensed and unlicensed doctors alike began to advertise in the 1850s, promoting false cures in competition with such time-worn yet orthodox practices as bloodletting. However, by then medical entrepreneurs such as Samuel Thompson (1769-1843) had emerged. Thompson developed a system of herbal treatments he franchised to thousands of practitioners, only to be pirated by some of his own salesmen who came to be known as "mongrel Thompsonians." Thus, his questionable remedies spread throughout rural America, but he was often cheated out of money his wayward disciples filched out of unsuspecting victims, leaving the swindler swindled.

Others were deceived by a more direct confidence game in which a first "doctor" was sent into a frontier town to find out who was ill with what symptoms. Soon, a second quack would arrive, and with seeming clairvoyance discuss the ailments of his new patients, just before taking advance payment and skipping town.[6]

None of this chicanery rivaled the amazing medical machines foisted on the public in 1904 by Thomas A. "Dash" Edison Jr., wayward son of the great inventor. Dash fronted for a company whose Magno-Electric Vitalizer was said to cure deafness, "paralysis, rheumatism, locomotor ataxia [sic], nervous prostration" and many other maladies with magnets and batteries. Postal authorities shut down the Thomas A. Edison Jr. Chemical Company for fraud with some assistance from his father, who gave an affidavit saying that Dash had no scientific talent at all.[7]

After leaving the prestigious St. Paul's Preparatory School without a diploma, Tom Jr. had worked for his father in a series of positions created just for him before striking out on his own as an inventor. One gullible reporter for the *New York Herald* claimed that Dash invented an incandescent light bulb superior to the one his father had invented.

Soon, young Edison landed a position in public relations at New York's Madison Square Garden, where his duties consisted mainly of supervising building decorations. After the Vitalizer fraud was revealed, the elder Edison told the *New American* that his son had refused to pursue higher education, since he wanted to become famous like his father and have it said that "he too never attended college." Eventually, the younger Edison sank into alcoholism and mental illness.

Dr. Albert Abrams: The Prince of Fakery

Young Brinkley's idol Dr. Albert Abrams was talented enough to become president of the San Francisco Medical Surgery Society, but made his fortune promoting electric medical machines in competition with Thomas A. Edison Jr.

As early as 1854, nine years before Abrams was born, Americans began to place great faith in electric gizmos, such as the Davis Kidder Magneto, which only caused minor body contractions by generating low-voltage electricity with a magnet, but was touted as curing both physical and mental illnesses.

The inventor Nikola Tesla created the Tesla coil, the supposed foundation for the Violet Ray machine, which became available in about 1915. Modern versions are marketed today on the Internet for the supposed cure of infections, baldness, and even poor circulation.[8] Such claims would have hardly bothered one behemoth of quackery.

In his day, Dr. Albert Abrams was described by the American Medical Association as the "dean of the twentieth century charlatans" and a "cool prince of fakery." Abrams was born about 1863 and trained at Cooper Medical College, a predecessor of the Stanford University School of Medicine.[9]

School records confirm his attendance there for at least one year before he was awarded the degree of Doctor of Medicine in 1883. Two years later he began a sixteen-year career at his alma mater as a Demonstrator, Adjunct, and finally a Professor of Pathology. Later he claimed additional degrees from the University of Heidelberg, Germany, and Portland University in Portland, Oregon, which were pure fiction. After leaving Cooper Medical College he became a surgeon and served as president of the San Francisco Medical Surgery Society in 1893.

In 1910 Dr. Abrams published a book on a spinal therapy technique he called "spondlyotherapy." A second book, *New Concepts in Diagnosis in Treatment,* published the year Dr. John Brinkley worked at a Kansas City slaughterhouse, described a concept that came to be known as the "electronic reactions of Abrams." Albert claimed that all matter contains vibrations and harmonics that can be manipulated.[10]

He then invented two machines, one for diagnosis and one for treatment. Abrams claimed the first, which he called the

Dynomizer, could diagnose every disease known to man from a single drop of blood. The treatment machine, which he called the Oscillast or sometimes the Radioclast, could be used to treat any human disease simply by dialing a particular frequency known only to Abrams and the other doctors he trained for a very lucrative fee.

The Five-Million-Dollar Demonstration

The secret to the massive fortune he soon accumulated was franchising. He only used the Dynomizer once for diagnosis, but by 1921 he had licensed some 3,500 doctors around the country to use his machines and techniques, for an individual fee of about $1,200. Abrams made a fortune that would be worth about $4.8 million today. Since his machines were extremely sensitive, his students were warned that the panels protecting the instrumentation inside should never be opened.

The medical establishment had begun to doubt Dr. Abrams' credibility some ten years earlier, when he introduced "spondlyotherapy." These concerns culminated in March 1922 when the fledgling *Journal of the American Medical Association (JAMA)* began criticizing his theories and practices, notably his claim that the religious beliefs and present whereabouts of a past patient could be determined by testing a single drop of blood.[11]

The Misadventures of Dr. X, Dr. Crum, and Urbane Barrett

A leading practitioner of the Abrams method, identified only as "Dr. X" was given the chance to restore his mentor's credibility, but failed miserably in two efforts to identify two vials containing pathogens prepared by the American Medical Association.

In another AMA test case, an Abrams practitioner using his devices claimed that a vial containing chicken blood contained evidence of human malaria, diabetes, cancer, and syphilis.

Dr. Abrams died in 1924, just before he was scheduled to testify on behalf of one of his disciples in a court case at Jonesboro, Arkansas. Nevertheless, his followers continued to battle for recognition of the Abrams treatments. These protégés included Dr. Heil Eugene Crum, who obtained degrees in naturopathy, chiropractic, herbal materia [sic], and electro-therapeutics following an exhaustive one-year course of instruction at the Indianapolis-based College of Drugless Physicians. Licensed in 1927, he invented and patented a co-etheter machine nine years later. Crum claimed that his machine could diagnose any disease, and perhaps of equal importance, fertilize any farm from as far as seventy miles away.

After Abrams' death, officials of the American Medical Association opened one of his devices and found "nothing but wires connected to lights and a buzzer." The later model created by his protégé Dr. Crum, offered an innovation; it contained the original bulb and buzzer as designed by Dr. Abrams, but ingeniously added twenty-six holes on the outside through which to watch the light and sound show.[12] Crum's career came to an end when the Indiana courts jerked his medical license on November 3, 1941.[13]

Earlier, during the 1920s, the Abramites competed for business with other medical hucksters, such as Los Angeles inventor Urbane Barrett, whose Natural Eye Normalizer shut out all light and massaged the eyelids. His inspiration had been Dr. William Horatio Bates, whose book *The Cure of Imperfect Eyesight by Treatment without Glasses* was published in 1921.[14] Barrett claimed for years that the Normalizer solved all eye maladies, but the courts saw things differently. Barrett was convicted of mail fraud in 1927.

The Rejuvenator

Three years earlier, a new clinic devoted to curing impotence appeared on the Western prairie. Dr. John Romulus Brinkley claimed that the problem could be cured by transplanting goat glands into otherwise sterile men. By 1930, his worldwide headquarters were not far from Junction City, Kansas, in tiny Milford. He boasted a PhD and four other degrees, all fakes.

On the morning of September 15, 1930, Dr. Brinkley demonstrated his technique, using one of his own goats for manhood-boosting testicular materials. The patient for the demonstration surgery was a fifty-five-year-old mail carrier identified only as "Mr. X." Even though the ten-minute procedure took twenty extra minutes, Brinkley brimmed with confidence as his still queasy patient staggered away, leaving twenty representatives of the Kansas Medical Association to consider what was to be done. Two days later, they revoked Brinkley's medical license. Later, the Supreme Court of Kansas described him as an imposter "quite beyond that of the humble mountebank."[15]

First Brinkley had impersonated a traveling "Quaker-doctor," a common swindle of the time, before relocating his practice to Knoxville, Tennessee, some ninety miles away from his rocky boyhood home in Beta, North Carolina. Beta is a picturesque place like so many others in the Smoky Mountains, where the poor have little more than pride. About 1907, at age twenty-two, with little education and some time as a telegraph operator, Brinkley continued his career in Knoxville with "Doctor Burke," who trained his staff in a one-day medical school, put them in starched white coats, and then expected a patent medicine sale to one of every ten visitors to his combination clinic-museum. Although the medicine wasn't really patented, the deformed male organs supposedly showing the effects of syphilis and other horrific displays of degraded manhood were designed to inspire the fearful. They purchased the surefire cure, priced at what the traffic would bear, but usually between $10 and $20 per bottle, which would cost between $228 and $455 today.

Young Brinkley had bigger dreams. Chicago beckoned, some five hundred miles to the northwest. Fortunes were being made there by the brash and the bold. Chicago boasted at least three medical schools that had been approved by the American Medical Association (AMA), which headquartered in the Windy City. Like many large cities of that era, Chicago also had an abundance of institutions training alternative medicine practitioners governed by their own protective boards. Allopathy, the AMA-endorsed discipline that advocated the use of pills and surgery for most medical ills, was on the rise, but had not yet emerged from the pack, which also included osteopathy, naturopathy, chiropractic care, and a host of others. Homeopathy, for example, had originated with a German physician in about 1796. Although some homeopathic ideas have been integrated into mainstream medicine, the last school teaching this discipline closed in 1920. Eclectic medicine was promoted by Dr. Samuel Thompson (1769-1843), whom we met earlier. Eclectics espoused the use of medicinal plants.

When Brinkley began his studies in 1908, he picked Bennett Eclectic Medical College, which did not demand that tuition be paid in full until the beginning of the fourth year. This plan worked perfectly for Brinkley, who borrowed his initial tuition payments from loan sharks and then worked nights as a telegraph operator to support his wife, Sally, and their children. Even so, he had to quit before beginning his senior year.

Brinkley left his family in Chicago about 1911 and apparently traveled around the Midwest the next two years, only to resurface back in Chicago. There he met James E. Crawford, a young man with similar ambitions five years his junior who had lost an arm in a hunting accident. They headed to Knoxville, where Crawford also matriculated from Dr. Burke's one-day medical school and served a brief residency.

They opened a new medical practice some 185 miles across the mountains to the southwest, in Greenville, South Carolina. Their parents might have been proud, had they used their own names. Instead, Brinkley and Crawford called themselves "Blakely and Burke" the "ELECTRO MEDIC DOCTORS." Their prolific newspaper advertisements promptly filled the waiting room with the sad and listless. The pitch was subtle enough: "Are you a manly man full of vigor?" the *Greenville Daily News* headline screamed, giving the partners abundant opportunities to collect twenty-five dollars per patient for each hypodermic needle filled with colored water injected into the buttocks of the hopeful.

Soon they appeared prosperous enough to paper the town with bad checks spread among some forty merchants, who were left holding the bag while the medicos skipped town.

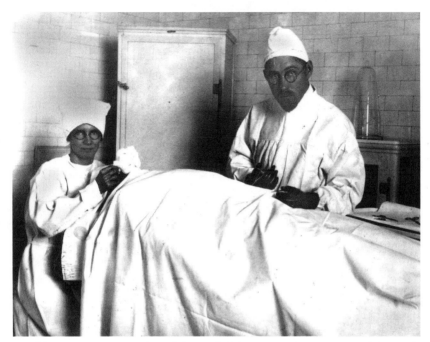

Brinkley in operating garb with his wife (The Kansas State Historical Society)

The next month, in late August 1913, Brinkley took a second wife. Minerva (Minnie) Jones was the daughter of a prominent Memphis doctor. Her parents were undoubtedly embarrassed when four months later young Dr. Brinkley was returned to Greenville in chains to face the merchants he had swindled. He promptly gave Crawford up, allowing the authorities to drag young "Dr. Burke" back from Kansas City. Crawford paid off most of the local merchants the partners had grifted, leaving a small amount for Brinkley to cover.

Brinkley spent a few weeks in 1916 as a physician at a Kansas City meatpacking plant, and then served two months in the Army, mostly in bed sick. After he was discharged, Brinkley and Minnie looked for work in Kansas. After false starts in two burgs, they arrived at Milford in October 1917. Milford was home to only two hundred souls on a busy Saturday, far from the bulging metropolis of two thousand that Brinkley had expected from the newspaper advertisement that lured him there. The most prominent building was a derelict exhibit hall, which had been freighted in from the 1904 World's Fair at St. Louis.

Two years earlier, Brinkley had purchased a diploma from the long-defunct Eclectic Medical University of Kansas City, which entitled him to practice in eight states under the lenient medical licensing laws of that era. Finally he could implement his plan.

Brinkley later claimed that the goat gland operations that made his fortune were not his idea. A local farmer named Bill Stittsworth complained of "sexual weakness" and asked Brinkley to transplant a goat testicle into his own body, Brinkley said. Mrs. Stittsworth promptly conceived, the word spread, and soon she asked for a goat ovary transplant. All of this heralded a promising new practice for Brinkley, who did not worry in the slightest when he flunked a surgery refresher course in Chicago, telling his instructor, "I have a scheme up my sleeve."[16]

Indeed he did. Yet male rejuvenation efforts dated back to ancient Egypt, and Brinkley was not the only modern practitioner pursuing the dream. Even widely respected physicians such as Illinois University surgery professor G. Frank Lydston were performing experimental transplants. Lydston used testicles harvested from condemned prisoners, with strong anecdotal reports of success, even as Dr. Serge Voronoff conducted similar experiments using smug, ill-mannered lambs and monkeys in Paris.

Thus it was no surprise when Brinkley opened a sixteen-room clinic in Milford dedicated almost entirely to goat gland transplants. And yet, he had to interrupt the goat gland gala for several months in 1918 due to the Spanish flu pandemic, which killed hundreds of thousands worldwide.

Brinkley attacked the local epidemic vigorously, patient by patient, bumping along the section lines to distant farm homes in an old Ford. These treatments gained him friendships and respect that endured for years on the Kansas prairie. His biographer Pope Brock described these months as "the finest achievement of his life."[17]

Perhaps it was inevitable that in the aftermath of such praise,

Brinkley would overreach. Wonder of wonders, he discovered that goat glands might cure some twenty-seven medical conditions, including insanity, flatulence, and even emphysema. Soon his claims of a 95 percent success rate drew the unwelcome attention of the American Medical Association back in Chicago, which sent out an undercover detective.

Still, things were going very well, what with childless couples around Milford conceiving, even as the first problems began to appear. Sure, a few goats around Milford simply disappeared—that was to be expected. And more than a few Brinkley patients were dying—if not during the goat gland procedure, then after their return home. Yet the immediate problem was not the claimed cures or the deaths; it was the advertising Brinkley had conducted in violation of AMA guidelines.

Years earlier, the American Medical Association had prohibited advertising by its members, which included Brinkley for a short period of time.[18] Perhaps professional jealousy of his success in mass advertising was also a factor.

Brinkley attempted to attend a human gonad transplant demonstration in Chicago during the early summer of 1920. When he was barred at the door, his enterprising new public relations whiz, H. Roy Mosnat of Kansas City, simply arranged a competing goat gland demonstration later at the Park Avenue Hospital, attracting so much attention he eventually performed some thirty transplants there.

His Chicago patients notably included seventy-one-year-old J. J. Tobias, chancellor of the University of Chicago Law School, who proclaimed himself "a new man, full of pep, strong, healthy and ready to go on with his work."[19] A photograph of Tobias clicking his heels in midair seen in newspapers coast to coast did nothing to hurt Brinkley's prospects for a growing practice.

However, in 1920, Dr. Max Thorek, the practitioner who had flunked Brinkley out of a surgery refresher course years before, was enthralled with monkey testicle transplants, and thus was quick to criticize the Milford miracle. Brinkley was unperturbed and began a New England tour the next year, just about the time he began to appear a little odd and unbalanced.

These were minor things to be sure, such as chasing patients out of the clinic with butcher knives, destroying cars with axes, and, if one rumor is to be believed, chewing the ear off of one unlucky Kansan.

Still, he financed a local church, was disappointed when it was not named Brinkley Methodist, but supported the Milford Little League team anyway. They were called Brinkley's Goats.

All of this was made possible by the goat gland transplants for which Brinkley had developed a price structure. The standard treatment cost $700, while the businessman's special, with all the extras, started at $5,000, about $59,000 today.

No one was surprised when Hollywood beckoned in the person of Harry Chandler, who had become publisher of the *Los Angeles Times* five years earlier, in 1917, upon the death of his father-in-law. Years earlier, Chandler orchestrated a successful effort to pirate water from nearby Owens Valley for Los Angeles as fictionalized in the film *Chinatown*.

The offer was quite simple. Brinkley was asked to shake the prairie dust from his white coat, then perform a goat gland transplant on a hapless *Times* editor of Chandler's choice, since the publisher was not available himself.

Los Angeles was then chock full of medicos, wizards, geomancers, and soothsayers, all devoted to serving the six hundred thousand inhabitants, many of whom who had come from the Midwest to improve their health.[20] Perhaps Brinkley thought he would find the acceptance denied him when he had briefly considered relocating from Milford to Chicago, headquarters of the AMA. The Los Angeles chamber of commerce reportedly offered to build a facility if he would find a site. Brinkley toured the new radio station Chandler was building, scouted out the Hidalgo Hotel in nearby Ensenada, and even found a goat supplier in Del Monte, but the relocation was not to be.

Enter Morris Fishbein: the Quack Buster

That very year Morris Fishbein, editor of the *Journal of the*

American Medical Association, attacked Brinkley's spiritual mentor, Dr. Albert Abrams. Eventually, Fishbein, a dapper, talkative doctor who preferred working as a journalist, ranked Abrams second only to Brinkley as a medical quack. Fishbein was born in Indianapolis, the son of a prosperous glassware merchant. Young Morris attended Rush Medical School, an AMA-approved institution. He once claimed that his career as a quack buster was inspired by the conditions he observed in cancer patients treated by Indianapolis doctor Benjamin Bye.

After a few months considering pathology and pediatrics, he chose neither. Fishbein accepted a temporary position with the *Journal of the American Medical Association*. Among his earliest associates was Arthur Cramp, a Milwaukee schoolteacher hired to lead the AMA Bureau of Investigation. Ever since his young daughter had died at the hands of a quack, Cramp's pursuit of medical charlatans was relentless.

Serious national attention to the problem began with a 1905 *Colliers* magazine series, "The Great American Fraud" by Samuel Hopkins Adams, which focused on the harm done by patent medicines. These articles and the Upton Sinclair meatpacking exposé *The Jungle* practically ensured the passage of the Pure Food and Drug Act in 1906, but at a price. Patent medicine had been a godsend for American newspapers and was the source of up to half their advertising revenue.

Fishbein became a man about town whose friends eventually included the journalist-poet Carl Sandburg and writer Sinclair Lewis, himself from a family full of doctors. In August 1922 Sinclair Lewis showed up in Chicago to meet the famous labor leader Eugene V. Debs who was under the care of Albert Abrams' disciple Harry Lindlahr. The Lindlahr sanitarium combined quack electrical devices with naturopathy treatments, which Fishbein detested equally. During a drunken midnight ride to visit Debs, Lewis, Fishbein, and investigative journalist Paul Dekruif discussed a story idea that became the 1926 Pulitzer Prize-winning novel *Arrowsmith*.

Such things were hardly of interest to Dr. Brinkley, whose time in Los Angeles had given him another vision. During the summer of 1923, he hired James O. Weldon of Dallas as chief engineer of Brinkley's new-fangled radio station "Kansas first, Kansas best," KFKB. Construction began as Brinkley departed on an Asiatic goat gland tour in which he circumcised the Prince of Siam.[21]

The charlatan business was booming, even for the patients. That March, Evelyn Lyons of Escanaba, Michigan, had astounded her doctors by surviving high-grade temperatures sometimes exceeding 118 degrees Fahrenheit, until it was discovered she had manufactured the publicity stunt by maneuvering thermometers onto a hidden hot water bottle during contrived coughing fits.

That very month an investigative reporter disclosed that the diploma Brinkley had received from the Kansas City College of Medicine and hundreds if not thousands like it were a fraud. Dr. Dale Alexander, who had signed Brinkley's diploma, was outraged to be charged with selling them for $200. "That is a deadly insult," he whined. "I never charged less than $500."[22] Brinkley then experienced his first adverse publicity ever. Worse still, he was indicted in San Francisco for buying the diploma, but this fraud was only the tip of the iceberg, since according to one estimate more than 25,000 American doctors held training certificates not worth the expensive paper they were printed on. Brinkley had applied for California licensing on the strength of the fake diploma, giving authorities in Sacramento a good excuse to arrest him. They demanded that Brinkley be returned to face the charges.

Kansas Governor Jonathan McMillan saw things differently and refused extradition, commenting, "We . . . get fat on his medicine. We're going to keep him here so long as he lives." Despite this reprieve, others were plotting against practitioners like Brinkley. Prominent among them was the journalist-publisher H. L. Mencken. The "sage of Baltimore" was himself the descendent of a quack buster who published a 1715 tome against charlantry. The second issue of his 1924 *American Mercury* magazine featured an article by Morris Fishbein, ranting against osteopathy.[23]

Fishbein was not popular with everyone. The June 1924 issue of *Pearson's Magazine* observed that he found quackery in every medical discipline except allopathy, the AMA-endorsed regimen of surgery and pills.

Some might say that the Fishbein campaign against quacks was not very successful. After all, only two years earlier, Brinkley had operated on the editor of the *Los Angeles Times*, a federal judge, and several Hollywood stars whose identities remain a mystery. By 1924, some 750 quacks touted gland rejuvenation across America, none more prominent than Brinkley and his wildly popular radio promotions. He was a natural huckster who eventually flogged his wares on the airwaves with the renowned country music Carter family and popular cowboy-singer Gene Autry. But for the moment, he got by with Roy Faulkner and Zapata's Novelty Troubadours. Brinkley also quickly adapted emerging public relations and advertising concepts pioneered by Edward L. Bernays in his book *Crystallizing Public Opinion*.

Yet there was something missing in Brinkley's pedigree—a credible diploma. In the summer of 1925, as the country followed the Scopes monkey trial in remote Dayton, Tennessee, Brinkley and his wife sailed for Europe. After institutions in Dublin, London, and Glasgow rebuffed his requests for an honorary degree, he finally found a friendly reception in Italy.

Pavia was a remote burg that had seen its most prominent days as capital of the Lombard Kingdom eleven hundred years earlier. Although its university dated back to 1366, Brinkley apparently dazzled the faculty with visions of rich endowments. The University of Pavia promptly granted him an honorary medical degree, which the dictator Benito Mussolini personally revoked later. No matter; Brinkley claimed the degree until the day he died.[24]

Andy Whitebeck of Council Bluffs, Iowa, probably didn't care much about degrees, although he wanted to be rejuvenated enough to bring Brinkley $550 he had raised by mortgaging his home. Since this amount was not enough for the goat gland operation, Dr. Brinkley asked for written assurance that Whitebeck's employer would withhold weekly sums from his wages until the $200 balance for the procedure was paid. The operation did no good, but the complaints of Whitebeck and many others made

little difference. Soon Brinkley enlarged his practice by announcing that the goat gland operations could also reduce the size of a
prostate gland.

Yet another source of prosperity was the Medical Question
Box Brinkley promoted during his radio programs. Some nine
assistants processed daily questions from listeners, always
recommending palliatives available only through the Brinkley
Pharmaceutical Association, a network of about five hundred
Midwestern drugstores. Brinkley suppressed bad publicity by insisting that his affiliates pay refunds to unhappy customers and
reduce what was owed him accordingly, at least in the beginning.[25]

Profits from the Medical Question Box operation averaged
$14,000 weekly by 1930, although other doctors sometimes had
to repair the damages caused by the Brinkley prescriptions. For
example, Dr. H. W. Gilley of Ottawa, Kansas, some 130 miles from
Milford, claimed that Brinkley's Reliable No. 50 liver medicine
nearly killed one patient.

By 1924 Brinkley had become a national phenomenon, making him a prime target for Morris Fishbein in Chicago. Fishbein
personally traveled to each state in which Binkley had obtained
permission to practice medicine, as well as to London where he
caused Brinkley's license to be revoked.[26]

This activity did not deter copycats such as retired vaudeville
magician Norman Baker, who ditched his partner, a clairvoyant
known as Madame Tangley, and began flogging patent medicines
in November 1925. Baker broadcast from KTNT ("know the na-
ked truth") in Muscatine, Iowa, on the Mississippi River. Eventually, he opened his own clinic there.

Morris Fishbein spent that New Year's Eve in Hollywood with
Chicago buddies and a host of movie stars. The next April he
began a new quack attack against Brinkley and Baker, threatening in the *Journal of the American Medical Association* to have
them both removed from the airwaves. Brinkley also faced formal
charges before the Kansas State Medical Board, which simply accused him of "gross immorality" and unprofessional conduct.[27]

Brinkley had another formidable enemy. He had defeated the
Kansas City Star radio affiliate WDAF in a battle over frequency

power. The *Star* gathered reverse testimonials against him from around the country. The critics notably included Cora Maddox, who claimed that Dr. Brinkley locked her in his clinic until her brothers could find another hundred dollars for an appendectomy.[28]

Brinkley responded to all this opposition with an initiative of his own. Morris Fishbein was served with a summons while attending the annual Kansas Medical Society convention in Topeka. Fishbein responded to the defamation suit by quipping that the AMA *Journal* would continue to brand Brinkley a quack. Eventually, the lawsuit was dropped.[29]

The goat gland doctor had other problems. The Federal Radio Commission soon conducted a hearing in Washington, and Brinkley's license was cancelled on June 12 by a three-to-two-vote, despite numerous testimonials on his behalf. About a month later, Brinkley and his opponents sweltered through a medical license hearing at the Kansas Hotel in Topeka. During the proceedings, his attorney almost brawled with investigative journalist A. B. McDonald of the *Kansas City Star*. The board witnesses against Brinkley were outnumbered significantly by Brinkley's pleased patients, but to no avail. Two days after watching a goat gland operation themselves, the authorities revoked his medical license.

Brinkley then channeled his efforts into a new field. He ran for governor and according to some observers would have won had the Kansas attorney general not imposed last-minute rules eliminating all write-in ballots not containing the precise wording "J. R. Brinkley."

In response to this setback he simply moved his operation to little Del Rio, Texas. The town welcomed him with open arms, but there was a problem. Officials in Washington, Kansas, and Missouri tried to have Brinkley indicted for mail fraud. They were thwarted by Vice President Charles Curtis of Kansas, who had been Senate majority leader. Curtis was bored with the vice presidency and saw an opportunity to regain his popularity back in Kansas by helping Brinkley. Somehow, the mail fraud prosecution threats against Brinkley disappeared, even as his $350,000 "border blaster" tower rose in dusty Villa Acuna, Mexico, just across the sluggish Rio Grande from Del Rio.[30]

The Depression brought even more business to Brinkley, who was ready to help husbands all over America struggling with bedroom blues supposedly caused by financial worries. Of course, Morris Fishbein and the American Medical Association also experienced an increase in business as the complaints about bogus patent medicines multiplied.

The new Brinkley station called XER went on the air with 1,000,000 megawatts of power, with a broadcast footprint covering most of the United States. Sometimes XER was heard as far away as Finland. Although he broadcast from Mexico, Brinkley still operated his Milford Clinic through two staff physicians and sometimes broadcast from there. XER also broadcast enough country music to make Del Rio a "Hillbilly Hollywood," with regulars Red Foley, Gene Autry, and Jimmie Rodgers.[31] Years later, the station would be operated by legendary disc jockey Wolfman Jack.

The Federal Radio Commission began removing mind readers, astrologers, seers, and quacks of all kinds from the airwaves in 1932. By then Brinkley had competition, notably from Norman Baker who had also been shut down by the Federal Radio Commission and reappeared at Nuevo Laredo, on 150,000-watt XENT from which he attacked Brinkley. By June, Brinkley was running for governor in Kansas again, but this time with a different, more somber style—one that left him some 30,000 votes short of victory that fall. The complaints that his first wife conveyed to the Kansas press about supposed neglect of his first family probably did not help his chances.[32]

In October 1933 he tied up a few loose ends back in Milford by taking most of the staff, the furniture, and even the better fixtures away in trucks bound for Texas. Brinkley closed the door just as the demolisher he had hired to level the place showed up. When the convoy reached Del Rio, the parties and dances went on for hours.

Still, trouble was looming. The federal government and American broadcasting industry representatives persuaded Mexican authorities to host a "North American Radio Conference" in June, but Brinkley and former U.S. vice president Charles Curtis stole the show. Brinkley was not even stopped when Mexican authorities shut him down in February 1934. He simply patched together a network of stations and continued operations until 1935, when the Mexican courts ruled in his favor and permitted XER to be reopened as XERA.[33] Brinkley reopened the Mexican station with a flourish. He announced that the goat gland transplants that made him famous were now a thing of the past, replaced by a simple vasectomy which he personalized with a squirt of Mercurochrome, coloring the urine. He also offered three levels of "prostate softening" ranging from the "poor folks" $100 regimen to the full-works $1,000 treatment.

Such good fortune allowed the Brinkley family to summer far from the Del Rio heat, sailing the ocean in a succession of three yachts, the last 172 feet long. The doctor dressed as an admiral replete with sword, met the Duke and Duchess of Windsor, and even brought in the largest tuna caught until that time in the Western hemisphere.[34]

The occasional goat gland operations still performed by Brinkley when the money was right, and the competing monkey gland method touted by Parisian doctor Serge Voronoff in Paris, faced strong competition from another quarter. Two European doctors working independently—one Swiss, the other German—successfully manufactured testosterone. No matter; Brinkley was bringing in an estimated $12 million annually at a time when medical specialists averaged $7,000 or less per year.

Life was good in Del Rio. The Brinkley mansion on the banks of the Rio Grande sported a large fountain complete with garish neon "Brinkley" signage in the circle drive. From the back, he could see the twin radio towers and mission-style XERA station.

In 1936, Brinkley and his wife did some more traveling. While returning from England on the luxury liner *Normandy,* Brinkley encountered Morris Fishbein, who was returning from a convention in Ireland. Fishbein looked up from a book to see Brinkley, who was so angry he could not utter a word and stalked off.

Fishbein resolved that day to settle Brinkley's hash once and for all, using a medical journal for the general public called *Hygeia* launched in 1923. Fishbein targeted Brinkley in a two-part article titled "Modern Medical Charlatans." Perhaps this was the beginning of the end for Brinkley, but trouble was brewing much closer than Chicago.

The Gangs of Del Rio and the Move to Arkansas

It was bound to happen.

The Brinkley operation attracted a cut-rate competitor in the person of Del Rio surgeon James Middlebrook. Soon the two medicos were using rival gangs of thugs to hook prospective patients arriving at the train station. And then things got ugly. Soon, peddlers arriving in town to sell plumbing fixtures and other merchandise were carried off to Brinkley or Middlebrook for vasectomies they had not requested. When Brinkley reminded city leaders that he had brought millions to Del Rio during the worst years of the Depression and asked for help, he was met with silence, prompting him to open a new clinic in Little Rock in early 1938.

Just a few months after Brinkley moved to Little Rock, his archrival Norman Baker got a new start at Eureka Springs, Arkansas, where a dilapidated old resort called the Crescent Hotel became the Baker Cancer Cure Center. Baker proudly displayed two machine guns in his purple-shaded office, where he was protected by bulletproof windows. Baker even invited Brinkley's old Del Rio competitor Dr. Middlebrook to join him, but Middlebrook declined.

In Chicago, Morris Fishbein celebrated Brinkley's move to Little Rock with the second installment of "Modern Medical Charlatans," which described the "filth and falsehood" of Brinkley's career. The *Hygeia* series described Brinkley as "a blatant quack" who "continues to demonstrate his astuteness in shaking shekels from the pockets of credulous Americans." Brinkley had earlier returned the favor, calling Fishbein and the AMA "the biggest bunch of grafters and the biggest bunch of crooks and the biggest bunch of thieves on the top side of this earth."[35]

More than one commentator has noted how Brinkley and Fishbein mirrored each other in ego, work habits, speaking skills, and native intelligence. And both were celebrities. Fishbein dined with the novelist Somerset Maugham and counted literary stars of that era such as Carl Sandburg and H. L. Mencken among his friends.

Time magazine described Brinkley as the "most widely maligned, and perhaps influential medico" in the country.

The Final Legal Battle

Later that spring, Brinkley announced he was suing for libel and $250,000 in money damages. This legal action was no surprise to Fishbein, who apparently offered himself as bait for just such a lawsuit.[36] Brinkley spent part of February 1939 in San Antonio, preparing for his libel trial against Fishbein with his attorneys. Late the next month, the trial started in the county courthouse at Del Rio under the stern eye of Federal District Judge R. J. McMillan. Brinkley drove to the first day of trial in his favorite, fire-engine-red Cadillac with his name stenciled in about a dozen places on the exterior. Although public seating was scarce, an entire section of the courtroom was saved for the Del Rio High School civics class.

Perhaps it was fitting that this clash occurred so close to the stomping grounds of Judge Roy Bean, the "Law West of the Pecos," who presided over rugged country only sixty miles to the northwest until his death thirty-five years earlier.

During the one-week trial, which began on March 22, Brinkley was represented by Morriss and Morriss, a local father-and-son legal team confronted by Clinton Giddings Brown, the former mayor of San Antonio. Will Morriss Sr. seemed to snarl even when he smiled. His first witness for Brinkley was a local newspaper stand owner who established that Fishbeins' statements against Brinkley had been published. Morriss then paraded staff members through the court to establish the credibility of the Brinkley procedures as best he could, and then called for the first of some twenty patients who were there to sing Brinkley's praises—the heart of the plaintiff's case. However, after hours of evidentiary wrangling and a night to sleep on it, McMillan decided that none of the patients on either side could testify, banning "some of the friskiest old roosters you ever saw in your life."[37]

And with this decision, Brinkley's side rested, however uneasily.

Brinkley appeared disinterested as he fidgeted with a gold toothpick during the testimony. Each evening, he broadcast commentary from his Del Rio studios. The first night he offered a $500 prize for the listener who provided the best explanation of why Brinkley was the world's best prostate specialist. Although Fishbein objected the next day, Judge McMillan let Brinkley continue broadcasting throughout the trial.

The defense produced a 1930 deposition given by Brinkley's old partner, James E. Crawford, then serving time in Oklahoma for an armed robbery he had committed at the Mayo Hotel in Tulsa.

Crawford explained the quackery he and Brinkley had perpetrated back in Greenville, South Carolina, more than two decades earlier, before they skipped town without paying their bills. Through the Crawford deposition, the defense established that the predecessor of the vaunted Brinkley Formula 1020 was nothing more than colored water.

The defense also presented a trio of Texas urologists who testified that Brinkley's prostate operations were worthless and the goat gland transplants nonsense. Morris Fishbein likened his campaign against Brinkley to "dissecting a malignant tumor." He discussed the hallmarks of quackery at length—the impossible claims of possible cures, fake degrees, and secret processes—in sharp contrast with the published articles disclosing the credentials and discoveries of legitimate doctors. He also noted that Brinkley charged his patients $400 for a prescription of Formula 2010 that cost $1.20 to produce.[38] On cross-examination, Brinkley's attorneys roughed Fishbein up a bit, establishing that he had advertised a book of home remedies while criticizing Brinkley for similar practices.

On rebuttal, Brinkley's attorneys led him through friendly questions designed to refute Fishbein's every contention—questions which would come in cross-examination. None of this courtroom maneuvering helped Brinkley much in the end. Two days of cross-examination came down to one critical question. Brinkley had claimed for twenty years that he had carefully "grafted" goat testicles into his human patients, but in the end he admitted that he had simply slit the human testicle open, popped in a goat testicle, and then sewed up the incision. And with that admission, his case died.[39]

After four hours, the jury exonerated Fishbein and the American Medical Association. One source claimed that the jury was

Cartoon of an old man and a goat referencing Brinkley's operations (The Kansas State Historical Society)

swayed by the testimony about Brinkley's use of colored water as medicine and his admission that the goat gland operation involved no grafting at all.

Several months later, Brinkley and his wife attended the premiere of *Gone with the Wind* in Atlanta, but everything had changed. The Fishbein decision had prompted some $3 million in malpractice lawsuits, including one filed by the Brinkley business manager. As if this were not enough, the move to Little Rock had not panned out at all. After layoffs and salary reductions for those employees who stayed, Brinkley was still in such deep trouble he could not relocate back to Del Rio.

He turned an old Kansas City shop into the Dilley Aircraft School, falsely claiming that the mechanics trained there could not be drafted in order to improve enrollment. Even with this incentive, the Dilley Aircraft School went nowhere. Brinkley was forced to file bankruptcy in early 1941.

Three months later, he offered his creditors six horses, ninety head of cattle, forty ducks, and even more questionable assets. By July, the Mexican government had seized his radio station on the grounds that Brinkley had broadcast programs sympathetic to the Nazis. Earlier, the Del Rio Wonder had come to admire Adolph Hitler and decorated the tiles around his pool with swastikas for effect.

Father Flanagan of Boys Town visited Brinkley three days after his July 24, 1941, heart attack, perhaps as a gesture to a once generous donor, even as the legal problems piled up.

The fifty-seven-year-old medico was served with a fifteen-count mail fraud indictment in August, while recuperating in a Kansas City hospital following a leg amputation caused by a blood clot. He did live long enough to see his archrival Norman Baker convicted of mail fraud before Brinkley died in his sleep in San Antonio. Perhaps the most telling eulogy uttered after Brinkley's death on May 26, 1942, was offered by an anonymous patient who admitted, "I knew he was bilking me, but I liked him anyway."[40]

CHAPTER 7

Patrick Henry: The Yazoo Land Grabber

*Were I to characterize the United States, it should be [as] . . .
the land of speculation.*[1]

—William Priest

Fourteen years after demanding liberty or death in a plain white church still standing in Richmond, Virginia, Patrick Henry was seeking his fortune through land speculation in the American West.[2] His bid for millions of acres west of Georgia may have been at a fair price, had he and his partners paid for it in real money. Instead, they tried to scam Georgia officials with depreciated state paper almost as worthless as Confederate money would be today. He lost the deal when he could not pay in gold or silver. This event started the first of three scandals collectively known as the Yazoo land fraud. A separate 1795 Georgia scandal known as the Pine Barrens fraud is also often conflated with the other three.

No one involved could have predicted that these scandals would eventually rock the foundations of the young United States and result in the first Supreme Court decision holding a state law unconstitutional. The failure of the first scheme set the stage for the second Yazoo land scandal, in which Georgia's western lands were sold to speculators who had bribed virtually the entire Georgia legislature. The third Yazoo land scandal was the resale of Yazoo lands to New England speculators on the very same day a newly elected Georgia legislature rescinded the second sale.

Patrick Henry was hardly the first to dabble in land grabbing along the Yazoo River, a long tributary of the Mississippi River, second only in length to the Ohio. The French explorer LaSalle reportedly named the Yazoo in 1682 for a small Indian tribe living near its mouth. Some surmise the word is Choctaw for "hunting ground." Others say it was named the "River of Death," in remembrance of the thousands of Choctaws who died of diseases attributed to Spanish explorers. The high bluffs and rolling hills of the Upper Yazoo inspired William Faulkner's fictional Yoknapatawpha County. The Lower Yazoo meanders through Delta soil rich enough to sustain cotton crops.[3]

The American composer Stephen Collins Foster (1826-64) waxed lyrical about the Yazoo in his 1851 tune "Old Folks at Home," until his brother convinced him it would be better to sing about times "way down upon the Sewanee River."[4]

Patrick Henry's Background

Gaunt, dark-haired Patrick Henry had piercing eyes that he put to good use. He was of middling Virginia gentry and began life in the social circle of Martha Dandridge Custis, the young widow who married George Washington.[5] He is best known today for two statements before the American Revolution attributed to him.

When he dared to mention King George II during a fiery 1765 speech in the Virginia House of Burgesses in Williamsburg, he was met with cries of treason. Henry is said to have responded, "If that be treason make the most of it." The second outburst, nine years later, "Give me liberty or give me death," is more remembered today.[6]

Above all, Patrick Henry was an outspoken country lawyer. A 1927 essay compared him unfavorably with George Washington, Thomas Jefferson, James Madison, and the Lees, yet to his credit, perhaps unwittingly, the critic described him as akin to "the artless Lincoln."[7]

He was politically allied with George Mason and fellow land speculator Henry "Light-Horse Harry" Lee, the father of Confederate leader Robert E. Lee. Light-Horse Harry was the eulogist who described George Washington as "first in war, first in peace and first in the hearts of his countrymen."

Patrick Henry first became governor of Virginia in 1776 and later succeeded his political ally Benjamin Harrison, who served as Virginia governor for two years beginning in 1782. Together with Governor George Clinton of New York and others, he led the fight against adoption of the United States Constitution. Clinton once threatened that New York would secede with the Carolinas and Virginia to form a "middle confederacy."[8]

Although his efforts to stop ratification of the United States Constitution in 1789 failed, Henry at least prevented Alexander Hamilton and others from wrapping President George Washington in royal dignity with a title such as "Your Excellency," "His Elective Highness," or "Your Majesty." Thanks in no small part to Patrick Henry, George Washington was simply addressed as "The President of the United States."[9]

The Mississippi Land Bubble (1720)

The Scottish financier and adventurer John Law (1671-1729) was among the first Europeans to envision settlement of the Yazoo region. He founded the French Compiegne d'Occident in 1717 to finance his Mississippi Scheme, a plan to populate the lower Mississippi River region, only to watch it collapse as the result of his own "oversubscription" of company stock three years later. The settlers fared little better in what later became the Yazoo district, finding themselves in the tender mercies of the hostile Creeks, Cherokees, and Choctaws who populated that region. A revolt and massacre in 1729 marked the end of the Mississippi Scheme, the very year Law himself was forced to flee Paris for Venice, where he died in poverty.[10]

Early American Land Speculation

Fifty-three years later, Benjamin Franklin boosted land speculation in his *Information to Those Who Would Remove to America.*

His pamphlet encouraged journeymen mechanics and tradesmen with the lure of selling more goods, farmers with the prospect of cheap land, and investors with "the promise [inherent] in the increase of land values as the growing population fills in and improves wilderness areas."[11]

Even then, Patrick Henry was dreaming of an empire of his own. One biographer has argued that Henry's part in the Yazoo land scandal was prompted by his intention "to form a new independent territory and secede from the United States."[12] These dreams were undoubtedly spurred on by Henry's need to provide for six sons, the last of whom was born only three years before the revolutionary patriot's death.

This was nothing new. George Washington himself had been involved in a huge land venture in the Ohio country nine years before the Revolution. The "Colony's charter described Virginia as extending two hundred miles northward and southward from the entrance to the Chesapeake Bay and within these boundaries *westward from sea to sea*." Not only this, but "on the flimsiest of patents—and only the sketchiest notion of American geography—Virginia gentlemen airily built their castles."[13] Indeed, George Washington was "one of the most active land speculators of colonial times."[14]

Indeed, by the middle of the eighteenth century, land speculation in America had become more attractive to some than farming. One observer noted,

> One could perhaps get rich more quickly and with far less effort by buying the land cheaply, holding it and selling it for a profit. The trick depended on one of two conditions. That the improvements of neighboring lands would increase the value of one's own unimproved acreage or that a fever of speculation would draw so many potential investors as to make prices temporarily soar. Either condition required that . . . one work indirectly on other people's confidence.[15]

George Washington's brothers Lawrence and Augustine had formed the Ohio River Company in 1748 with Governor Robert

Dinwiddie and others petitioning the king for 200,000 acres near the forks of the Ohio.[16] They had petitioned to offer free passage to indentured servants who would clear and improve farms and homesteads with the prospect of earning rents from the new settlers.[17] They hoped to acquire another 300,000 acres for their efforts after seven years.

Washington was much taken with this wide-eyed vision of western lands, proclaiming to one friend in 1767 that anyone "who neglects the present opportunity of hunting out good lands and in some measure marking and distinguishing them for their own will never regain it."[18] Four years earlier, Washington had joined with Jack Washington and four Lees to form the Mississippi Land Company and acquire 2.5 million acres at the confluence of the Mississippi and Ohio Rivers.[19]

The very next year in 1768, Patrick Henry had organized an expedition to survey western lands he had acquired from his financially distressed father-in-law John Shelton at bargain prices. Shelton's interests were part of a land company headed by two prominent Virginia land brokers: James Patton and Dr. Thomas Walker.[20]

Thus, it is no surprise that the British characterized the Americans as suffering speculative fever at the dawn of the Revolution.[21]

Post-Revolutionary Land Speculation

In 1786, Henry "Light-Horse Harry" Lee; Wilson Cary Nicholas, a future Virginia governor; George Keith Taylor, a brother-in-law of future Chief Justice John Marshall; and General John Preston conveyed a 300,000-acre tract of Virginia land to certain Connecticut businessmen for $30,000. When the investors discovered that the tract contained only 133,874 acres, an arrest warrant was issued for poor Harry, who was jailed in Boston en route to the West Indies. Eventually, Lee gave up part of his Pennsylvania holdings in reparation for the fraud. Similarly, one Oliver Phelps purchased 100,000 acres near present-day Charleston, West Virginia, from sellers who had no title.[22]

After American independence, the individual states vied with each other, the occupying tribes, and the Spanish for the lands west of the original thirteen colonies.

No state distributed questionable titles to these western lands more generously than Georgia, which refused to cede such claims to the United States government as had Connecticut, New York, and Virginia. Some thirty-five million acres, representing most of present-day Alabama and Mississippi, were thus ripe for the picking.

The western lands in question were controlled by the Cherokee, Creek, Chickasaw, and Choctaw Nations, which periodically attacked white squatters who had settled there. The tribes hardly needed the occasional encouragement they received from the Spanish, who claimed lawful possession.[23]

Initially, such Georgia lands were granted to those who had settled in the organized eastern counties and cultivated crops in allotments of a thousand acres or less. Eventually, these thousand-acre limitations were simply ignored. Governor George Walton usually favored land speculators over bona fide settlers and sometimes granted individuals parcels of as much as 50,000 acres.

By 1794, his successor, Governor George Mathews, dramatically exceeded that amount, granting 1.5 million acres to one individual. Two years later, about twenty-nine million Georgia acres had been granted in twenty-four organized counties containing only nine million acres.[24]

The First Yazoo Land Sale

The secretive Combined Society was formed in 1785 to obtain large grants of land from the state of Georgia. South Carolinians and Georgians organized the Bourbon Company to develop part of the Yazoo country. When the Bourbon Company failed, it was reorganized as the South Carolina Company, whose owners included Creek Chief Alexander McGillivray and "Major Thomas Washington," who was hanged as a counterfeiter at Charleston, South Carolina, in 1791.

In November 1789 Patrick Henry joined six other Virginians to form the Virginia Land Company, to acquire eleven million acres in northwest Georgia at less than one cent per acre, as did the Tennessee Land Company and the South Carolina Land Company. The companies then contracted to acquire some sixty-one million acres in the western territories claimed by Georgia, constituting most of present-day Alabama and Mississippi traversed by the Yazoo River.

This activity concerned President George Washington. In 1790 he warned that the Yazoo land possessed by the Five Tribes pursuant to treaties with the United States was not to be disturbed.

Patrick Henry and his associates contracted to buy the eleven million acres from the Georgia legislature for $200,000. The Virginia Company lost the deal and never received title to these vast lands, since Patrick Henry and his fellow speculators made initial payments in old, nearly worthless state certificates and Georgia officials insisted that the final payment be made in gold or silver specie. This did not stop the admiring biographer Henry Mayer from contending that Henry "bought an interest in a huge Georgia tract, only to lose it through fraudulent manipulations by that state's legislature."[25] The Georgia legislature had passed a resolution directing the state treasurer to accept only silver or gold, leaving Patrick Henry and the first Yazooists holding state scrip and other paper money of questionable value.

The South Carolina Company fought these decisions in court with no success. Their efforts to recover for breach of contract were frustrated by a Supreme Court decision holding that under the eleventh amendment to the United States Constitution, individuals could not sue states in federal court.[26]

Thomas Jefferson was not bashful about criticizing Henry as cheap and greedy.[27] Later, Jefferson wrote that Henry

engaged in the Yazoo speculation and bought up a great deal of depreciated paper at 2 and 2/6 on the pound to pay for it . . . The Georgia legislature having declared that transaction fraudulent and void, the depreciated paper he bought up to pay for the

Yazoo purchase was likely to remain on his hands worth nothing,
but Hamilton's funding system . . . came most opportunely to his
relief, and suddenly raised his paper from 2/6 to 27/6 to the pound.
Hamilton became his new idol.[28]

Henry's principal early biographer William Wirt acknowledged
that the old hero was not entirely free from censure in the Yazoo controversy. He opined without elaboration that "the Yazoo
proved not to be the fraudulent enterprise [for] which John Randolph of Roanoke would later excoriate on the floor of Congress
the guilty and allegedly guilty participants." Henry himself later
complained "of the interference with the sovereign right of the
state" and deception by the federal government.

According to Meade, "The land was subject to Indian title and the
company was to pay Georgia $93,750 within two years, including a
small payment at an early date in paper money. But the Georgia legislature drastically increased the terms of payment and the Virginia
Yazoo Company was unable to make a satisfactory adjustment."[29]

And so, Patrick Henry's dream of building an empire along the
Yazoo, free from financial rule by his old enemies the Federalists,
was over.

The Second Yazoo Land Sale

The second Yazoo land scandal in Georgia began in November
1794 when prominent Georgians and Pennsylvanians bid $250,000
(about $3 million today) "to purchase a part of the unlocated [sic]
territory of the state." There were four companies in all. The Georgia
Company was led by Georgia's United States Senator James Gunn.
The Georgia-Mississippi Company, the Upper Mississippi Company,
and the Tennessee Company were controlled by Georgia and Pennsylvania speculators. These included Pennsylvanian Robert Morris,
who was also involved in the Pine Barrens speculation; Representative Thomas P. Carnes of Georgia; Representative Robert Goodloe
Harper of South Carolina; and James Wilson, a justice of the Supreme Court of the United States. Wilson reportedly carried about

$25,000 in bribe money to Georgia when efforts to obtain the second Yazoo land grant began.[30]

United States Senator James Gunn of Georgia may have had advance inside information that Spain would soon surrender all claims to the Yazoo tracts. It is known that the next year the French ambassador advised his government that James Gunn was one of two United States senators bribed to approve the Jay Treaty.[31]

Eventually virtually the entire Georgia legislature was bribed for passing the Act of January 5, 1795, granting the speculators 3.5 million acres. This was about two-thirds of Georgia's western lands, sold for $500,000, about $6 million today. Cash bribes or stock in the grantee companies reportedly ranged from $600 to $1,000. An investigation the next year revealed that land grant bribes varied from 56,000 to 112,000 acres for each legislator involved.[32] One scholar claims that "when one representative, Thomas Raburn, was jokingly criticized for selling his vote for a mere $600 while his colleagues were getting $1,000, he blandly replied that 'it showed he was easily satisfied and was not greedy.'"[33]

Governor George Mathews signed the second Yazoo land grant bill on January 7, 1795, after vetoing a virtually identical bill the prior month.[34] There is no direct evidence that he was bribed.

When the public learned what had happened, Gunn was burned in effigy in several locations across Georgia. The legislature and the governor were promptly thrown out of office.[35]

Traditional accounts relate that Georgia voters rose as one in opposition to the second Yazoo sale. Their leader was James Jackson (1757-1806), a wily, hot-tempered duelist and land speculator then serving with Gunn as Georgia's other United States senator. Jackson had migrated from England to Savannah, Georgia, in about 1772, served as a militia officer and at age twenty-three killed the lieutenant governor in an "affair of honor." Later, in 1802 he dueled with Colonel Robert Watkins, one of the few Georgia legislators who voted for the 1795 Yazoo sale without being bribed, buttressing his reputation as the "Prince of Savannah duelists."[36]

Jackson did not initially challenge the sale. In fact, about twenty days after the second Yazoo grant was approved by the Georgia legislature, he asked the United States Senate to support a treaty with the occupying tribes to extinguish their titles to such lands. Jackson also remained silent in early March of the next year when President Washington sent a message to Congress warning of potential conflicts between the Indians and the Yazoo settlers.[37]

Perhaps this was so because there were practical reasons to initially acquiesce in the second Yazoo sale, however tainted by bribery. The second group of speculators who purchased the Yazoo tracts had to compete for title not only with the Native Americans in possession but also with Spain, which also claimed the land. Henry Adams noted in his *History of the United States of America* that "the State would have been *fortunate* to make it a free gift to any authority strong enough to deal with the Creeks and the Cherokees."[38]

Yet by late March 1795, Jackson reversed course and became an activist who opposed the second Yazoo sale, perhaps as a favor to John Wereat, who had acted as Jackson's legal guardian in his youth. Wereat had outbid the Gunn group by $300,000 for the Yazoo tracts late in the process, but his bid was rejected, supposedly because the successful Yazooists provided better security.

Faced with serious opposition and ruination, the second Yazooists and their purchasers turned to Alexander Hamilton. His legal opinion, published in March 1795, argued that "every grant from one to another, whether the grantor be a state or an individual is essentially a contract." Hamilton also contended that a legislature could not revoke the grant without impairing a contract protected by Article X, Section 1, of the United States Constitution, even if the grant were procured by corruption or bribery.[39]

Senator James Jackson was not intimidated. Despite his own record as a land promoter, Jackson famously railed against "the vile Yazoo speculation." He also led efforts to defeat legislators who had voted for it. Jackson was elected to the Georgia legislature in November 1795. He immediately attacked the "Tories, Federalists and land grabbers" involved and engineered legislative repeal of the Yazoo land sale law signed by the new Georgia governor on February 13, 1796.[40] After the repeal bill was signed later that month, the original and every copy of the bill granting the second Yazoo land grant was burned in Louisville, a small town near Augusta which then served as the Georgia state capital. John Randolph, a young student from Roanoke, Virginia, visiting a schoolmate was among the crowd that watched the fire.[41]

Years later, one observer noted that rescission of the second Yazoo sale by the Georgia legislature did not cause "disillusionment but a fresh round of speculation over whether or not the new [federal] government would rescue investors by backing up the rescinded scrip."[42]

Clearly, this provided a battleground for Federalists largely based in New England and their Jeffersonian opponents whose political support was more broadly based. Most Federalists opposed the Georgia repeal of the second Yazoo sale on general principle. They placed a strong value on property rights and opposed the right of state legislatures to declare previously passed laws unconstitutional. The Anti-Federalists on the other hand were more geographically broad in popular support and believed that the Yazoo land sale repeal was a legitimate expression of popular will by a sovereign independent state.[43] Although George Washington was a Federalist, he was concerned that the Yazoo sale might affect relations with the Indian tribes in the territory as well as Spain. He suggested in 1795 that the United States Senate should investigate the legality of the sale.[44]

The Pine Barrens Scandal (1794)

At about the same time, the Pine Barrens land scandal of 1794 was perpetrated by a second group of speculators, which included Robert Morris, a signer of the Declaration of Independence and delegate to the Constitutional Convention from Pennsylvania. Morris and his North American Land Company sold sandy, barren acreages in Georgia to fellow Northerners and European purchasers. Such promises were satirized by one wag, who distributed a circular (flyer) offering "ten millions of acres of valuable pine barren land . . . for gentlemen of the speculative class."[45]

The Pine Barrens fraud was never resolved. Generations later, descendants of the Pine Barrens purchasers searched in vain for the "land traversed by streams and clothed with oak, walnut and hickory trees" that had been promised.[46]

The Third Yazoo Land Sale (1796)

Meanwhile, in February 1796, the very day the second Yazoo land sale was nullified in Georgia, in a "wave of gullibility," the New England Mississippi Company purchased most of the Yazoo holdings of the Georgia Mississippi Company for $1,138,000 (about $14 million today), representing a 650 percent profit on the Georgians' original investment. Most of the New England Mississippi Land Company investors lived in and around Boston. They had no idea that the title of their sellers had been invalidated. The land in question covered eleven million acres in the southwest section of the Yazoo tract.[47]

Not all of the third Yazooists were in Boston. Abraham Bishop was a Connecticut lawyer who initially lost his Yazoo investment when the Georgia legislature nullified the sale. Abraham, his father, and seven other Connecticut residents purchased 550,000 acres of Yazoo land from Georgia speculators. The Abrahams acquired 200,000 acres of these lands for $4,000 in cash and $12,000 in promissory notes, none of which they were able to recover in litigation. Although Abraham recovered about $5,700 from the federal government on his claim in 1818, his principal contribution to the controversy was a pamphlet entitled *Georgia Speculation Unveiled*, which he published in October 1797. In a precursor to Woody Guthrie's Depression-era lament that some men will "rob you with a fountain pen,"[48] Abraham described the Georgia land speculators as

> aiming with feathers [pens] to cut throats and on parchments to seal destruction—*these are the robbers of modern days*—They bring desolation among our farmers—they spread distress in our towns—they scorn the paltry plunder of pocket books, and watches—they aim at houses and lands—strike at the foundation of many generations—and would destroy families root and branch.

Formerly, the enemies of man frequented the public roads—put pistols to the breasts of unsuspecting travelers and robbed them of the valuables they had about them; but the sufferers could return to their houses and lands, and by industry repair the loss. We live to see robbery in a more refined style. Men who never add an iota to the wealth or morals of the world . . . aiming to cut throats.[49]

The third Yazooists deftly swapped horses in 1800, when the Federalists led by Alexander Hamilton had been defeated by Thomas Jefferson and the Republicans, the political ancestors of the modern Democrat party.

Two years later, Georgia finally ceded its western lands to the United States for $1,250,000, but five million acres were reserved to resolve the Yazoo land scandal claims.[50] The third Yazooists were on the verge of having their claims resolved, but were opposed by Representative John Randolph of Roanoke, Virginia, who years before as a student had watched the hated 1795 Yazoo land grant documents burned in Louisville, Georgia.

Randolph's philosophy was a curious mixture of agrarian and elitist principles. Having acquired large estates himself, he opposed the Yazooists' efforts to acquire large parts of Alabama and Mississippi, characterizing them as financial capitalists. He also opposed federal recognition of the original Yazoo claims as contrary to the right of the Georgia legislature to repeal the second sale as a matter of state's rights. And of course about three-fifths of the New Yazooists were based in New England, not Virginia.

Randolph was as picturesque in opposition to the New Yazooists as James Gunn had been as their leader and advocate. Tradition says both Randolph and Gunn enjoyed carrying formidable whips about during legislative sessions for dramatic effect.[51] Although nominally a Jefferson administration ally, Randolph blocked the indemnification of the New Yazooists' investments—tacitly approved by the Jefferson administration—after a colorfully savage floor flight featuring challenges to duels and fisticuffs.[52]

In 1805, while charges of bribery floated around Congress, efforts to compensate the third Yazooists floundered. Georgia Senator James Jackson was the most prominent Anti-Yazooist, but he had acquiesced in negotiations between the federal government and Georgia as an accommodation to Thomas Jefferson. Despite this situation, efforts to obtain compensation failed in four consecutive sessions of Congress, in votes largely divided along sectional lines. The third Yazooists were persistent, since they held questionable title to about 10.5 million acres, for which they paid about seven times as much as had the original purchasers.[53]

The Yazooists Go to Court

The conflict between Yazooists who favored the sale and Anti-Yazooists who opposed it was finally resolved in *Fletcher v. Peck*, the first decision in which the Supreme Court of the United States ruled that a state law violated the United States Constitution.[54] The case had started as a friendly 1803 lawsuit that was dormant for three years in Massachusetts. The litigants were New Hampshire investor Robert Fletcher and Bostonian John Peck from whom Fletcher had purchased Yazoo land.

One scholar described it as a contrived case, "constructed in such a way to test every single question of interest to the New England Yazooists."[55] After a jury handed down a nearly undecipherable special verdict requesting assistance from the two sitting judges, the federal circuit court ruled for the seller John Peck in October 1807. The court decided that Georgia's title to the Yazoo land had been good, the 1795 sale was valid, and the subsequent legislative repeal was not.

When the case was first argued to the Supreme Court of the United States in early 1809, John Peck and the Yazooist interests were represented by John Quincy Adams, former president of the United States, in his last appearance there before the *Amistad* slave ship controversy. Luther Martin of Maryland represented the buyer Robert Fletcher, who claimed he had been sold an invalid title. Martin was an early Anti-Federalist who had switched sides and appeared regularly before the Supreme Court. The Supreme Court first reversed the decision on a technicality on March 11. Fletcher and Peck avoided having the matter returned to the circuit court by entering a stipulation that some have insisted was highly unusual and suggests collusion.[56] When the case was reargued in 1810, John Quincy Adams had been replaced by Joseph Story, whose in-laws were New England Yazooists. The buyer Robert Fletcher was represented by Luther Martin, who appeared so drunk that the chief justice adjourned the proceedings so that Martin could regain his sobriety—the only known such incident in the history of the Supreme Court.[57]

The high court ruled that Peck had conveyed good title, speaking through Chief Justice John Marshall on March 16, 1810. The court rationale was largely consistent with a legal opinion written by Alexander Hamilton in 1795, a similar view expressed by John Goodloe Harper the next year, an argument Harper made in Congress during the 1798 session, and two substantially similar state court decisions.[58] The court specifically ruled that state legislation could not be overturned by state courts merely because the legislation had been obtained by bribery, further noting that "if the original transaction was infected with fraud, these purchasers did not participate in it." Finally, the court ruled that the Georgia repeal act violated the provision of the United States Constitution prohibiting "the impairment of obligations of contracts."[59]

Any Yazooist who believed he would get speedy justice following this 1810 Supreme Court decision was surely disappointed. Since the eccentric John Randolph had been brought home by Virginia voters in 1812, only Representative George Troup of Georgia stood in prominent opposition to efforts of the Yazooists to obtain compensation two years later, warning in March 1814:

> Do not believe, sir, that the corruption in which this transaction was engendered was a corruption of the ordinary character; it was a corruption without example in history; may it never find a parallel! Not merely were the corrupted by corrupters—the corrupters cheated the corrupted—the corrupters cheated one another, and the corrupters . . . cheated these claimants.[60]

In spite of such eloquence Troup lost. A compensation bill was passed by Congress and signed by President James Madison in early 1814. Thus, Yazoo claims originally purchased for $500,000 were settled by the government for $4.3 million, largely with speculators who had bought the claims at a deep discount.[61]

President James Madison signed the Yazoo compensation bill into law on March 31, 1814. Under the terms of the legislation, the Yazoo claimants largely centered in New England were required to file documents releasing their claims for $5 million in U.S. stock certificates financed by the sale of the five million acres reserved under the 1802 agreement between Georgia and the federal government. The Yazooists who preferred land could then trade their U.S. stock certificates for land in the new Mississippi Territory. The $4.2 million disbursements made from the $5 million compensation fund included about $1 million paid to the New England Mississippi Land Company for the benefit of its shareholders. Individual awards included $2,857 to George Blake, $67,104 to Samuel Dexter, $14,880 to William Sullivan, $13,771 to Samuel Sewell, and $9,150 to the estate of James Sullivan.[62]

The scope of the swindle was enormous. The second Yazoo land sale still stands as the largest land fraud in American history. Beyond this fact, in the opinion of one historian, the Yazoo scandal "left many in the South with a deep hatred of the federal government and an equally deep yearning for secession from the United States."

None of this controversy benefited two of the most prominent early Georgia land speculators. Like John Law, the promoter of the Mississippi Bubble who had to flee from Paris to Venice in 1720, Robert Morris, "the financier of the Revolution," found himself in distress when his Pine Barrens scheme collapsed. After barricading himself in his Philadelphia mansion he was eventually frog-marched off to the Prune Street debtor's prison. He died a free but financially destitute man in 1806.[63]

Patrick Henry might have taken some comfort from this matter had he lived long enough. However, in 1799, seven years before Robert Morris died, the old patriot took one last chance, at least according to one biographer. While seriously ill, Patrick Henry was offered a dose of liquid mercury, which his doctor believed would either kill him or prolong his life. He prayed, drank the concoction, and promptly lost the wager.[64]

CHAPTER 8

P. T. Barnum:
Godfather of the Frontier Swindlers

*I don't believe in duping the public, but I believe
in first attracting and then pleasing them.*[1]

—P. T. Barnum

The mark was prosperous beyond his wildest childhood dreams. He had relied on audacity and the latest advertising innovations to rise from the streets of New York to one of America's great fortunes. He became the first millionaire—yet he was clipped in a land swindle that he never saw coming, just after being taken by a wastrel cousin for $46,000.

He had signed some $500,000 in promissory notes for his business partner in a plan to transform some vacant land into a thriving metropolis—or so he thought, before learning that he had been taken for eleven million dollars in today's money. The sucker was Phineas Taylor Barnum of Bridgeport, Connecticut. And for the moment, he was bankrupt.

Barnum saw little of the American West as we know it today, but he was the godfather of the confidence men who plied their trade on the frontier. Among his contemporaries were four dour Californians who built the Central Pacific railroad east to Promontory, Utah, and connected with the Union Pacific, creating the transcontinental railroad. They also bilked the federal government out of millions of dollars in overstated mileage and construction costs. Naturally, they kept most of the profits for themselves.

Barnum started his career as a storekeeper, as had all of the Big Four—the former peddlers and frontier merchants who had built the Central Pacific as quickly as possible to maximize profits.

Charles Crocker, Mark Hopkins, Collis P. Huntington, and Leland Stanford had one thing in common with P. T. Barnum and many Western entrepreneurs—supreme confidence.

At the dawn of the nineteenth century, Timothy Dwight, the president of Yale University, wrote that "men who begin life . . .bargaining for small wares will almost invariably become sharpers [swindlers]."[2] This description easily fits P. T. Barnum, today remembered largely as a circus and museum owner.

An Age of American Confidence

Barnum began his professional life at age fifteen as a storekeeper and lottery peddler in Bethel, Connecticut, carrying on a tradition started by his well-to-do grandfather, lottery entrepreneur Phineas Taylor. By 1828, young Barnum was engaged full time in the lottery. Barnum claimed later that he clipped suckers for five hundred to two thousand dollars each day at the "Temple of Fortune," his grandfather's carriage house that the young entrepreneur used rent-free.

About five years later, the poet-journalist Walt Whitman described Barnum as an engaging character with "flashing gray eyes." He was of medium height and struggled with portliness his whole life. And although Barnum never said, "There's a sucker born every minute," a maxim probably uttered by notorious confidence man Joseph "Paper Collar Joe" Bessimer, he easily might have.[3]

While one biographer saw Barnum as "one of the outstanding figures of our national life," another saw him as a "brash huckster."[4] Still another said Barnum "seemed the supreme symbol . . . of his age, independent, successful and audacious." One of his fondest biographers recognized one secret of his success. "He used deceit and exaggeration, deception and disguise to make his fortune." Little wonder then, that Barnum labeled himself the Prince of Humbugs early in his career after "a succession of spectacular frauds he foisted upon his gullible patrons."[5]

His own description of "humbug" was telling. Barnum defined

it as putting on glittering appearances so as "to suddenly arrest public attention and the public eye and ear."[6] It is no surprise then that shameless hoaxes perpetrated by Barnum early in his career helped make him famous.

Barnum's Four Frauds

He first learned of Joice Heth, "the 161-year-old nursemaid of George Washington," in 1835. Soon Barnum traveled to Philadelphia, where he watched her entertain visitors with stories about "dear little George." He was so impressed that he decided to start a new venture. Barnum promptly sold his interest in a New York store he owned with John Moody, whose grandson founded Moody's Investment Service. The twenty-five-year-old was on his way to a new career.[7]

Barnum had learned from exhibitor R. W. Lindsey that Heth's owners, the Bowling family of Kentucky, had discovered a bill of sale dated February 5, 1727, in the Virginia Records Office. According to the document, Augustine Washington had sold fifty-four-year-old Joice Heth (Heath) to a sister-in-law. Barnum examined the bill of sale and promptly talked Lindsey into selling him twelve months of exhibition rights for $1,000, far from the $3,000 Lindsey had asked.[8]

Barnum began his first exhibit in New York, and then took Heth on a New England tour. When the audiences did not meet expectations, he spread the rumor that she was an automaton; crowds of earlier visitors began filling a concert hall at Boston to see if they had been swindled. When Joice died on the road unexpectedly on February 19, 1836, Barnum had her examined by a prominent New York physician who declared she was no more than eighty years old. No matter, Barnum had realized at least $10,000, worth about $200,000 today, during the brief tour.

Barnum later told at least two versions of his role in the Joice Heth swindle. He once supposedly confessed to the English journalist Albert Smith that he had concocted her story himself. Barnum told Smith that he even aged and forged the bill of sale.[9] His second story, published some six years later, claimed that Barnum himself was defrauded by the original exhibitor. Whatever the truth, Barnum launched his career with this exhibit by using newly invented lighted transparencies to publicize Joice as a "facile conversationalist." After her death, Joice was buried in a lost, long-forgotten pauper's grave at Bethel, Connecticut. R. W. Lindsey eventually fell into obscurity.

Not so the "Feejee Mermaid" that Barnum discovered in 1842. Today, the mermaid supposedly resides in the Peabody Museum of Archeology and Ethnology at Harvard University, although some believe she was filched by a Franciscan friar in 1950.[10] Her provenance was even more questionable than her current whereabouts. A British sea captain supposedly embezzled $6,000 from his employer in 1817 to purchase her in Calcutta, and then spent the rest of his life repaying debts incurred in a disastrous European exhibition tour.

Barnum learned about the mermaid from Moses Kimball, who owned the Boston Museum and supposedly purchased it from the sea captain's son. The specimen was undoubtedly a monkey's head sewed on the body of a fish—a real crowd-pleaser, which had been seen ten years earlier in Charles Willson Peale's American Museum at Philadelphia.

Kimball and Barnum often exchanged exhibits, information, and advice. The Boston impresario agreed on June 18, 1842, to give Barnum exclusive use of the mermaid for as many as eight weeks at $12.50 per week, at which time it would be returned to Kimball for twelve weeks. After that, the two men were to share profits for up to two years of exhibits.

Soon after this agreement was signed, New York newspapers began to receive curious letters from places as far away as Montgomery, Alabama. They reported that a Dr. Griffin of London was progressing through the United States toward New York with a "veritable mermaid captured in the Feejee [Fiji] Islands." Dr. Griffin was none other than Barnum's assistant Levi Lyman.[11]

The mermaid that arrived in New York was hardly the buxom

beauty depicted in the eight-foot transparency just outside the American Museum. Barnum himself described the mermaid later as "ugly" and "dried up," carefully neglecting to mention her origins. Even so, she thrilled most New York audiences, although some skeptical medical students secretly placed a cigar in her mouth. Southern journalists found her far less captivating when she appeared in Charleston, South Carolina. The mermaid was secretly shipped back to New York, exhibited years later on April Fools' Day in 1855, and then placed in storage.[12]

Barnum first began exhibiting "Colonel Fremont's Woolly Horse" while the famed Western explorer John C. Fremont was briefly missing during a late 1848 expedition into the Rocky Mountains. The showman claimed the animal was an admixture of sheep, deer, horse, buffalo, and camel ancestry capable of leaping high in the air. Barnum had the woolly horse displayed in Washington, DC, until Fremont's father-in-law, Senator Thomas Hart Benton of Missouri, had Barnum's exhibitor arrested for taking money under false pretences.[13]

Barnum's fourth and perhaps his most audacious fraud was the Cardiff Giant, a "petrified man" that he "discovered" more than two decades later in 1870.

The Confidence Man: Prince of Swindlers

The first known mention of a confidence man in America appeared in the July 8, 1849, *New York Herald,* which reported that one William Thompson, late of Sing Sing prison, "would go up to a perfect stranger in the street, and being a man of genteel appearance, would easily command an interview." After a brief conversation, Thompson would simply ask, "Have you confidence in me to trust me with your watch until tomorrow?" A Mr. Thomas McDonald of No. 276 Madison Street lost his $110 gold watch to Thompson in William Street, on May 12, only to encounter the swindler that July 7 in Liberty Street. Thompson was frog-marched off to the Tombs prison where he was lost to history.

Herman Melville popularized the term "Confidence Man" as the title of his last novel, which was set in the American West. The book was released during the financial Panic of 1857, two years after P. T. Barnum published the first version of his autobiography. During a time when most banks would not even honor their own notes, Melville described a mysterious, anonymous stranger who boarded a Mississippi River boat on April Fools' Day, then, like William Thompson nine years earlier, asked a series of victims for signs of "confidence" in one of several disguises, including, appropriately enough, that of a stockbroker.

The "First Consul" of Counterfeiters

Stephen Burroughs would have been completely comfortable in the world Melville described, perhaps even as an exhibit huckster, like P. T. Barnum. He was a counterfeiter, land speculator, and scholar who published his best-selling memoir in 1798, twelve years before P. T. Barnum was born. Seducer, counterfeiter, trickster—Burroughs was all of that and more. He lived and worked on two frontiers. Burroughs frequented the disputed border between Canada and Vermont only thirty years after the Declaration of Independence was proclaimed and also explored the new frontier of economic freedom. America was then a place with burgeoning markets, little governmental control, and even less gold and silver available for business transactions—a perfect environment for counterfeiters.

Years later, a Vermont sheriff named Mike Barron wrote of how he stormed Burroughs' house in Canada during the spring of 1806 and then trundled the counterfeiter off to Montreal, only to have Burroughs escape in November.

Burroughs' widely distributed 1798 autobiography described his early years. He was the son of a New Hampshire Presbyterian minister who sent him to Dartmouth, but only briefly. Burroughs' real calling was confidence games. He first posed as a physician, but then became a minister, using a set of canned sermons stolen from his own father. His first congregation was in Pelham,

Massachusetts, where Burroughs used the Sunday collection to fund an alchemist who claimed he could convert copper into silver. Burroughs tried to recoup his losses in this scam by partnering with Glazier Wheeler, whose coin counterfeiting skills left something to be desired. Burroughs tried to pass Wheeler's coins in Springfield, Massachusetts, but was captured and imprisoned until 1788. He was released, married a cousin, then dallied with young female students while he was supposed to be teaching and was forced to flee south.

He found employment in Georgia with the Philadelphia financier Robert Morris during the Yazoo land speculations discussed earlier. Somehow, Burroughs had accumulated enough money to loan some to his employer, who promptly went bankrupt when a crooked lawyer took the Morris investment and fled. And with this reversal of fortune, Burroughs turned back to making money—this time, with his own equipment.

Burroughs operated in the wild country north of Vermont known then as Lower Canada. His reputation as an early American outlaw prompted one wag to describe him as "just another banker."[14]

The spring after he was captured by Sheriff Barron, Burroughs was robbed of $53,000 in printed money—legitimate or otherwise—by Canadian bounty hunter Oliver Barker, who carried a commission as a justice of the peace. Eventually, Burroughs had Oliver arrested on bogus charges, but was himself captured after two successful jailbreaks. Burroughs died a free man in 1840, the year before P. T. Barnum purchased the New American Museum in New York in a bid for legitimacy. Curiously, in Britain and most of Europe, counterfeiting had long been considered treason.

Posters and circulars widely distributed in England often proclaimed, "To counterfeit is death." However, in America, the law was more lenient, in part because the United States Constitution defined treason very narrowly.[15] This was very lucky for the kind of confidence men Melville wrote about.

Many of Melville's readers were probably familiar with a cheap pamphlet called a "counterfeit detector" with which his "mysterious stranger" and thousands of Americans tried to analyze doubtful bank notes and avoid traps laid by men like Burroughs. When Melville's character decided that the authenticity of the notes was "*kind of uncertain,*" most readers in 1857 would have hardly blinked an eye.[16]

The issuance of bad bank money was a regrettable yet perhaps necessary boost to the development of a vibrant, emerging economy as Americans moved west. Confidence was then "the indispensable basis . . . of business transactions," at least according to Melville's mysterious stranger. John Neal, a merchant of that era, would have agreed. He once remarked that in his experience, counterfeit bills, if discovered, "were always put back in the till."[17]

The Panic of 1837 twenty years before publication of *The Confidence Man* started when banks in New York City suspended payments on their notes, while nearby Barnum began shamelessly touting "George Washington's Nursemaid." Over a quarter of then-existing banks in the young United States failed. Former President John Quincy Adams considered currency swindlers a better sort than bank directors, noting that at least counterfeiters showed "evidence of superior skill and . . . modesty . . . the counterfeiter at least does his work in the dark, while the suspenders of species payments [bankers] are brazen in the face of day."[18] Gold and silver specie became so rare that tradesman began printing their own money, helping to erode the already shaky distinction between genuine bank notes and fraudulent currency.

Books and pamphlets listing characteristics of counterfeit money had first become available a few years before the 1837 Panic, but were somewhat unreliable. One canal boat passenger that year carefully consulted a "counterfeit detector" like one described later by Melville to change a five-dollar note, only to be arrested later for passing it.[19]

This was nothing new. Practically from the very beginning, American bankers often tolerated known counterfeit money. In 1818, one newspaper editor remarked that "we seem about to become *a nation of counterfeiters.*"[20]

The Original Wildcatters

I didn't have much else to do, so I rented an empty store build-
ing and printed 'bank' on the window. The first day I was open
a businessman came in and deposited one hundred dollars. The
second day another deposited two hundred fifty dollars and so
along the third day I got confidence enough in the bank to put in
a hundred myself.[21]

In the early years of the American republic, counterfeit money
typically came from one of two sources. Fictitious banks such as
the notorious "Merchant Bank of Utica" existed only in the criminal underworld; wildcat banks were located in remote areas just to
make the exchange of bank paper for gold or silver difficult, if not
impossible.[22] The term "wildcat bank" entered the American cul-
ture in the 1830s, describing any bank "that did not have anywhere
near enough gold or silver specie on hand to redeem its outstanding notes."[23] During that era, the sheer number of wildcat and non-
existent banks on whom notes were printed blurred practically all
distinctions between legitimate banking and outright fraud.[24]

The Kirtland Anti-Bank: A Rank Wildcat

The Kirtland Safety Society Bank of Kirtland, Ohio, was not
intended to be a wildcat bank but became one soon after it was
founded by Mormon leader Joseph Smith.

Prior to 1836, Smith had borrowed $15,000 and was extended
credit for another $60,000 in goods. Starting a bank to liquidate
this debt was not an unusual strategy in those days. A historian
has noted that "because of frenetic land speculation in that era
. . . all that was required to start a bank in the West was an unlimited amount of nerve and the necessary capital to pay the en-
graver and printer for making the notes." One library association
chartered itself as a bank using its book collection as the only
collateral. Equity in the new Kirtland bank had been paid with
town lots generally valued at five to six times their normal value.[25]

Smith purchased bank note plates and paper for the Kirtland bank from a Philadelphia firm before his state banking charter had been approved by the Ohio legislature. Again, this was hardly a novel approach. Prior to the 1850s, in most states, when a bank went bankrupt, copies of the plates and dyes used to print bank notes were sold to the highest bidder, no questions asked.[26]

When the charter application was denied, Smith simply printed and issued notes for the "Kirtland Safety Society *Anti-Banking* Company," secured by overvalued real estate, which sank in value during the Panic of 1837. Later, Smith's enemies claimed that boxes in the bank labeled $1,000 each contained lead, sand, and even combustibles under a thin top layer of fifty-cent pieces.[27] Burroughs would have shrugged.

The First American Outlaws

Counterfeiters like Stephen Burroughs were among the first American folk heroes in the West, many years before Jesse James was born. "Long before the outlaws of the late nineteenth century seized the popular imagination, tales of individual counterfeiters became the [lens] through which people experiencing the market revolution could project their hopes, fears, anxieties, envy, and admiration."[28] One economic historian characterized early American confidence as "the engine of economic growth, the *mysterious sentiment* that permitted a country poor in specie [gold or silver] but rich in promises to create something from nothing."[29] The Brown family was good at that sort of thing.

The Boston Bankers

The American West of 1848 included much of the present-day South and Middle West, whose borderlands were often inhabited by counterfeiters; the most notable were brothers James and Daniel Brown Sr. of Boston, Ohio, near the Cuyahoga River.

These were tough men. In 1829, the year young P. T. Barnum started a newspaper, James was struck by lightning outside his general store, yet lived to tell the tale. Together with Canadian counterfeiters William Ashley and William G. Taylor, who each called themselves "Colonel," the Brown brothers became known as the Boston bankers. During the Panic of 1819, which had been caused by a run on the Second Bank of the United States, the fake currency issued by the Browns fared much better than some legitimate bank notes, since the Boston bankers cared enough to counterfeit notes from the very best and most stable banks.[30]

Thirteen years later, tragedy struck the Boston bankers. A failed counterfeiting venture in New Orleans left Daniel Brown Sr. imprisoned. After Daniel died in 1832, James became the premier counterfeiter of the West. His untimely death on a canal boat while traveling to a court hearing left only one Brown to carry on the family tradition.

Daniel Brown Jr. was only one of many counterfeiters who emerged in the California goldfields after fleeing St. Louis to avoid several indictments. He became "Tom Lacey" for his new ventures, which included ranching, storekeeping, and counterfeiting. He copied the bank notes of the State Bank of Missouri, a particular favorite with the many Missourians then in California seeking their fortunes. Brown traded worthless currency for a reported $100,000 and fled to the family home in Ohio, where he died of apparent consumption in January 1851, just before a delegation of justice-seeking miners arrived from California.[31] They disinterred poor Daniel for proof of death, and then skulked away.[32]

The Land of Speculation

Everybody is speculating and everything has become an object of speculation . . . from Maine to the Red River . . . The principal objects of speculation are those subjects which chiefly occupy the calculating minds of the Americans . . . cotton, land, city and town lots, banks and railroads.[33]

—Michael Chevalier, French economist traveling in America, 1834

Like many Easterners, Yale University president Timothy
Dwight was critical of the westward movement. He claimed that
expansion loosened people from settled values and divorced profit
from effort.[34] British and European observers noted that "the optimistic note of promise became the American note and confidence
became an icon of the developing society." These tendencies continued well into the twentieth century as one Florida land investment company officer noted in 1925, "Lots were bought from
blue prints. They look better that way. Then the buyer gets the
promoter's vision, can see the splendid curving boulevards, the
yacht basin, [and] the parks lined with leaning coconut trees."[35]

Despite the occasional bust, land speculation promoted westward expansion by tying up thousands of acres of tillable soil for
quick sales. "The large land companies could provide well-spotted
lands, transportation and credit for potential settlers." One researcher has noted that "for all their . . . unreliability, land speculators were important agents in the development of America."[36]

The historian Henry Brooks Adams, the son of Charles Francis Adams, would have agreed. Unlike the European travelers who
were outraged at the obvious lies and swindles of American land
boomers, Henry Adams recognized "how readily the new immigrants adopted the promoter's vision instead of feeling deceived."
He noted that within a moment *they saw the gold and jewels,
the summer cornfields and the glowing continent.*" He considered
these immigrant visions a creative force in American history.[37]

The currency counterfeiters and bank wildcatters also helped
develop the West. During the 1830s, land speculation was largely
fueled by an increase in the availability of bank notes from the
nearly six hundred banks then in operation, some of which were
even solvent.[38]

Among those often in the forefront of land speculation were the
Scots-Irish. Few Ulster Scots owned land. And landlords demanded compensation for improvements their tenants made. This experience in Northern Ireland hardened the traditional Scottish
belief that revolts against authority were morally justifiable and
that the principle of revolution could be applied by the individual

in civil disobedience. The Scots-Irish tended to move three or four times before settling permanently. In America, their initial push was to the western reaches of North and South Carolina. They carried the ability to combine efficient homesteading with the military skills needed to defend themselves. Appalachia was a maze from which the more adventurous broke out into Kentucky, Missouri, Texas, Colorado, and California.[39]

Taming the Great American Desert

The area now called the Great Plains, which stretches from Texas to the Canadian border and west to the Rockies, was promoted by speculators who organized into companies that began colonizing Kansas, Nebraska, and the Dakota Territories. Although the railroads were initially slow to develop the alternate sections they owned along their rights of way, the government could sell any sections in this checkerboard system once construction of the adjoining tracks was completed.

Westward movement was accelerated with the passage of the Homestead Act of 1862 even as the Civil War raged in the East. This law provided that a person twenty-one years of age or the head of a household could settle a quarter section of unoccupied public land and obtain a patent in five years. The homesteader could also purchase 160 acres at $1.25 per acre after six months. Former Confederate soldiers could apply for homesteads beginning in 1866.

Five years later, Clinton C. Hutchinson published his promotional gazette, *Resources of Kansas: Fifteen Years Experience,* which ridiculed the very concept of an American desert. "Many an eastern farmer would gladly turn the flocks and herds onto this desert," Hutchinson proclaimed.[40] The railroads were ready to sell their land and often cherry-picked the best, most optimistic comments available from recent settlers about cheap lands that produced abundant crops for their land promotion pamphlets.

Hutchinson's pamphlet also claimed that "railroads and telegrams . . . cause more frequent showers, perhaps by promoting

a more even distribution of magnetic forces." He also said that
planting trees and crops would increase rainfall. Perhaps this
claim would have seemed as ridiculous as it seems today were it
not for the similar opinion of Ferdinand V. Hayden, who was in
charge of the U.S. Geological Survey of the Territories.[41]

Sadly, farmers soon learned that although they could obtain
320 acres under the Preemption Act of 1841 or the Timber Cul-
ture Act of 1873, twice as much land was often needed for a profitable operation.

Worse still, a July drought in 1874 with temperatures reaching
110 degrees in some parts of Kansas drove many farmers back
East. Some stopped for a word or two with Henry Worrall, an Eng-
lishman whose primitive sketch *Drouthy Kansas* oozed abundant
fruit, corn, and other symbols of prosperity that had helped lure
thousands into the unrelenting prairie sun. He probably told very
few of his visitors that he had sketched *Drouthy Kansas* as a joke
for the entertainment of some friends. Many sodbusters had seen
the sketch in a late 1869 issue of *Kansas Farmer* used by railroads to promote westward migration. More than a few pilgrims
returning East claimed that Worrall's sketch had ruined them.[42]

Farmers who stayed but needed financing soon found that borrowing money was fraught with danger. Lenders often required
borrowers without final patent to their homesteads to offer their
livestock and crops as collateral. Banks were often little more than
merchants with safes and a little extra cash. The banker often discounted the note the farmer signed to borrow money by as much
as 10 percent, giving seventy cents on the dollar, while charging
12 percent interest for a five-year term. Little wonder then that in
a bad year more than a few farmers disappeared in the night with
their livestock, sometimes even taking their small cabins.[43]

Town Lot Fraud

Active town promotion was made possible by the Federal
Townsites Act of 1844, which allowed the sale of 320 acres for

each occupied townsite at $1.25 per acre. Organizers could establish a town company to buy the land and thereby obtain the rights to adjoining quarter sections for $1,400; these could then be sold when needed.

The story of three such townsites illustrates the fine line between town speculation and fraud. Oread, some forty-five miles west of Lawrence, Kansas, was planned by promoters before the townsite had even been identified. Several Lawrence businessmen discussing the news one winter day realized that town lot certificates were circulating just as freely as wildcat bank notes, secured by nothing more than hope. Once the town company was organized, shares sold briskly. Soon, three log cabins were located at the head of a creek, but later that year the Panic of 1857 swept little Oread away.[44]

Cities in the Mist

Some boosters did not bother with a mere town. "Between 1854 and 1857, many new towns in Nebraska and Kansas Territories had the word 'city' appended to their names to make them sound important . . . whether this really helped a town to grow and prosper is doubtful."[45]

The *Kansas Chief* published at White Cloud noted on June 4, 1857, that "there is scarcely a store or tavern in the Union in which there is not posted in a conspicuous place town plats of some large city in Kansas or Nebraska, a majority of which do not contain a single house." While traveling the plains about two years later, prominent Eastern journalist Horace Greeley observed, "It takes three log houses . . . to make a city in Kansas, but they begin calling it a city as soon as they have staked out the lots."[46]

Since the prospects for profit were high, many town promoters became wanderers looking for a quick sale and a fast horse. Some were able to take the money without breaking a single law, as did the promoters of Curlew, Nebraska, a registered townsite widely advertised in the Eastern states. Money was collected for town lots, but not a single settler traveled west and no homes were built, allowing the promoters to collect $150,000 at little cost. Worse yet, one Nebraska land promoter sold $120,000 in lots without registering the townsite, much less buying the land.[47]

Of course, some settlements survived hard times. Dodge City, Kansas, was one endangered cow town that simply refused to die when the expansion of railroads began to make cattle drives from Texas to Kansas less necessary. A *Dodge City Globe* editorialist commented in August 1885 that although land "could not be developed while it was held for stock ranges . . . the recent absorption of the public domain by settlers, the removal of the cattle trail and the rapidly disappearing cowboy have now thoroughly convinced our people that a permanent commercial metropolis at this [location] is demanded by the needs of the country."

Far and Away: Boomers, Sooners, and Land Grabbers

Oklahoma's frantic land runs expressed the last hurrah of the spirit that believed 'there's always something better beyond.'[48]

Five years before that *Dodge City Globe* editorialist expressed such unqualified optimism about the future, railroads and farm implement manufacturers began to promote settlement south of Dodge City in Indian Territory. They hired lawyers who gained the support of the *Wichita Eagle* in Kansas and organized prospective settlers in Kansas, Missouri, and Texas. David L. Payne, destined to become the most notorious squatter in Oklahoma, charged the "boomers" twelve dollars for a certificate guaranteeing future ownership of a quarter-section in Indian Territory. The boomers had established illegal settlements as far south as present-day Oklahoma City long before Payne died in 1884.

Finally, in 1889, President Benjamin Harrison ordered the first of seven land runs culminating eighteen years later in the new state of Oklahoma.[49] The first and most famous was called "Harrison's Horse Race." The last-chance event eleven years later liquidated Comanche, Kiowa, and Apache lands in present-day southwestern Oklahoma.

These land runs were conducted to distribute the lands not occupied by the Five Tribes—the Choctaws, Creeks, Cherokees, and Seminoles in eastern Indian Territory and the Chickasaw people west of the Choctaw Nation. Many years earlier, settlers in the present-day southeastern United States had deemed them "civilized" because of the relative speed with which they adapted American legal principles, social customs, and slavery.

Much of the land not occupied by the Five Tribes had been illegally leased for ranching years before, in a few rare instances with the best of intentions. The federal agent at the Kiowa-Comanche reservation signed such a lease in 1882 to sustain Indians receiving government rations that could no longer be supplemented by buffalo hunts.

Some boomers had invaded Indian Territory lands west of the Five Tribes long before 1880, prompting the creation of Oklahoma Territory ten years later. They were followed by Sooners—invaders who came in after the land runs were announced, but before the starting pistol was fired. Years later, historians noted that the land runs west of the Five Tribes set the stage for some of the most blatant land frauds in the making of the American West.

The Dawes Commission was established in 1893 to negotiate the sale of Choctaw, Chickasaw, Creek, Cherokee, and Seminole lands. Non-Indian occupants of town lots were allowed to purchase them outright at a fraction of their value. This encouraged speculators to dig a well or plant a single tree as an "improvement" allowing purchase at low prices. For example, a 2,383-acre tract within Muskogee, then one of the larger communities in Indian Territory, was appraised at $238,835 for purposes of sale, but was worth $1,584,788 two years later. Such opportunities encouraged fraudulent dummy purchases of multiple town lots, using individuals who promptly conveyed the lots to pre-arranged purchasers.

The Dawes Commission officials generally avoided self-dealing, with one very significant exception. Investigations in 1903 confirmed the earlier complaints of the tribes that the Dawes Commission chairman and "nearly all Federal employees in Indian Territory were purchasing town lots."[50] Also, white settlers were often allowed to buy and sell town lots in the name of non-resident relatives.[51]

The Creeks had little success stopping such sales. After years of litigation, only twenty-seven lots in Muskogee and twenty-two lots in Tulsa were recovered—nearly thirty years after the sales.[52]

Guardianships presented good opportunities for mostly non-Indian speculators to obtain oil or timber interests cheaply. One scheme stopped by Choctaw attorneys would have resulted in a single individual obtaining guardianship over 350 children whose timber holdings could have been liquidated. Other young Indian allottees were the victims of forgery, kidnapping, or worse at the hands of speculators seeking oil-bearing lands around Tulsa. Two black children were murdered as they slept so that speculators could secure their oil interests in the fabled Glenn Pool field near Tulsa. Equally disturbing, a number of Choctaws died shortly after deeding their land to dealers in exchange for life pensions.

And north of Tulsa, Osage Indians were sometimes murdered for their oil royalties. Between 1902 and 1936, the Osage Nation and its members received $252 million under a unique arrangement. The Osage collectively owned their subsurface mineral rights and received quarterly payments for their leases. Each man, woman, and child of the original 2,229 individuals on the tribal roll had a share or "head right," which in 1923 was worth $13,200. [53]Average Osage families of that decade collected $69,000 in royalties annually, which would be an annual income of almost $750,000 today. Thus the Osage became the richest Indians in the world, and new targets for exploitation and murder.

Among the worst of the predators was William K. "Bill" Hale, who plotted to acquire Osage Indian property by killing the relatives of Mollie Burkhart, his nephew's wife. Hale apparently planned to then kill Mollie herself and perhaps even his nephew, Ernest Burkhart. In all, at least five Osage were killed before Hale and Ernest Burkhart were convicted. Hale lived to the ripe old age of eighty-eight.[54]

The Prisoner of Wilshire Boulevard

Another swindling victim of sorts was simple-minded Jackson Barnett, a three-quarter-blood Creek who had been allotted some of the worst farmland in the Creek Nation.

Jackson Barnett sitting, looking like his true self (Research Division of the Oklahoma Historical Society)

When his rock-rich allotment turned out to be smack-dab in the middle of the oil-rich Cushing field, Barnett became "the World's Richest Indian." During the Teapot Dome scandal covered in a later chapter, Department of the Interior Secretary Albert Fall split a million dollars of Barnett's assets between the Indian's young fortune-hunting wife and a favorite Harding administration charity, in January 1923.

Shortly thereafter, the Barnetts departed for Los Angeles, where Jackson Barnett spent much of his time pretending to direct traffic in front of his swanky mansion on Wilshire Boulevard. Fifteen years later, Jackson's gold-digging widow was tear-gassed out of the place, but only after she brandished a hatchet and tried to kill one of the law officers sent to evict her.

Los Angeles: A City of Oil and Water

Such antics were hardly novel in Los Angeles, whose very transition from a remote, dusty village to major metropolis was promoted with an underhanded water swindle. Some of the richest men in California, notably including railroad magnate Henry Huntington of Union Pacific fame, became known as the San Fernando Valley Ring after optioning some 16,000 dry acres there in 1905 for next to nothing. They had inside information about a simple plan then underway that would make the San Fernando Valley bloom.

Farmers in water-rich Owens Valley, some 250 miles north of Los Angeles, were persuaded to surrender their water rights to the United States Bureau of Reclamation for a local water development project. Instead, the Bureau of Reclamation allowed the Owens Valley water to be pipelined south to Los Angeles. Had this not happened, the City of Angels might not have grown beyond a population of 250,000.[55]

A good supply of water had been critical to the growth of that early oil boomtown. Albert Fall's patron and early New Mexico mining associate Edward L. Doheny, whom we shall meet again in a later chapter, was the first oil prospector to successfully challenge the quirky geology in Southern California. He had noticed local Hispanics using oily chucks of tar they called *brea* to waterproof wood and lubricate machinery.

Doheny leased a vacant lot in East Los Angeles and promptly hand dug his first oil well to 155 feet. Since no oil spurted up, he whittled the end of a eucalyptus tree into a point, scratched his way down another 300 feet, and brought in the first Los Angeles gusher on November 4, 1892.

The boom was on. Eventually, oil was found in two other residential developments. Huntington Beach had been so unattractive that local door-to-door hucksters would give potential customers a vacant lot there if they bought a set of encyclopedias. Some of these lots became oil leases.

Oil was also found in 1921 at Santa Fe Springs, a neighborhood some twelve miles from downtown Los Angeles. Canadian Courtney C. Julian used the Santa Fe Springs oil field to raise thousands of dollars in $100 units under the "common law trust" scheme first developed in the Texas oil fields. This system had virtually none of the safeguards afforded common shareholders. In the beginning no one seemed to care.

The Sucker Tent

Los Angeles became a haven for oil stock swindlers. Department of Justice investigators later estimated that these confidence men were netting as much as $100,000 each week, using old tricks that had been perfected during the mining frauds of bygone days.

The Julian promotions were unique in that they catered to the concerns and prejudices of small investors afraid of being taken by confidence men and corporations. Julian rightly boasted to gullible buyers that he had "no boards of directors at fat salaries to juggle [take] your profits." This was true enough—in the early years, he had no directors at all.[56]

Other swindlers were not quite so concerned about public relations. A worse-than-average oil well could be transformed into a

Barnett struck oil on his land (Research Division of the Oklahoma Historical Society)

Jackson Barnett all dressed up (Western History Collection, University of Oklahoma)

gusher by connecting a small pipe to an air compressor. Worse, Southern California real estate promotion techniques relying on tent shows and a free lunch offered to tourists arriving in Los Angeles were promptly adopted for use in oil field confidence games. The chumps gawked at Los Angeles "oil mansions" from buses later driven through thriving oil fields and beyond to marginal prospects represented as being "in the heart of the oil field." Busy, well-attended Sunday shows featured brass bands, airplanes, and even parachute jumps.

When the slaughter of the lambs began, $100 units could be purchased in installments, much like time shares sometimes are today, often with a 5 percent down payment.

The Julian technique differed from many of these run-of-the-mill swindles in its cautionary tone, which eventually made Julian "the king of the sucker tents." His newspaper advertisement headlines sometimes screamed: *Julian refuses to accept your money unless you can afford to lose! Widows and orphans, this is no investment for you.*

The first Julian promotion netted him $600,000. After five months, he had netted nearly one million dollars in sales. His first well, Julian No. 1, was pumped in at an unspectacular yet respectable 1,600 barrels a day. Julian No. 4 reportedly *flowed in* at 6,200 barrels a day. Three months later, Julian moved his wife and two daughters from a modest apartment to a mansion surrounded by five acres of prime Los Angeles real estate. He frequently used newly received investment revenue to pay earlier investors in the tradition of his spiritual mentor and contemporary Boston confidence man Charles Ponzi.

Yet this was only the beginning. Julian and his partner S. C. Lewis eventually took in movie moguls Louis B. Mayer and Cecil B. DeMille, as well as fire-breathing right-winger H. M. Haldeman, grandfather of Watergate figure H. R. Haldeman. Some of their investors demanded and received reimbursement. Louis B. Mayer eventually got his $50,000 investment back, right down to a thirty-nine dollar underpayment he demanded and received by separate check.

Julian's enemies were formidable. He was targeted by "Iron

Mike" Daugherty of the California Department of Corporations and radio evangelist Robert "Fighting Bob" Schuler, father of the like-named contemporary television preacher. Neither of these opponents really measured up to Charlie Chaplin, the comedic movie star, who decked Julian during a 1924 nightclub fight. At the time, Chaplin was accompanied by has-been actress Mary Miles Minter, whose promising career had been derailed by her supposed implication in the mysterious and still unsolved murder of director John Desmond Taylor two years earlier. The fight was dramatic and well-publicized enough that a local prizefight promoter publicly offered to feature a rematch on his Saturday night boxing card. Both men declined the offer.

Before his 1934 suicide in Paris, Courtney C. Julian had become the premiere oil field swindler of his age. Altogether, the boodle Julian and his partners may have collected during that brief, eleven-year period might have exceeded $150 million, some $1,837,260,000 today.

Tulsa Turmoil

Not all the fraud in the West was committed by non-Indians. Some was perpetrated by tribal members, such as the young Creek in Tulsa who signed forty-three different deeds to the same tract before attaining adulthood.[57]

In 1895, a federal judge ruled that Tulsa, Indian Territory, could incorporate. A city charter was granted on January 18, 1898, but not before a rip-roaring fight between certain Tulsa citizens who proposed to buy the land from the Creeks and the rest of the town. The Curtis Act of 1898 was intended to protect the owners of legitimate improvements whose efforts had helped build the towns in Indian Territory, but it also encouraged lot jumpers.

Tulsa lots were sold by a federal townsite commission at one-half to two-thirds of the appraised value, without regard to the value of the improvements. The improving party had a right of first refusal to purchase the lot. If the improving party chose not to buy, he was entitled to all proceeds that the lot bought at sale exceeding the appraised unimproved value. Sale proceeds below the appraised unimproved value were paid to the Creek Nation.[58] Just before the townsite survey began, oil was struck nearby at Red Fork in late June 1901. Before that date, Tulsa boasted some 1,400 hardy souls dependent upon salty, polluted water wells. Suddenly, even as surveyor J. Gus Patton converted muddy quagmires on the east side of Main Street into "avenues" named for refined cities on the far side of the Mississippi, hustlers, promoters, and legitimate businessmen began streaming into town.

When Patton was finished in December, the town site consisted of 655 platted acres, for which the Creek Nation received only $659, a pittance of $17,000 in modern money, due to the artificially low lot valuation methods used. Six years later, the Creeks recovered the unimproved market value of a few lots. However, even as lot sales continued, white settlers and others illegally harvested timber near Tulsa along the Arkansas River without paying the Creeks. The timber was shipped away on the railroads that had come to the area only two decades earlier. And only twelve years before that time, East and West were bound together by iron, "from sea to shining sea."

The Transcontinental Railroad

The building of the Union Pacific Railroad . . . was a massive series of swindles, but it was also a great feat of engineering skill and capitalist expansion.[59]

In the spring of 1862, a visionary named Theodore Judah began lobbying Congress for the creation of a transcontinental railroad, with the help of four hard-nosed California merchants. The Pacific Railroad Act passed that year authorized the creation of the Union Pacific Railroad, the first corporation chartered by the federal government since the Second Bank of the United States was created forty-six years earlier. The Union Pacific was chartered to build the railroad west from Omaha, Nebraska, and meet the Central Pacific, an earlier existing railroad company constructing track from California to the East.

The original Union Pacific shareholders included Thomas Durant, a physician who preferred Wall Street speculation to medical practice. Later, Congressman Oakes Ames and his brother Oliver Ames joined the enterprise. The Central Pacific was owned by "the associates": Leland Stanford, Charles Crocker, Mark Hopkins, and Collis Huntington. Theodore Judah recruited the four associates and then watched them take over the project.

Railroad Construction Swindles

The transcontinental railroad was a monumental challenge that provided vast opportunities for fraud. The federal government gave the transcontinental railroads every other section of land along the right of way, varying in width from two to ten miles, as had been granted in earlier railroad construction during the 1850s. The railroads also received government bonds at the rate of $16,000 for each mile constructed through the plains and $48,000 for each mile constructed in mountainous areas. The bonds eventually were to be repaid out of railroad revenues.[60] From time to time, the railroad engineers added curves that were not really needed and billed the government to cross mountains that were invisible to others.

The real power behind the Union Pacific board of directors established in 1863 was Dr. Thomas "Doc" Durant. He believed that Union Pacific profitability would come primarily from construction operations. And so, Durant and his partner George Francis Train acquired the dormant Pennsylvania Fiscal Agency, originally chartered in 1859, which became an infamous symbol of nineteenth-century theft and corruption known as Credit Mobilier.

The name is something of a mystery, since "credit mobilier" was a general term for a joint stock company created for the construction of public works with loans secured by personal property rather than land. The Pennsylvania Fiscal Agency was renamed Credit Mobilier of America in 1864 and used to enrich inside investors at the expense of smaller outside investors and the government.

This was done through the use of overpriced construction contracts between Credit Mobilier and the Union Pacific to secure extraordinary profits. The largest investors had interests in both companies. Construction operations were structured so that the insiders would profit whether a train ever ran or not. "For the insiders it meant excess profits."[61] The creation of Credit Mobilier also "tended to vest control of the Railroad in the hands of the chief stockholders of the construction company."[62] This was hardly anything new. The railroad baron Jay Gould once bought a nearly worthless railroad and used it to threaten his own railroad into purchasing shares at an inflated price.[63]

Still, "when the Union Pacific Railroad was proposed" it was considered "a wildcat venture . . . They [the chief shareholders] played a great game . . . for either a complete failure or a brilliant prize."[64]

The Union Pacific began building west from Omaha, Nebraska, in 1864. Three years later, Mormon leader Brigham Young met with Credit Mobilier director, Sidney Dillon; Ohio Senator John Sherman, brother of General William Tecumseh Sherman; and Governor Jacob Cox, of Ohio, a Union Pacific investor. The group wanted Young's cooperation in building the railroad across Utah, which they got in exchange for certain promises the railroad kept—eventually.

The financial strategy that allowed Credit Mobilier to scam the federal government was fairly straightforward. The Union Pacific entered construction contracts with individuals who in turn contracted with Credit Mobilier. The Union Pacific issued checks to Credit Mobilier, which in turn issued stock to the Union Pacific at par value and sold its stock on the open market at huge profits. There is no evidence Brigham Young was directly involved.

Credit Mobilier paid a series of generous dividends to its shareholders, mostly directors and principal shareholders of the Union Pacific, beginning in 1867. Holders of ten Credit Mobilier shares received cash and stock options constituting a 67-percent return on their investment.

Well-placed congressman and United States senators also benefited from the scam. Oakes Ames, a principal shareholder of both Union Pacific and Credit Mobilier, placed 160 shares with nine congressmen and two United States senators for $16,000 in 1867 and again the following year as a means of promoting "a general favorable feeling."[65]

In late December the following year, Credit Mobilier trustees declared a 200-percent dividend payable in Union Pacific stock, even as Union Pacific operating officers Oliver Ames and Doc Durant claimed they were strapped for cash and needed to build tracks into Ogden, Utah, before the Central Pacific.

The Union Pacific and Central Pacific crews came within sight of each other in late September 1868. The next month, Brigham Young began Herculean efforts to collect about $750,000 that the Union Pacific owed his followers for work performed over a nine-month period. Young was still waiting to be paid in November 1869, but Credit Mobilier and the Union Pacific had larger problems.

The Pacific Railroad Ring

Charles Francis Adams, the great-grandson of one president and grandson of another, exposed Credit Mobilier in an article that appeared in the January 1869 issue of *North American Review*. Adams claimed that a Pacific Railroad ring, consisting of congressmen, bondholders, trustees, directors, and contractors, were involved in gouging and self-dealing, right up to the pockets of their fancy waistcoats.[66] Adams had uncovered the largest political scandal in nineteenth-century America:

> The money that flowed from the Union Pacific into the Credit Mobilier and what was done with it—which wasn't to pay the contractors the subcontractors or the laborers who had gotten the railroad from Omaha to the Utah border—was further enriching a relatively few already wealthy men who milked the corporation, the government and ultimately the people for their fat and ill-gotten profits.[67]

Even as the competing Union Pacific and Central Pacific crews came within sight of each other, Credit Mobilier of America became much more visible than its founders had ever intended. Nevada

Senators William M. Stewart and James Nye highlighted the shortcomings of the Union Pacific and its affiliates for political gain, perhaps not realizing that the scandal would eventually also damage their political allies in the competing Central Pacific leadership.

A compromise between the competing railroads was reached on April 9. The Central Pacific would reimburse its competitor for track laid between Ogden and Promontory, Utah, where the railroads would meet. Yet, the federal subsidy was so rewarding that the Central Pacific and Union Pacific actually passed each other and kept building, until the federal government directed the two lines to finish the job.

The financial struggle between Union Pacific and Central Pacific was over. Within a few days, Union Pacific engineer Silas Seymour said it all—there was "nothing like it in the world."[68]

On May 10, 1869, a golden spike signifying completion of the transcontinental railroad was driven into place by a workman after two railroad officials bungled the job. The spike was later rushed off for safekeeping elsewhere, even as souvenir hunters began to whittle away at the first of six railroad ties placed where the two railroads met that day.[69]

Whatever his public pronouncements, Brigham Young surely stewed about the money the railroads still owed. The Mormons were finally paid, but in materials, not cash. They accepted payment in rails, bolts, and railroad cars valued at about $600,000 to be used for their own railroad in September 1869. And what happened to Credit Mobilier?

Three years later, the *New York Sun* renewed the attack begun by Charles Francis Adams, decrying Credit Mobilier as the "King of Frauds." Oakes Ames, the congressman who distributed $16,000 of Credit Mobilier stock among his colleagues in 1866 and the following year, was a natural target of congressional investigations that inevitably followed the publicity. Someone had to pay for the folly and the graft.

One noted historian has argued that the scope of the corruption involved in the development of the transcontinental railroad has been overstated, although,

The men who held stock in the Credit Mobilier . . . got rich from it. In large part this was done by defrauding the government and the public by paying the lowest possible wages to the men who built the lines and by delaying or actually ignoring payments of bills to subcontractors and the workmen . . . they used their power to guarantee profits for themselves.[70]

The amounts grifted by the railroads and their affiliates are staggering even today. Charles Crocker's Contract and Finance Company, by one estimate, received a total of $79,000,000 in stocks, bonds, and cash—$36,000,000 in excess of reasonable costs—a rip-off of $573,000,000 in modern money.[71]

No one seemed to be paying attention, "not the friendly government inspectors who turned their eyes away [from excessive costs], nor the stockholders and directors of the Credit Mobilier in New York and Washington, nor the homesteaders who cried for railroads" and least of all, the country "which had received daily news of these things flashed along the new telegraph lines to the world press."[72]

Two of the more prominent profiteers, Oakes Ames and James Brooks, were censured by Congress and died within a week of each other in May 1873. Doc Durant of the Union Pacific was already long gone from the public spotlight by then. The business records of the Charles Crocker Contract and Finance Company, which had extracted millions for the biggest Central Pacific shareholders, were burned.[73]

These reversals barely affected the continuing corruption associated with railroad construction. According to one account, in early May 1878, Jay Gould and other Texas and Pacific Railroad shareholders offered one member of Congress $1,000 cash and another $5,000 in cash and $10,000 in bonds when certain legislation was passed.[74]

Ohio Republican James Garfield, one of the congressmen who benefited from largesse distributed by Oakes Ames, became president of the United States in 1880, only to be mortally wounded by an assassin eight months to the day following his inauguration.

The Prince of Humbugs began "P. T. Barnum's Greatest Show on Earth" the next year. Ten years later, he died a multimillionaire at his Bridgeport, Connecticut, home. Barnum was born eleven years after the death of Patrick Henry and died the year before a brash young historian named Frederick Jackson Turner claimed that the American frontier *had closed*, starting an argument about the West that endures to this day. No one would have disagreed with Turner more than Phineas Taylor Barnum, whose bold and sometimes fraudulent schemes set the standard for counterfeiters, wildcat bankers, town lot swindlers, and land grabbers in an age of American confidence.

CHAPTER 9

James Addison Reavis: Perchance to Dream

After taking someone else's sleeping berth in a mix-up, James Addison Reavis arrived in Tucson on the Southern Pacific Limited under virtual arrest. His reason for being there on September 3, 1882, was already known:

> Months earlier, Arizonians had begun to hear of this man Reavis and his Peralta Grant from stories in California papers. It appeared that the fellow claimed ownership of the whole Salt River Valley in central Arizona, and heaven only knew how much of the territory besides.[1]

Eventually the whole claim, complete with lengthy documents in Spanish, surfaced. Reavis claimed land as far east as New Mexico. The Phoenix reporter from the *Arizona Gazette* noted that on the train, Reavis related "the story of his acquisition of the Spanish grant and his future course when it is fully confirmed by the Congress. Mr. Reavis is in no hurry to effect a settlement with those who occupy his broad acres."[2]

Tucson was then the largest city in the territory, even though the capital had been moved away to Prescott earlier that year. Phoenix then had its own pretensions, although less than five years earlier, six men had been shot to death during one hot summer week, and the shooting was followed promptly by a lynching. A competing Phoenix newspaper reported:

> The tone of society which even during our frontier days was not bad is now of a high order and improving every year. There is probably no more social place in Arizona. Scarcely a week passes

without bringing a private or public entertainment of some kind.[3]

Early the next month, Reavis asked the local probate court in nearby Safford to order that the estate of his old friend and business partner Dr. George M. Willing be sold. This was but the opening salvo in his battle for the Peralta Land Grant, which relied on a bundle of moldy papers and a few photographs.

Yet another journalist noted that there was little danger of an immediate sale but warned that "Reavis is determined to fight every inch of ground to obtain the land, and doubtless has some powerful backing behind him. He is not purchasing a law suit for the mere gratification of a whim . . . but is systematically working to obtain proper and lawful title to the old Spanish grant."[4]

After the Graham County probate court denied his motion, Reavis retreated to California but returned in March 1883. He filed a formal claim against the United States for the Peralta grant at Tucson on March 27, supported by a barrelful of old deeds, wills, and photographs. It was obvious that Reavis claimed all of Arizona and part of New Mexico—the desert, the mountains and streams, the towns and mines, the entire incorporated city of Phoenix, hundreds of miles of Southern Pacific railroad track, and the fabulous Silver King Mine—all of it.

Who was this guy?

A Man with a Claim—and a Plan

James Addison Reavis was a skinny six-footer with reddish hair and a long prominent nose. He was reportedly born near Clinton in Henry County, Missouri, in 1843. Fourteen years later, his father established a store at Montevallo, Vernon County, Missouri. During the Civil War, young James joined Hunter's Regiment, Eighth Division of the Missouri State Guard, which fought for the Confederacy. He reenlisted the next year at Springfield in Lowe's Company.

Perhaps in Springfield, he discovered the skills of forgery he employed in later years to build his "empire," but for the moment he just needed to escape military duty. A newspaper reported many years later that Reavis left Lowe's Company using furlough papers and surrendered to the Union Army.[5] Years later, Senator Thomas Catron of New Mexico reportedly remarked that Reavis had joined his artillery regiment, but requested and received furlough to marry, and never returned.[6]

After the war, he migrated to Brazil, but then settled in St. Louis, Missouri, perhaps as early as 1866. Reavis worked as a traveling salesman in clothing and other goods, then as a street car conductor on Olive Street; but his real passion was buying and selling real estate with his meager savings. Eventually he was able to pursue real estate ventures full time from a small office on Olive Street. The forgery skills Reavis learned during the Civil War did not go unused. On at least one occasion he cured an imperfect title with a few flourishes.[7]

And then a conversation changed his life.

Dr. George M. Willing Jr. appeared at the Reavis real estate office in 1871 seeking his advice and help. Years earlier, Willing had left his family and his medical practice to pursue gold in California and the mountain West. His brother, a Captain Willing, was acquainted with James Reavis and suggested that George Willing seek his help with a little real estate problem.

Dr. George Willing claimed he owned the massive Peralta grant supposedly covering a good part of Arizona Territory, which then included present-day New Mexico. The good doctor even had a deed of sorts to support this tale, although it was scrolled on "greasy pencil-marked camp paper," whatever that might have been. The grimy deed was dated October 20, 1864, though circumstantial evidence later established that if it was valid at all, it had been written three years later.

Willing related that he paid Miguel Peralta $20,000 in gold dust and prospecting equipment near Prescott to acquire the grant. Willing also had an 1853 letter from President Santa Anna of Mexico to Miguel Peralta transmitting copies of all Peralta grant documents in the Mexican records.

Reavis was not the first prospective partner to hear this story.

Willing had initially offered a half-interest in the massive land grant to settle a forty-dollar livery stable bill in Prescott in 1867, James D. Monihan later recalled. Monihan refused the offer and insisted on cash. Willing paid the bill by selling his horses, before departing for New Mexico.

Years later, Reavis claimed that after discussing the Arizona prospect with Dr. Willing for several months in 1871 and 1872, he sold his real estate holdings in St. Louis and Illinois, and then departed for the West to pursue the Peralta claim with his new partner. Perhaps, but by his own account, Reavis never saw Dr. George M. Willing again.[8]

Willing apparently departed St. Louis in late 1873 and arrived in March of the next year back at Prescott, where he recorded a deed to himself from Miguel Peralta. He was found dead, face down, the next day at a boarding house. A local newspaper reported on March 20, 1874, that Willing had arrived in Prescott the evening of March 18, telling stories of his adventures in New Mexico and elsewhere.

"His object in again visiting the Territory was to secure title to some mines claimed by the Willing mining and exploring company in the vicinity of Black Canyon creek, and a Spanish land grant on the Gila River." The *Arizona Weekly Miner* eulogized that "he had his faults, not the least of which was the habit of stretching the truth, but was, on the whole a bold adventurer and intelligent man. He leaves a wife in the east."[9]

Willing was hardly the first in the Southwest to stretch the truth where land claims were concerned. One dispute over a fictitious land claim erupted in Spanish colonial days between descendants of Don Fernando Duran y Chaves and others over a tract known as Las Cirvelas near Albuquerque in present-day New Mexico. The Spanish governor eventually set aside the claim.[10]

Reavis married Miss Ada Pope of Montevallo, Missouri, on May 5, 1874, just before departing for the West. The lovers met only once again six years later. They reportedly divorced in 1883.[11]

He had a succession of jobs in California during the next few years. Reavis taught school at Downey from 1875 to 1876 before finding the only thing other than land claims that he was interested in—journalism. He was a correspondent for two reputable San Francisco newspapers and even started the *Sacramento Advertiser*, before leaving for Arizona in early 1880. Reavis climbed down off the stagecoach in Phoenix that spring and walked toward the nearest livery stable, owned by the same James D. Monihan who had declined to become Dr. Willing's partner in Prescott thirteen years earlier. Once again, Monihan was regaled with tales of the Peralta land grant, and this time the improvements Reavis planned for the desert. Monihan took Reavis on a buggy tour of the area, but was no more impressed than he was by Dr. Willing.

He warned Reavis that any attempt to impose his "floating land grant" (a concession of lands with no specific location or boundaries) on the hardy Arizona pioneers could be a fatal mistake.[12] Reavis assured him that he would not bother the homesteaders, but simply make a claim against the federal government for the land that it had sold, an assurance he reneged on just a few years later. The next day Monihan learned that Reavis had fled Phoenix without paying his hotel bill.

Reavis quietly arrived at Prescott, one hundred miles away, representing himself as a newspaper correspondent, and then found the old lawyer who was serving as probate judge when Willing had died. He produced documents granting him the widow's permission to retrieve Willing's personal effects.

He then returned to California seeking a power of attorney and deeds in the possession of Floral Massal, who had once financed a Willing prospecting venture as a favor. Reavis convinced Massal to tender the deeds to "certain Arizona mines" and a power of attorney in exchange for a promise to pay the $3,000 that Dr. Willing owed, with interest.

Next, according to his own account, Reavis traveled to Washington, DC, where he obtained the "will of the first Baron of Arizona," as well as all right, title, and interest to the Peralta grant on May 1, 1882, in exchange for a promise to pay the widow Mary Ann Willing $30,000.[13]

Thus, by 1883, Reavis had an impressive set of documents ready to file with the surveyor general's office in Tucson—fictitious documents that told the stories of the first and second Barons of Arizona, a father and son each named Miguel Silva de Peralta. The process Reavis faced was daunting.

After acquiring parts of Arizona and New Mexico in the 1854 Gadsden Purchase, Congress enacted a procedure for Mexican or Spanish land grantees, their descendants or assignees to file their claims with the surveyor general for Arizona or New Mexico. In due time the surveyor general would file a report and recommendation with the secretary of the interior, who in turn submitted a recommendation to Congress for special legislation approving the grant.

Although the large Maxwell grant in New Mexico had been approved, no significant Arizona grant had been approved by 1883. Secretary of the Interior Carl Schurz had noted three years earlier that fewer than 150 claims had been submitted and only 71 acted upon.[14]

Later, Reavis told a Phoenix reporter that he would ask no more than three dollars per acre from the homesteaders occupying his domain, despite early assurances to Monihan and others that he would make claim only against the federal government.[15]

However, George M. Willing Sr., the father of Dr. Willing, challenged the Reavis ownership of the Peralta claim to protect his grandchildren, or so he said, in a January 1883 letter to Arizona newspapers.[16] The *Phoenix Gazette* told its readers early that month, "The Willings have opened an office in Phoenix, and like the Bean-Pole Baron, are endeavoring to sell deeds to the present land-owners at small figures. Those who purchase deeds from both . . . will act in haste and repent at leisure."[17] The Willing family litigation was initiated by St. Louis attorney Britton Hill, who advanced money to carry on the suit in exchange for a half-interest in the property to be won.

Reavis and his brother William then began traveling their grant, selling quitclaim deeds conveying any rights that Reavis owned to settlers. The enormous Peralta grant was said to consist of some "19,000,000 varas of Arizona dirt,"[18] equal to about 18,500 square miles. In effect, the quitclaim deeds bought by the victims were a form of illicit title insurance, protecting their rights if the outrageous Reavis claim was affirmed by the authorities.

Reavis could be generous, sometimes giving his dinner hosts along the road a quitclaim deed just for the cost of a meal as he wandered about the Salt River Valley.

Although he was derided in the press, area businesses began purchasing their own quitclaim deeds from Reavis. Even the publisher of the *Gazette*, which had called upon the Arizona citizenry to rise up against Reavis in July, quietly bought his own Reavis quitclaim in November for sixty dollars.

When this purchase was discovered, a citizen boycott of the *Gazette* was quickly organized, causing the shame-faced publisher to return the deed to Reavis. The competing *Weekly Phoenix Herald* noted, "This community is not as blind as a bat nor as dumb as an ox that it can neither see nor hear, and it is no wonder that so much indignation is now entertained at the conduct of the land grabber's organ."[19]

Even so, the land-grabbing business must have been good, since Reavis spent the last two months of 1883 in Mexico, returning early the next year. He traveled there with Mr. R. C. Hopkins, a senior clerk of the surveyor general's office, to examine documents supporting the Reavis claim. Amazingly, while there, Reavis somehow discovered a key document dating to December 1748 that supported his claim. Later, the surveyor general found fault with Hopkins' positive assessment of the Reavis claim, commenting that the documentation was superficial at best.

Worse still for Reavis, Hopkins had not found a single mention of the Peralta claim or Miguel Peralta beyond the documentation provided by Reavis himself. Reavis did not help his cause by suggesting to third parties that he was a friend of newly appointed Surveyor General Royal A. Johnson. He then began to argue publicly that the federal government had no right to sell the land covered by the Peralta claim.[20]

Refreshed and enthusiastic, he turned his attentions to Florence, a mining town in Pinal County, where he was met with fierce opposition in the person of Tom Weedin, editor of the *Enterprise*. He also ran afoul of Southern Pacific officials, who in October 1884 refused to pay him for quitclaim deeds covering their own coal deposits nearby.

In January 1884, Johnson was under some pressure to reject the Peralta claim, but simply reported that he had other claims to process and would deal with Reavis in due course. Arizonians were less than enthusiastic about this even-handed approach, and one newspaper even accused Johnson of favoring the claimant.[21]

In February 1884, Clark Churchill, territorial attorney general, filed a quiet title action against Reavis to clarify ownership of Churchill's own Phoenix real estate. Reavis was forced to give a deposition before trial, in which he admitted paying Mrs. Willing only $100 and unspecified small amounts against the $30,000 she was owed for the Peralta grants.[22]

During the deposition, he also claimed to have received $5,000 each from Charles Crocker of the Southern Pacific Railroad and James M. Barney of the Silver King Mining Company, giving the impression that they backed him.[23] In the end, the trial judge found for Churchill and against Reavis, casting a massive cloud of doubt on the Peralta claim.

By 1885, George M. Willing Sr. intensified efforts to sell quitclaim deeds in the Phoenix area in competition with Reavis. The *Gazette* quipped that anyone who purchased deeds from either Willing or Reavis "will act in haste and repent at leisure."[24]

A mass movement opposing Reavis then formed. In April 1885, citizen committees were launched in Phoenix, nearby Pinal County, Florence, and the Gila Valley. The *Weekly Phoenix Herald* resolved on April 20, 1885, "No more fraud, rascally Reavis must go." Land Commissioner W. A. Sparks ordered Johnson to cease work on the Peralta claim that May, but Reavis remained confident. While soldiers in Arizona tried to capture Geronimo that summer, Reavis was on his way to find documentary support for the Peralta claim in Spain.

Reavis returned to Tucson in late August 1887, with a new look and a personal retinue. He took the best suite at the San Xavier Hotel, accompanied by two servants, two mysterious Spanish ladies, and his uncle, John Reavis. He also sported a new name, James Addison Peralta-Reavis, which complemented the new land claim he was about to file.

Strangers on a Train

His wife claimed to be Dona Sophia Micaela Maso Reavis y Peralta de la Cordoba, the third Baroness of Arizona. A California journalist had interviewed her at length on August 5 at the Glenwood Hotel in Riverside. She appeared to be about twenty-six years old and spoke English quite fluently.

The baroness related that her father Jose Ramon Maso (Jose Maso) had married a Ms. Peralta in Mexico and left her behind to take care of some business in Spain, never to return. In 1877, the baroness met her husband, James Addison Reavis, on a Central Pacific train going to Sacramento. Incredibly, Reavis immediately recognized her as a member of the Massol (Massal) family of Sacramento. The young couple fell in love and married quietly on December 31, 1882. Three years later, they traveled to Spain, where they celebrated their marriage in a grand *fiesta* given by her Peralta relatives.[25]

Remarkably, following the *fiesta*, Reavis researched the Spanish archives and found the will of the second Baron of Peralta, which left the fabled Arizona grant to none other than Sophia herself.

None of this was known to the good folks in Sherwood Valley, where Sophia was commonly thought to be the cast-off child of John Treadway and a mysterious Indian woman with no apparent Spanish title or inheritance for Sophia.

Reavis Files His Claim to Fame and Fortune

Reavis filed the first Peralta claim in his own name with no reference to the baroness at all in March 1883. After two years, he traveled with Baroness Sophia to Spain, with as much as half a million dollars raised promoting the claim. At least $50,000 of this amount may have come from the Southern Pacific Railroad, controlled by Charles Crocker of San Francisco. On September 17, 1881, Reavis signed an agreement with the Pacific Improvement Company, a Southern Pacific affiliate. In exchange for the money, Reavis was to assign Charles Crocker half of the lands Reavis secured. Reavis later claimed that he acquired the contract and the funds by offering to block the efforts of the Texas and Pacific Railroad, which was competing with the Southern Pacific in a track-laying race across Arizona, New Mexico, and West Texas. The race path crossed the southwest corner of the Peralta grant.

Reavis granted the Southern Pacific a two-hundred-foot right of way across the Peralta grant on February 21, 1883, and a short time later the contract was cancelled after Crocker reached an "accommodation" with the Texas and Pacific.

Of course he had expenses. Reavis had promised to pay the widow Willing $30,000, but so far is as known, he gave her only $600 in cash, $100,000 in stock in a company Reavis had created, and a few fancy dresses.[26]

Between 1883 and 1885, he sold quitclaim deeds and other interests in the grant, scoring as much as $25,000 from the fabled Silver King Mining Company. According to his own estimation, Reavis also realized between $1,000 and $20,000 each year as a newspaper correspondent.

Two other possible sources of funds are worthy of mention. Reavis signed an agreement with M. M. Herr of San Francisco in November 1885 to form a stock company capitalized at $25,000,000. Reavis was to receive a monthly salary of $250 to pursue the Peralta grant, which was to be conveyed to Herr.[27]

On December 18, 1885, just before Reavis departed for Spain, John W. Mackay, a Virginia City, Nevada, miner who had struck it rich in the "Big Bonanza" of 1872, agreed to provide $500 each month while Reavis searched for records supporting the Peralta grant—a sum that allowed the baron and baroness to travel and live in great luxury.

Reavis claimed later that agents of the United States followed him to Spain and through a series of misfortunes all of the documentation brought from the United States was lost. Eventually, against all odds, the documents surfaced at his hotel in Madrid. Between parties and family gatherings, Reavis searched through page after page of dusty archival material. Finally, he found a crucial piece of evidence—the will in which Don Jesus Miguel left his Arizona lands to young Sophia. The baron and baroness returned to the United States in November 1886.[28]

The next August, Reavis and his retainers began exploring for the cornerstone of the Peralta grant. Fortunately, they had an account of the ceremony in which the cornerstone was laid by a Father Pauer, which led them to the eastern base of the Estrella Mountains south of Phoenix. The cornerstone rested on its side, but nevertheless provided an excellent background for an impromptu photograph of the smiling, triumphant Sophia Micaela Maso Reavis y Peralta de la Cordoba, the Baroness of Peralta.

As husband of the baroness, it was time for Reavis to once again pursue the land claim. Through his acquaintance with Charles Crocker, he roped some New York notables into his scheme. These included attorney Robert G. Ingersoll, with whom Reavis incorporated the Casa Grande Land and Improvement Company of Arizona in November 1887 to replace two earlier corporations bearing similar names. Capital stock for the 1887 venture was stated to be $50,000,000. Casa Grande would invest in internal improvements, including the development of roads, railways, and canals. Water rights were to be granted in the amount of $2,000,000.

This business accomplished, Reavis and his entourage began to travel regularly between San Francisco, New York, and Washington. He began to spend more time in meetings with other businessmen interested in developing Arizona, prompting the baroness to focus some of her affections on an orphan she adopted and named Fenton, for Reavis's father.[29]

As Reavis began to travel more and more, organizing stock companies to develop his huge Arizona land grant, some accounting errors were bound to occur. The *Tucson Citizen* reported on

October 5 that one local merchant had accepted drafts in the amount of $395.75 on the Casa Grande Land Company that had been returned protested. The Tucson paper promptly ridiculed Reavis for claiming to have $5,000,000 in the bank while refusing a check for less than $400.

Perhaps Reavis was slightly embarrassed, but his confidence was unshaken. Soon he had added former United States senator Roscoe Conkling to his stable of lawyers. Conkling took the Reavis case on a contingency, which was unusual at the time, expressing confidence that the documents he had seen "show Mrs. Reavis to be the person she believes herself to be, namely, the lineal descendent of the original grantee."[30]

Conkling died during the great New York blizzard of 1888, but by then Reavis had other legal talent available, namely Robert G. Ingersoll, also of New York. Although three years earlier he had discounted Reavis and his Arizona claim, in 1887 former congressman James G. Broadstreet of St. Louis had joined Conkling and Ingersoll as counsel to Reavis. Broadstreet described Reavis as "a man of remarkable energy and persistence."[31]

Reavis Files Lawsuits

Reavis was also a man of some patience who probably thought he had every reason to be optimistic as 1890 began.

Reavis filed a lawsuit in the Court of Claims as J. A. Peralta-Reavis with his wife as Dona Sophia Loreta Micaela Maso Reavis y Peralta de Cordoba. He listed some $145,900 in payments he had received from those who supported his claim or at least wanted assurance that he would not take their land if successful. According to his court filing, Reavis had been paid $50,000 by the Southern Pacific Railroad, $25,000 by the Silver King Mining Company, $5,000 by one B. Barney, and $65,900 in payments ranging from $10 to $2,500 by other grantees.

In September 1889, the acting commissioner of the Land Office asked Johnson, then surveyor general of Arizona, for a report as to "the exact condition of said [Peralta] grant as shown by records and papers in your office and all the information you can obtain in regard to it."[32] Johnson had been studying the matter for years, and submitted his findings on October 12, entitled *Adverse Report of the Surveyor General of Arizona Royal A. Johnson Upon the Alleged Peralta Grant, a Complete Exposure of its Fraudulent Character.* His predecessor had hardly been any more favorable to the Peralta claim. Before leaving office, Surveyor General John C. Hise had refused to do a survey of the Peralta claim. Worse yet for Reavis, Hise wrote a brief, adverse report on the claim just months before leaving office, summarizing many of the deficiencies that Johnson then amplified.[33]

Johnson did not mince words in his own conclusions:

> Speedy and final action should be had on this base claim in order that the people of this territory may enjoy their homes with peace of mind. And parties guilty of forgery or the fabrication of papers that have caused so much trouble should be vigorously prosecuted by the government and that without delay. I recommend that the alleged grant should not be confirmed as is prayed for, it being to my mind *without the slightest foundation in fact and utterly void.*[34]

Johnson noted numerous deficiencies and indications of forgery. None were more significant than the observation that virtually the entire body of Reavis documentation from the eighteenth century was written with a steel pen, not in common use until 1800. He also found abundant proof that the entire Peralta grant had been surreptitiously inserted into the Mexican and Spanish archives without permission.

Beyond this evidence, Johnson had initiated a search of the Spanish archives through the American Department of State in which not a single document pertaining to the Peralta claim was found. He also appended an argument from Reavis's old nemesis Clark Churchill, in which Churchill argued that documents supposedly prepared by the prime minister of Spain contained basic errors of grammar and usage more consistent with the writing of an

American speaking bad Spanish than a high government official. Johnson even recruited the historian Hubert Howe Bancroft, who had just published a history of Arizona and New Mexico. Bancroft opined that "the title is plausible enough on its face, but it is somewhat remarkable that annals of the province, as recorded, contain no allusion to Peralta."[35] Finally, Johnson noted certain inconsistencies between the claim Reavis filed for himself in March 1883 and the one that was filed for his wife the baroness.[36]

The Johnson report was praised by many of the same journalists who had earlier criticized the delays caused by his thorough and painstaking investigation. The *Weekly Phoenix Herald,* which in earlier years had criticized Johnson, now enthusiastically proposed a public reception in his honor, which was held by the governor in the spring of 1890.

The March 27 issue of the *Herald* noted that Johnson "was most deeply moved by the canvas clad farmers who stepped within the brilliantly lighted Executive Chambers last Saturday night for one glance only at the somewhat careworn features of the man who had removed a great shadow from off a weary land."[37]

Reavis and his bride then filed an eleven-million-dollar lawsuit against the federal government in the United States Court of Claims.[38] His attorney Harvey Brown, who also represented the Southern Pacific Railroad, began taking sworn testimony in October from witnesses supporting the Peralta claim.

Alfred Sherwood was one critical witness. He remembered little Sophia being brought to his home as an infant, attended by her grandmother and a nurse. According to Sherwood, the grandmother frequently told the little girl that someday she would inherit a vast estate. Reavis also produced John Snowball, who had adopted little Sophia at age eight, as well as Miguel Lauro Peralta y Vasquez, who recalled traveling years earlier with the second Baron of Arizona, Sophia's grandfather. W. W. "Bill" Jenkins testified he was an intimate friend of Sophia's father, Jose Masol, and had been in the Agua Mansa district (later Riverside, California) when the Peraltas arrived in 1862. Jenkins also testified he personally knew the elderly grandfather, Baron Don

Miguel, from whom young Sophia inherited the Peralta grant. The spring of 1892 found Reavis in the mission church at San Bernardino, California, seeking further documentation for the Peralta claim. Miraculously, he found baptismal records for Sophia and her twin brother who died at birth with their mother as well as the burial records documenting that sad event. A trip to Guadalajara soon thereafter was even more fruitful. Reavis found absolutely nothing until he was referred to a local historian, who helped find some easily overlooked documents that solidly confirmed the Peralta claim. First, Reavis uncovered the probate record of the first Baron of Peralta and then discovered four critical *cedulas* (royal decrees). The first two appointed the first Baron of Peralta a captain of dragoons, while the third expressed the king's intention to make the baron a grant of land confirmed in the fourth *cedula*. Reavis had certified copies made and bound with a portrait of his wife on the title page.[39]

After the birth of twin sons in March 1893, Reavis accompanied his attorney James O. Broadhead, a former congressman and former president of the American Bar Association, to produce further testimony on behalf of the Peralta claim back in California. Fortunately, Miguel Noe recalled his close friend, Sophia's father Joe Maso, as well as Maso's father-in-law, the second Baron of Arizona, and visits with little Sophia.[40]

The baron also produced Andres Sandoval, who recalled knowing the Masos and the second Baron of Arizona in San Francisco in the 1860s, when they gathered daily at the Sandoval restaurant and boarding house.[41] Broadhead was reportedly so satisfied with the testimony that he left before the proceedings were over.

Reavis was then ready to begin a second lawsuit against the United States. Congress had established the Court of Private Land Claims in March 1891 to deal with the Arizona land controversies. The court consisted of five judges empowered to settle all grants of land made by Spanish or Mexican governments within the borders of the United States.

Reavis appeared in Santa Fe, New Mexico, in February 1893 to file the second lawsuit. One court employee later recalled that the array of boxes, packages, documents, and portraits that accompanied the Reavis petition covered three large tables.[42] Since neither the Casa Grande developments nor the hundreds of letters sent to Salt River Valley residents offering releases for cash had produced any significant income, the next month Reavis was forced to accept help with the litigation expenses. A San Francisco syndicate provided $30,000 at a rate of $2,500 per month, on the promise the investors would be compensated in land once the claims were successfully established.

Nine months later, in November 1893, the Peralta-Reavis family returned to Arizona. They were accompanied by J. B. Whitney, a California engineer with whom Reavis crossed the desert planning a massive irrigation system. The prior month, a second syndicate had been formed by J. B. Whitney and Dr. E. T. Sherwood to deal with the enormous litigation expenses Reavis incurred in pursuing the Peralta claim. The syndicate advertised a headline proclaiming the "Barony of Arizona Open to Settlement." Prospective investors were assured that "in November last, the United States Court of Private Land Claims finally determined the exact boundaries of the estate, and thereby practically sealed Mrs. Peralta-Reavis' claim. A clear title to any or all of the property is thereby assured."[43]

Yet all the court had really done was permit Peralta-Reavis to slightly amend the precise boundaries of the claim. One newspaper reported that at least $10,000 "had poured into the coffers of Reavis & Co. and in return for every half dollar received, they gave title to an acre of land."[44]

Reavis even planned two dams, one near the very spot where the Roosevelt Dam was completed in 1910. He described his plans during an interview from his executive offices:

> I am about to undertake the colonization of the Peralta Grant
> . . . I do not wish to appear in the light of a man who praises his
> own property . . . but all who have ever traveled over the Barony
> must admit that its resources are superb . . . I am now organizing
> a company to aid me in the work of constructing dams on the Salt
> and Gila rivers.[45]

Government Special Counsel Severo Mallet-Prevost began

investigating the documents of grant on file in Tucson and Santa Fe in January 1894 to prepare the government case. Mallet-Prevost was a New York lawyer born in Zacatecas, Mexico, who spoke fluent Spanish. The lawyer obtained the assistance of the governor of Zacatecas to facilitate his examination of documents pertaining to the Peralta claim in the National Archives at Mexico City. In Guadalajara, he examined the Peralta papers on file there. Mallet-Prevost was soon convinced that a fraud had been perpetrated.[46]

He moved on to Madrid, where red tape delayed him for two weeks. Eventually he learned that "Reavis had, in August 1886, been to Seville and there attempted to insert false documents into the Archives of the Indias."[47] Reavis had clumsily attempted to insert an obvious forgery into the record on the very day a clerk assigned to watch him had been home ill. The clerk was quite certain that earlier, he himself had searched the very group of documents in which the Reavis discovery had been made and found nothing of the sort.

Beyond this fact, the questioned document was the only one in the document group that had been in an envelope. The document was not numbered as had been the other documents in the archives group, did not read like an authentic document of the era in question, and had been found folded in a peculiar manner in an envelope. Reavis was so strongly suspected of having tampered with the archives that criminal charges were filed against him at just about the time he left Spain for the United States.[48]

In early September 1894, Mallet-Prevost reported his findings to Matthew Given Reynolds, the government attorney in Santa Fe who would act as lead counsel in the Peralta trial.

Following the procedures of the time in such cases, Mallet-Prevost then traveled in October to Mexico with Judge Thomas C. Fuller of the Private Land Claims Court to take testimony from officials of the Mexican record offices Reavis had visited. Reavis was not represented by counsel in these proceedings. One key official examined was the Archivist of the Public Registry, who did not find any Peralta documents filed where they should be, but discovered obvious Peralta forgeries filed elsewhere.[49]

The investigation had moved to Spain by January. Mallet-Prevost and Judge Stone took testimony from archives officials through March, with no Reavis representative present, presumably because the claimant did not have the funds to send one. Lead government counsel Reynolds had been following other leads in the meantime, preparing for the May 30, 1895, trial.

In late 1893, Reynolds had received a very curious letter from San Francisco attorney W. W. Allen, who had been one of Reavis's attorneys. Allen claimed he had an "original contract" in which Reavis and his wife had promised a contingent fee of $50,000 to Miguel Noe if Noe testified to certain facts. Reynolds sent government documents and photographic expert William Tipton to interview Allen, who by then had written a second letter transmitting the contract in question.

Later, Tipton reported that Allen had referred Reavis to Miguel Noe. Allen thought Noe would provide the necessary connection between Reavis and the original grantee.[50] In 1893, testimony supporting Reavis, Miguel Noe recalled his close friend, Sophia's father Joe Maso and Maso's father-in-law, the second Baron of Arizona, as well as visits with little Sophia.[51] During Tipton's interview, Allen also signed a statement claiming Reavis had coached Noe on his testimony until Allen discovered what Reavis was doing and terminated their relationship.[52] Tipton believed that Allen was playing both sides and could not be trusted.

Reynolds then hired detectives Peter Brady and Levi Hughes to pursue California leads for the government case.

The Hiram Hatch Testimony, December 1894

That December an early Sherwood Valley acquaintance of John Treadway named Hiram Hatch gave his testimony regarding the early life of Baroness Peralta. He testified that John Treadway was the father of Baroness Sophia and that her mother was a Native American born far from Spain.

Beyond this testimony, critical Peralta claim witness Alfred Sherwood, who had served as the guardian of young Sophia, recanted

his earlier testimony claiming that little Sophia had been born elsewhere, then brought to his home attended by a Spanish grandmother
and a nurse. Sherwood then testified that Sophia was born in March
1863 in California.

He related that Reavis had asked him for an affidavit and later
for testimony given October 16, 1890, which had followed an outline Reavis had created. Then, Jennie Mack, who had lived with
Alfred Sherwood in the 1860s, corroborated and supplemented his
1894 testimony, adding that Sophia's mother had abandoned her.[53]

Others corroborated that Sophia was the daughter of Treadway. They did not remember anyone named Masol or Peralta.
Sophia had been taken away from the Treadway house at a young
age by John Snowball. Later, notary Charles Mosebach, who had
possession of the records of the official who supposedly notarized
the will left by the second Baron of Peralta, testified that notary
Thibault left no record of any such document.

Rufus C. Hopkins testified that Reavis brought Sophia to board
at his own home in September 1883; so far as he knew she spoke
but a few words of Spanish.

By the time the government depositions had concluded in late
1894 only one California witness still supported the Reavis claim.
Miguel Noe still insisted that he personally knew Carmelita Maso,
Jose Maso, and Don Miguel Peralta.

The Trial Begins . . . and Ends

The Peralta claim thus did not look promising when the trial
began in the Court of Private Land Claims at Santa Fe on June 3,
1895. Several key Peralta witnesses had renounced their testimony
in earlier depositions, while in March of the previous year the court
had thrown out several other large Arizona land grant claims. The
once impressive Reavis legal team had been reduced to Reavis himself as, one by one, his lawyers withdrew from the case.

Reavis did not show up for the first few days of the trial. The
only lawyer on the Peralta side of the case to appear was J. T. Kinney, who represented Peralta descendants who had hoped to ride

the Reavis shirttails to riches. Kinney promptly washed his hands of the case, advising the court that the "grant upon which Reavis relies . . . is a fabrication."[54]

The trial then began without Reavis. William Tipton, the government handwriting expert, pointed out numerous signs of fraud in the Peralta claim documents, which included made-up words that were not Spanish at all, grammar and usage errors uncharacteristic of educated high government officials, and suspicious new documents that suddenly appeared in archives created fifty years earlier. Mallet-Prevost also testified to signs of obvious forgery, such as fictitious cross-references and fabricated probate proceedings recorded on paper entirely different from authentic contemporary documents. After all this, it is no surprise that lead government attorney Matthew Reynolds was cooperative when Reavis telegraphed a request for a five-day continuance to the court on June 5.

Reavis tried to delay the proceedings even further when he finally appeared on Monday, June 10, solemnly shaking hands with each judge present. The court denied his motion to sever his own case from that of the Peralta heirs and his request that the case be immediately appealed to the Supreme Court of the United States, before giving him the afternoon to prepare.

The proceedings began on Tuesday with Reavis himself answering the questions of lead government attorney Reynolds. Again and again, Reavis gave lengthy meandering answers with irrelevant minute details, perhaps to avoid directly answering the questions.

He fooled no one. Reynolds methodically destroyed the Peralta claim, document by document, dismantling the Reavis arguments, the clumsy forgeries, and even the testimony of the baroness herself, as her young twins looked on from their play area beneath the feet of the indulgent judges. Among the last government witnesses was the former bishop of Tucson, then serving as the archbishop of Santa Fe, who was called to address the supposed 1788 will of Miguel Peralta. Reverend John B. Salpointe related that while researching the record books of the San Xavier Mission to write a history, he had found no such document.[55]

Reavis then played one last card in desperation. He explained there was a perfectly good reason that no Peralta had been found in the all-important land records. The name Peralta was simply a *nom de plume*—the family name was really Santisteban. Just as this argument was concluded, a large, ornate leather trunk was brought before the court. From within the trunk, Reavis drew what he called "the first oil portrait . . . of Don Miguel de Peralta de la Cordoba as a child," urging the court to acknowledge the "remarkable resemblance between [the portrait] and one of his twin sons."[56]

The judges reassembled on June 19 and pronounced the claim for some 12,456,000 acres in Arizona and New Mexico "wholly fictitious and fraudulent . . . the various documents . . . each and all of them forged, manufactured and . . . surreptitiously entered into the records and archives." The word "dismissed" had scarcely stopped echoing through the courtroom when Reavis bounded out the door and into the plaza, perhaps walking toward the hotel. Almost immediately, he was taken into custody by a U.S. marshal to face charges of attempting to defraud the United States.[57]

Even while he languished months in the Santa Fe jail for the want of a $500 bond, Reavis continued talking to reporters about irrigation projects he was planning with "important capitalists," much as a young child might talk of imagined playmates, claiming the businessmen were "very glad to have the grant beaten back and the land disposed of under United States laws,"[58] for reasons that still remain unclear.

However, Reavis still had a few supporters. Dr. A. T. Sherwood, a relative of the perjurer Alfred Sherwood, insisted, "It is impossible that any one man could have forged all the signatures in this case. Reavis would have had to forge over 200 Spanish documents . . . it is the most improbable thing conceivable."[59]

The Last Days of Baron Reavis and His Dream

About a year later the Reavis criminal trial began in June 1896. Andres Sandoval, who years earlier had recalled the fictitious Peraltas and Masos visiting California in the 1860s, confessed to perjury, while Miguel Noe, the only witness to stand by Reavis in depositions taken before the civil trial, apparently beat a quick path to Mexico.[60]

The former baron had two years in the New Mexico Territory Prison to consider all this activity following his fraud conviction on June 30, 1896. After his release, he spent most of his few remaining years wandering the West, seeking sponsors for Arizona irrigation projects. He admitted the best known parts of the fraud in an article published on March 26, 1899, in the *San Francisco Call* but still gloated that he had "thwarted government agents at every turn." Indeed.

His twin sons served with the U. S. Army in France during the First World War and were alive when their mother Sophia died in early April 1934 in Denver, some thirty-two years after divorcing James Reavis for desertion. Her parentage and background are unknown to this day. Treadway, who could have been her father, apparently died six months before she was born. The Court of Private Land Claims commented that she appeared to be of Spanish heritage, but made no further determination.[61]

James Addison Reavis, the former Baron of Arizona, died from complications of bronchitis five days before Christmas in 1914, having spent part of the prior year on the Los Angeles County California Poor Farm.

Perhaps in those last days, he recalled his vision for Arizona—lush green valleys and developments in the desert, irrigated by dams that he himself had proposed.

Dreams that Reavis conceived, but others fulfilled.

CHAPTER 10

Philip Arnold: The Diamond King, and Other Mining Grifters

Ten eager Californians found what they were looking for near Brown's Park, in northwest Colorado, that June of 1872. They discovered about 285 diamonds within an hour. And they owed it all to Philip Arnold, a Kentucky adventurer who had approached mining impresario George D. Roberts with this prospect about two years earlier.

Arnold, his cousin John Slack, and Roberts worked together in the earlier "Mountains of Silver" promotion near Ralston, New Mexico, with Asbury Harpending. Promises to English investors had been made and broken then, but this seemed to be a good prospect.

The Kentucky kinsmen were among the vast throng that had come to California for their share of wealth, turning up around Sacramento during the Gold Rush fourteen years earlier. Somehow, Arnold found about $50,000 before returning to his home in Elizabethtown, Kentucky.

He was born in Hardin County in about 1830, some twenty-one years after Abraham Lincoln was born at Hodgenville, twelve miles away. Arnold and his kinsman John Slack had both served in the Mexican War, but only Slack saw battle.

When Roberts examined the stones Arnold and Slack brought him in 1870, he was excited enough to contact a banker— and not just any banker—William C. Ralston, the man who controlled the Bank of California, one of the biggest financial institutions in the state.

Ralston invested in everything from hotels to mills. He even helped finance the Central Pacific Railroad started by the Big Four—Collis Huntington, Leland Stanford, Mark Hopkins, and

Charles Crocker, the Associates who eventually cut him out of the action. Ralston had also grubstaked much of the Comstock Lode play, and was hungry for more mining adventure. Roberts also contacted longtime mining promoter Asbury Harpending. Roberts reported that, by December 1870, Arnold had discovered even more "show."

There had been no significant American diamond discoveries to date, despite the reports of Kit Carson and other mountain men, although the Arizona and New Mexico terrain seemed to promise an eventual discovery. Arnold would not reveal the location of his find, and with good reason—even the walls had ears in mining-crazy San Francisco.

The cousins had asked Roberts to quietly hide the sparklers in his wall safe at home that first night, but despite his assurances, the word got out.

Investors William Lent and General George S. Dodge somehow learned about the find. John Slack was not particularly greedy; he only wanted $50,000—about $838,000 in modern money—to share the discovery, and he got it after a June 1871 meeting in San Francisco. Yet, some still thought that Arnold and Slack had just been lucky.

Several months later, they met Harpending at the Lathrop train station east of San Francisco. Arnold and Slack seemed "travel stained and weather beaten" as if they had been on a long and arduous journey. Harpending noticed that while Arnold slept, "Slack stayed grimly erect" as if to guard a treasure.

Harpending gave them a receipt, and then took their samples home, where prospective investors were standing by. While the others watched, Harpending spread the contents on a billiard table. He later described the stones as something "like a dazzling, many-colored cataract of light."

And with that, the San Francisco investors decided it was time to bring in the Eastern financiers.

In early 1872, New York corporate lawyer Samuel Barlow hosted a crucial meeting at One Madison Avenue in the heart of the city. The select group of investors present included General

George McClellan and Congressman Benjamin Butler, a former Union general who later earned a significant piece of the action by arranging a minor change to the federal mining laws. Charles Tiffany was then the most famous jeweler in the country. After Harpending opened the bag, Tiffany sorted the stones, casually knocking rubies, emeralds, and sapphires to the side in the silence. "Gentlemen, these are beyond question precious stones of enormous value,"[1] Tiffany intoned. He insisted that his own experts examine them more closely, and when they did Tiffany reported back to the group that the stones in his possession were worth $150,000, about $2.6 million today.

Soon, William Ralston was calling Arnold's prospect "the American Golconda," for the rich diamond field discovered years earlier in India. There were only two other major fields, one in Brazil and the other in South Africa.

Back in San Francisco, several of the choicest stones had been displayed by William Willis, one of San Francisco's most prominent jewelers.

Of course, Arnold's partners did not know how the diamonds were really found.

One account says that Arnold was a bookkeeper for the Diamond Drill Company, a San Francisco business that made drill bits tipped by industrial-grade diamonds. Another researcher says that Arnold associate James B. Cooper was the bookkeeper, and yet another has Cooper as a bookkeeper with Arnold as his assistant.

Whatever the arrangement, Arnold acquired a collection of industrial-grade diamonds and began mixing them with other stones acquired from an Arizona Indian. These were the stones originally used to lure in George D. Roberts and his more prominent California associates. The second, heavier bag of stones used to hook the Eastern financers had been purchased in three lots for $20,000 in London, using the $50,000 that General George S. Dodge had initially paid John Slack.

The next year at the "diamond butte," which Arnold and Slack had selected for its remote location, when the investor's mining engineer Henry Janin asked for someone to take sand and gravel batches to a nearby stream, Philip Arnold and John Slack quickly volunteered. They found 1,600 carats of diamonds and four pounds of rubies in four days.

After Janin estimated the value of the find to be four million dollars, Arnold easily collected $150,000 from the mining partners, sold his shares in the company to William Lent and Harpending for $400,000, and returned to Kentucky.

The promoters then planned to recruit seventeen companies which would each invest five million dollars for exploration rights. This approach would yield the San Francisco-New York group a cool $85 million. Another more immediate source of cash became available after they incorporated on July 20, 1872, as the San Francisco and New York Mining and Commercial Company.

A diamond and ruby glass case display at the Bank of California brought in $850,000 from new shareholders within two weeks. The publicity accelerated when the San Francisco partners refused to reveal the location of the discovery—prompting South African diamond miners to close their diggings in fear of lower prices, even as hundreds of American prospectors rushed to imaginary diamond fields from Kansas to Utah.

Naturally, the inevitable cranks also began to emerge. Thomas Miner announced a major Arizona gold strike and then claimed that the San Francisco-New York group had stolen it. The Arizona citizenry saw through his strategy, and Miner barely survived a lynching. Soon, a San Francisco group agreed to back a diamond expedition lead by Miner, while their own prospectors plundered Miner's earlier Pinal County, Arizona, mining claim.

The Leopold Keller Affair

Then, a diamond broker named Leopold Keller told the *London Times* and the *London Telegraph* about mysterious strangers from America who bought large quantities of inferior uncut diamonds from him. This news brought Keller few glowing tributes in America. The *Mining & Scientific Press* described the Keller revelations as the desperation of threatened monopolies, even as disinterested London experts somehow obtained some of Arnold's diamond samples and confirmed their inferior quality.[2] Keller described some Americans who visited him on three different occasions in July 1871, and purchased large quantities of inferior stones.

The first visitors were undoubtedly Arnold and Slack, using the fictitious names "Aundel" and "Burcham," John Slack's middle name. The pair paid about $20,000 for some industrial-quality diamonds. The third visitor is a mystery to this day.

According to some, Asbury Harpending was part of the swindle, although he denied this accusation his entire life and even wrote a book to clear himself. Keller told the press about the third man, who purchased yet another bag of inferior stones. Although Harpending was then in London and seen with Arnold there, no one has ever established whether Harpending was part of the swindle or just another victim.

Despite the Keller disclosures, everyone in the country wanted to know where Arnold's diamonds were found. Arnold or someone impersonating him told conflicting accounts about the find to newspapermen in Laramie, Wyoming, and Denver. Arnold even went to Laramie to confront his imposter. However, local reporters identified Arnold as the same man they interviewed earlier.

Ten days before that event, Asbury Harpending created a diversion designed to lead the curious away from the new but undisclosed diamond field. Harpending hired former sheriff Mike Gray to lead an expedition in search of the diamond field.

Apparently Gray did not know that his guide, a shadowy figure known only as Mr. Jones, would be leading his expedition far away from northwest Colorado. Harpending even paid the expedition expenses. The party left San Francisco in late August 1872 and eventually detrained in Pueblo, Colorado, some 1,400 miles away. Soon the adventurers were astride horses journeying toward Four Corners, a remote and arid place in the southwest corner of Colorado that touched New Mexico, Arizona, and Utah, some four hundred miles south of the Arnold diamond field.

After they mounted up, Mr. Jones had some good news for the

expedition, which was being followed at a distance by unidentified riders. In a matter of days, they would arrive at a goldfield that Mr. Jones and some partners had discovered. Jones told them that this earlier expedition picked up about $1,000 worth of gold each day they worked, until Indians found them and massacred everyone but him.

Regrettably, after some thirty days, Jones took them right back to the place they started, prompting the riders behind them to bitterly complain they had been tricked. Jones promptly disappeared, leaving the fortune-seekers to survive by their own wits. A Navaho volunteered to lead them to Fort Defiance, Arizona, but dragged them through a series of small villages where they were forced to slowly trade away their horses and mules for measly rations.

And so, the Gray Expedition to Nowhere rode on, even as Harpending and the other inside investors in San Francisco and New York sold more stock to the public, just before announcing in October 1872 that operations were being suspended until spring. Although the *Arizona Citizen* editor was suspicious and said so, no one else seemed to notice—except Clarence King.

King had graduated from Yale and used his contacts to become leader of a geological survey that followed the new transcontinental railroad from Cheyenne, Wyoming, to the California state line. King thought he had finished the survey that fall, but by then was not so sure. The newly discovered diamond field was smack dab in the middle of land he had surveyed. If King had missed such a significant geological feature, his career would be over before it had really begun.

King and his crew were alarmed enough to discuss this news even as they compiled their field notes in San Francisco that fall. The rumors actually pointed to the probable location—a particular peak and butte just south of the Colorado-Wyoming border. The question was whether they could get there and back before snow or even blizzards engulfed the area.

King's advance party consisting of geologist Samuel Emmons

and topographer Allen Wilson left on October 19, 1872, bound for Fort Bridger on the Green River in Wyoming. The pair arrived there five days later in sub-zero weather. King was close behind. They left Fort Bridger on October 29, crossed into Colorado, and arrived at the Arnold site five days later.

The exploratory pits, claim stakes, and diamonds that could so easily be sifted from the dirt covering the flat butte all seemed to confirm the public reports about the discovery. And so they began to crush the underlying sandstone and pan the steams nearby for the clusters of diamonds that should have been there—but were not.

There was another surprise. A mine operator and four other diamond hunters who had followed them at a distance and hidden themselves suddenly appeared from nowhere, wanting to know what King had found. He told them.

Since King's reputation was on the line, he raced to Black Butte Station, Wyoming, and then on to report the news in San Francisco and save the public from yet another mining swindle. When his train arrived in San Francisco, he immediately found poor Henry Janin who had been had again. The previous year, Janin had unwisely relied on fake ore samples provided by a California mine superintendent and led a group of English investors into an expensive swindle.

By early morning, the young geologist had convinced Janin that something had to be done.

On the morning of November 11, King told the story again—this time to the suckers. George D. Roberts and Asbury Harpending had directly or indirectly brought the rest into the swindle. Little wonder then that they were the only promoters who disagreed with King's conclusions.

To his credit, the young geologist refused to suppress the news. To do so would have allowed the inside investors to recoup their losses or even make money by selling their own stock short into the decline. King did give them two weeks to deal with the crisis, but the promoters had to stop issuing new shares.

Henry Janin and General David D. Colton returned to the Arnold diamond field to confirm King's findings. Two days later, the investors were convinced they had been swindled. California newspapers published the story on November 26, 1872. Civic leaders slowly realized that San Francisco would not be the diamond capital of the world, even as the Gray Expedition plodded back to San Francisco, short two prospectors who had died of exposure along the way.

Clarence King was an instant hero to everyone but his boss, A. A. Humphries, whom King eventually replaced. Only then did the broad outline of the Arnold and Slack swindle become clear. The two grifters had fooled some of the smartest people in the country with a bucketful of third-rate stones.

The Frobisher Fraud

Mining frauds in the American colonies started with English sea captain Martin Frobisher, who returned to London in 1576 with an amazing black rock that contained enough gold to convince the authorities to sponsor two more expeditions to the New World.

Of course, the gold in the black rock was not found by the first assayer, or even the second. Finally, the third, Giovanni Agnello, simply shrugged and handed Frobisher a small pouch with gold powder supposedly extracted from the black rock.

When Frobisher returned from the second expedition, it took another three attempts to find an assayer who would approve the new samples, extracted near the Baffin Islands, between Greenland and Canada. Agnello strongly recommended Jonas Schultz, who indeed found gold in the sample ore. Lucky that, since the major investor in the enterprise was Queen Elizabeth I. The Cathay Company, which Frobisher had chartered with his money man Michael Lok, was secure for the moment.

But when the third expedition brought back more than a thousand tons of rock from the same general area with no gold content at all, the English authorities discovered that Agnello and Schultz had provided false assays. Alas, some of the last shipment of ore was used to repair country roads. Most was simply dumped in the ocean.[3]

The Mears-Gardiner Claims

One of the earliest American mining frauds actually originated in Mexico. The Treaty of Guadalupe-Hidalgo, which had ended the Mexican War in 1848, provided abundant opportunities for swindlers. One treaty term provided that the United States would compensate American citizens for war-related claims against the Mexican government.

A claims commission impaneled in Washington approved two large claims developed by twenty-something American dentist George Gardiner before adjourning forever in 1850. Gardiner had claimed $700,000 for the loss of a silver mine in the state of San Luis Potosi, some 520 miles south of Austin, Texas. The commission was suspicious, but his earnest testimony convinced them to award Gardiner $429,000, about $11 million today.

Not only that, but the commission awarded him another $154,000 for a mercury mine claim that Gardiner had purchased from fellow medico John Mears, who was still in Mexico.

Gardiner wrote Mears letters boasting of his Washington connections, particularly with General Winfield Scott, whose Mexican War translator had been George's brother John Gardiner. Through these contacts, George had hired a Mexican diplomat who provided blank sheets with official stamps easily converted into deeds, receipts, and affidavits substantiating the bogus silver and mercury claims.

None of this documentation impressed Charles Davis, the government official charged with closing the records of the Mexican Claims Commission. He knew Mears was a swindler and had spent enough time in Mexico to suspect that the lost mine that Gardiner claimed was not among the fabled mines of the San Luis Potosi region. Davis sent a letter of inquiry about the claim to the attorney general, who did nothing.

Finally, an on-site investigation of the Mears-Gardiner claims began, but only after the attorney general and Davis were hauled in front of President Millard Fillmore and his cabinet to debate the issue. John Gardiner had married into a politically prominent

Washington family, but this relationship did him little good. Both brothers were indicted for fraud in July 1851; George eventually posted a $40,000 bond after a second grand jury indicted him for forgery.

The national press then had a story with legs. The Democrats used the publicity to attack Whig senator Thomas Corwin of Ohio, who had represented George Gardiner earlier during the claim process. Like all congressmen of that era, Corwin was free to also practice law in his spare time. The adverse publicity prompted Whig President Millard Fillmore to send future baseball impresario Abner Doubleday and other worthies on yet another fact-finding junket to Lagunillas, Mexico, in late 1852. The politicos did not find the Gardiner mine, but located a wealthy landowner whom George Gardiner had somehow forgotten to include when the grift money was divided up. The *patron* had plenty to say. He also provided the investigators with incriminating letters from the Gardiner brothers.

None of this evidence was enough to convict Gardiner, who was saved by a deadlocked jury. However, when a second trial concluded in March 1854, George Gardiner was convicted, and then promptly sentenced to ten years in prison. Finally, the suave dentist pardoned himself with a fatal dose of poison. Neither of the two Johns—John Mears or John Gardiner—was ever seen again.

Beware of Guinea Pigs

Mining swindlers in England and America often employed "guinea pigs," famous men questionable corporations invited to join their boards of directors to lure in the suckers. One such dependable guinea pig was Benjamin "Beast" Butler, one the victims in the 1872 Diamond Hoax. Butler was the general who managed the Union occupation of New Orleans during much of the Civil War.

The high-handed manner in which Butler treated Southerners endeared him to the prosperous Northern victors who flocked to any mining deal that bore his name. Finally, by July 30, 1892, the *Engineering and Mining Journal* warned that Butler's name on any mining prospectus should be fair warning to any savvy investor.

Another common trick was to bribe journalists for favorable press reports. Samuel Clemens became Mark Twain covering Nevada mining operations as a reporter for the *Territorial Enterprise* in 1861. About ten years later, he was very candid about the bribes that were available for newspaper reporters willing to take shares in new mines, measured in feet.

> New claims were taken up daily, and it was the friendly custom to run straight to the newspaper offices and give the reporter forty or fifty 'feet' [of the claim] and get them to go and examine the mine and publish a notice about it.[4]

Clemens readily admitted his own participation in such practices in letters written to his family back in Missouri.[5] After all, this was the wild and woolly Comstock Lode of Nevada, which was named for a swindler.

Comstock's Bluff

June 1859 found Peter O'Riley and Patrick McLaughlin mining for gold on Mount Davidson, twelve miles northeast of what became Carson City, Nevada. They dug some nuggets out of the ground, had them assayed at $3,876 per ton, and were promptly confronted by Henry Tompkins Comstock, a lounge-about from Canada who claimed to own the entire mountain. "Old Pancake" was charitable that day—he bought them out for forty dollars, a bottle of whiskey, and a blind horse.[6]

Old Pancake shot himself in Bozeman, Montana, eleven years later. Certainly, by then it was obvious that Comstock bought low and foolishly sold that way too. The Comstock Lode would eventually yield about $400,000,000 over the next thirty years, after he sold out for about $10,000.

Virginia City eventually was established on Mount Davidson, high above the mines. The camp eventually offered fifty-one saloons, two opera houses, and all the usual pleasures, at C Street dives such as the Bucket of Blood, Sawdust Corner, and the Sazerac. The local whores included Virginia "Buffalo Joe" Dodge and dear, genteel Julie Bulette.

When Samuel Clemens arrived in Virginia City in 1861, with his brother Orion, the welcoming committee included Jack Harris, a local bandito born in Maine as Amos Huxford. Harris politely excused himself to harass a witness about to testify against Jack in a stage robbery trial. Eventually, Wells Fargo hired Harris to stop his robberies. That day he got himself shot in a gunfight as the Clemens brothers watched and then rode away, clutching three bullet wounds with two hands.

Harris was so thoroughly shot to pieces after years of banditry that he died in 1875—the same year that Patrick McLaughlin, co-discoverer of the Comstock Lode, died a pauper in San Bernardino, California. Both survived Peter O'Riley by about a year.[7]

The Ore Milling Swindle

Two Ohioans with strikingly different personalities began to manipulate Comstock market conditions to their own advantage in 1865. One was William C. Ralston, who was later swindled in the Arnold and Slack diamond hoax.

After investing in Comstock Lode companies and serving stints as treasurer of two mining companies, William Chapman Ralston founded the Bank of California in June 1864, with Sacramento businessman Daniel Ogden Mills, in San Francisco. The bank was capitalized at $2,000,000 and thus instantly became the largest in the state.[8]

Ralston soon salvaged fellow Ohioan William Sharon, a bankrupt flatboat captain and cardsharp who made a small fortune playing poker in his spare time. Sharon became Ralston's representative in wide-open Virginia City, Nevada. Sharon persuaded Ralston and Mills to open a Bank of California branch there, even though the price of silver was low and local business activity even lower, in the post-war depression of 1865.

The bankers acquired several mining companies and virtually all local milling operations in the Comstock Lode through foreclosure, which presented a unique swindling opportunity. Sharon recognized that extraordinary cash flow could be generated even in those depressed times, adding rock and debris to the ore crushed in the milling process. And this was so even when the Bank of California held controlling interest in the mining company being swindled, because the mining fees were an expense deducted before any dividends paid to the shareholders. A superintendent later owned up to the grift: "I mixed waste rock with the Yellow Jacket Ore, till it would scarcely pay for crushing, when the company [Yellow Jacket, which Bank of California owned] might have been paying dividends for years."[9]

Ralston's main Comstock rival, Adolph Sutro, had figured out another Ralston strategy years earlier. "Everybody speculates, every miner or chambermaid or washerwoman, and soon as they get into one stock, they want to speculate on another stock and they have to pawn it and the Bank of California, a regular pawnbroker shop, loans money on them. [Eventually] all this stock stands in the name of the 'Bank of California.'" Ralston, Sharon, and their cronies soon owned so much of the Comstock Lode that their detractors called them the "Bank Ring."[10]

William C. Ralston played Father Christmas in San Francisco, helping to develop the city, while in Virginia City miserly William Sharon did everything he could to squeeze out profits for the Bank of California. They had begun their partnership when the Comstock Lode was in decline, yet still made money working together—until they didn't.

William Sharon began to separate himself from Ralston in December 1874. The previous year, Sharon and Ralston had purchased stock in the Ophir Mine. That month, as the price of shares in the Ophir soared, Sharon began to make a killing by selling short on his own account in a maneuver that promptly put Ralston in a financial tailspin.

Ralston's bank accounts had already been damaged by his own excesses—like having an expensive ballroom built for a special event and then torn down the next day.[11]

Surely, Sharon understood how much trouble Ralston was in

when he was offered controlling interest in Ralston's pet project—the Palace Hotel—which was still under construction. Sharon turned him down in May 1875. Only two months later, the Bank of California avoided a crisis when Ralston had two million dollars placed in a vault, and then returned to the lender just hours after a board of directors committee looked at the cash and sighed with relief.

From that moment on, Ralston seemingly could do nothing right. He bought controlling interest in the Spring Valley Water Company, which proposed to harness Alameda Creek and provide fresh water to San Francisco, only to be criticized by the media for trying to make a paltry $9 million profit on the deal.

When the stock market fell again in August, Ralston piled the bank counters high with twenty-dollar gold pieces, but fooled no one. As the cock crowed a second time on August 26, his former protégé William Sharon deposited the money he had made, liquidating his Comstock holdings—with Wells Fargo.

The Bank of California board of directors may have been fooled earlier when Ralston borrowed two million dollars for one day, but this time they dug deeper into the books. They discovered Ralston owed the Bank of California $4 million. The next day he signed a deed of trust assigning his entire estate to Sharon for the benefit of Ralston's creditors, resigned that afternoon from the bank, and left for a swim at North Beach.

He never came back. After putting on a swimming suit in the Neptune Beach Bath House and greeting a friend, Ralston dove in and was soon found floating face down—dead at forty-five. Ralston was popular enough in San Francisco that two newspapers that criticized him in death were attacked by mobs.

Perhaps he died of heart failure, but one astute associate didn't think so. "Best thing he could have done," Bill Sharon later said, according to Sharon's granddaughter. Best, perhaps, for Bill Sharon, but not for Ralston's widow. Sharon cajoled her into settling for a relatively modest $85,000 and kept the rest of the estate, estimated to be worth at least $3 million.

Sharon would need the money, if only to satisfy the claims of the lady friends he collected when he became a widower. Sarah Althea Hill was thirty years younger than Bill Sharon, yet she became his wife, at least according to a document that surfaced when she sued him for adultery, naming nine female rivals. Old Bill fought Sarah A. Hill up to his death, in November 1885, following sordid divorce proceedings decided against Sharon by the California Supreme Court.

The next year she married yet another, elderly, rich widower. Judge David S. Terry had been one of the lawyers representing her in divorce proceedings and related lawsuits against William Sharon. United States Supreme Court Justice Stephen J. Field ruled against her in a related federal matter, while sitting on a three-judge panel.

On August 14, 1889, Judge Terry slapped Supreme Court Justice Field in a train station dining room and was promptly shot dead by Field's bodyguard. Poor Sarah was committed to an insane asylum three years later and died in 1937.[12]

The Bonanza Kings

Four Irish-Americans known as the Bonanza Firm were among those who competed with William Sharon and William C. Ralston in the Comstock Lode. Two of the four, James C. Flood and William S. O'Brien, spent their time speculating on the stock exchange in San Francisco, far from Nevada.[13] They first partnered in a San Francisco lunchroom called the Auction frequented by miners and mining speculators.[14] The other two, James "Slippery Jim" Fair and John Mackay, were mining superintendents who had a keen eye for the quick buck. The formal name of their operation was Flood and O'Brien, but they became known as the Bonanza Firm after their rich 1872 discovery at the Consolidated Virginia mine, often simply called the Con Virginia—and with good reason.

Three years earlier they had quietly accumulated enough shares to take control of the Hale and Norcross mine from the two Bills—Ralston and Sharon—and then delighted the shareholders by increasing dividends, at least for a while.

They had a major problem back at the Con Virginia; the mine intersected with the original Comstock Lode and could not go any lower than that point. This situation did not prevent Slippery Jim Fair from falsely claiming a wide seam of ore in the 1875 Consolidated Virginia annual report; even as the partners began to quietly unload their own shares.

James R. Keene, former publisher of the *San Francisco Examiner,* somehow learned about this double dealing and began selling short himself. Keene collected his boodle and moved on to Wall Street after disclosing the whole fraud to the public in April 1876.

The Bonanza Kings had one last trick left at the Consolidated Virginia. They lowered the mine to the maximum depth, and in March 1877, a group of boosters led by George D. Roberts toured the mine and sang the praises of the rich ore they found.

It didn't work. Nineteen months later, Consolidated Virginia fired nearly everyone working at the mine. John Mackay sadly announced that the Con Virginia had played out.

Another shareholder, Squire P. Dewey, also believed that the shareholders had been misled. He sold a hundred shares to *San Francisco Chronicle* reporter John H. Burke, who became the nominal plaintiff in a fraud case. Burke and Dewey proved that Flood and O'Brien had defrauded the Consolidated Virginia shareholders of $926,000. Rather than appeal the case, Flood and O'Brien paid Dewey and Burke an undisclosed amount in 1881, leaving their fellow shareholders with nothing.

Eventually the Bonanza Kings retreated to San Francisco and safer investments; by the time the Comstock Lode began to lose its luster in the mid-1880s, they had accumulated fortunes estimated at fifteen to twenty million dollars each. In a sense, there is a monument to their shenanigans—the Pacific Union Club at Mason and California Streets, once owned by Flood.

The Bucketeers

By the late 1880s, thirty mines in the Comstock remained open only to encourage stock speculation. The final Comstock swindle was called bucketing. Stockbrokers asked to buy ever declining Comstock shares "on margin" often pocketed the 50 percent down payment and simply filed the order away. Such brokers assumed that in those rare instances where a buyer later ordered a sale, the stock could then be purchased much more cheaply. The customer would never know the difference. And often the dishonest brokers were right. In 1880, the once powerful Gold Hill Branch of the Bank of California near Virginia City closed. Three years later, the last editor of the *Gold Hill Daily News* noted in his diary that a house he had built there for $8,000 years earlier had just sold for a few hundred dollars.

Requiem for Mining Heroes and Swindlers

Clarence King, the hero who unearthed the Great Diamond Hoax of 1872, died in 1901 at a small cottage in Phoenix. His many friends, including Abraham Lincoln's Secretary John Hay, Henry Adams, and other Easterners, noted that King never wrote a work of fiction, as they had hoped, although his *Systematic Geology* and *Mountaineering in the Sierra Nevada* are considered classics to this day.

And what happened to Arnold and Slack?

Slack first moved to St. Louis and used his $30,000 boodle to purchase a coffin manufacturing firm. He moved on to White Oaks, New Mexico, in 1880, about the time that booming little mining camp became a favorite haunt of a scrawny youngster called Billy the Kid. Poor Billy had his favorite horse shot out from underneath him by a posse near White Oaks, on November 20, 1880, but he killed one of them, former Texas Ranger James N. Bell, about five months later. Slack became an undertaker and died in White Oaks sixteen years after arriving there. He died with an estate of $1,611.[15]

Arnold returned to Elizabethtown, Kentucky, with oodles of cash and an alibi of sorts. He claimed that the diamond field he "discovered" did contain diamonds. Of course it did—he should know, because he left them there. So far as Arnold was concerned, the value of the diamonds was for others to argue about. Unhappy investor William Lent wanted to argue about the $350,000 Arnold lifted from his back pocket, and sued him in Kentucky. Finally, Arnold settled with Lent for $150,000 and invested the rest in a new bank. After a competing banker shot him in an 1879 gunfight, Arnold contracted pneumonia and died.[16]

CHAPTER 11

Dr. Richard C. Flower:
A Scandal at Spenazuma

Sickness is a toy in his hands.[1]

Centuries ago, a legend said the Aztec prince Spenazuma had lived near a dramatic Arizona outcropping that bore his name. Later, an old Mexican, in his eagerness to repay the kindness of Professor T. A. Halchu from Longhorn, Montana, revealed a major source of Aztec wealth during his last hours.

Some hopeful Kansans had organized Spenazuma Mining Company in 1898, and then sold out to a forty-nine-year-old doctor back East. The mine was located near Blackrock Canyon in southwestern New Mexico Territory, near the Arizona border.[2]

The first thing Dr. Richard C. Flower did after purchasing the mine was make up a yarn about an Aztec prince named Spenazuma, whoever he was. Flower soon replaced most of the company directors, and then moved the Spenazuma Mine to a better location some 180 miles away, near Solomonville, Arizona. This was supposedly a better place because it was near an outcropping that Flower thought matched an Aztec profile. The nearest train stop was in Geronimo, Arizona.

The third group of Spenazuma investors hailed from Missouri, New York, and other places scattered from Dallas to Boston. They arrived in May 1899.[3] Dr. Flower had arranged some entertainment, but Graham County sheriff Bill Duncan spoiled it all.

Duncan had raced to the spot where several hired stage robbers were ready to ambush the investors on their way to the mines, but the spoilsport sheriff sent them back to the saloons in Geronimo where Flower's henchman "Alkali Tom" had found them earlier.[4] Soon, the visitors stepped down from their stage-coaches into a noisy, boisterous mining camp. Had they asked a few questions back in Geronimo, they likely would have heard nothing discouraging. After all, the Spenazuma was a source of employment for a few locals—and more temporarily when investors visited. Many of those who visited that day invested in the mine when they returned home.

An *Arizona Republican* reporter named George Smalley had arrived in Geronimo from Phoenix at about the same time, but did not visit the mine with the investors. Smalley had already written some unkind things about the mine for his newspaper in Phoenix and decided to take Sheriff Duncan when he visited himself—just in case.

The scene awaiting Smalley and Duncan was far different from the one the investors saw only days before at Spenazuma. Things were quiet and the staff downright unhelpful. The two visitors could not even get candles to inspect the mine works until Sheriff Duncan stole several in the company store. When no one was watching, Smalley and Duncan confirmed what Smalley's paper and the *Arizona Citizen* in Tucson had already opined to their readers: the Spenazuma mine was a fraud.[5]

Earlier, after the acquisition was complete, Flower had offered one million shares to the public at a dollar per share. Then he made some special arrangements before allowing the first investors to visit months before Smalley had arrived.

They were urged to pick up a rock at random and watch the camp assayer test their samples. Rock after rock proved to contain a high percentage of gold or silver, no matter how unpromising it might look.[6] The second crew of visitors was equally lucky, but this time, the new company assayer was puzzled.

Each prospective investor gave him a nondescript rock that tested positive for gold and silver. And then he discovered why—someone had doctored his chemicals.

Flower took no such chances with the marks that arrived just before Smalley and Sheriff Duncan. Since the Spenazuma really was not a working mine, he simply bought some good ore else-where and had it dumped next to the fake mine openings. Alkali Tom, the local who had arranged the fake stage holdup for Dr. Flower, learned that Smalley had talked with the mine owners who had supplied ore for the third group of visiting inves-tors. He provided Smalley a stolen horse for the return trip to Geronimo, knowing that if Smalley were spotted, he would prob-ably be shot by the owner. Later, Smalley claimed that he simply outraced his pursuer, and then told his Spenazuma tale in the May 17, 1899, issue of the *Arizona Republican.*

Flower and his captive board of directors did their best to dis-credit the story; they threatened to sue the *Republican,* offered Smalley a $5,000 bribe, and gathered testimonials from pliant Graham County businessmen.[7]

None of this activity dissuaded the Arizona territorial gover-nor from targeting the Spenazuma in a June 1899 proclamation against mining swindles. The entire adult population of Tivoli, New York, claimed to have been victimized by the Spenazuma swindle. The Tivolites had invested some $50,000, about $1.3 million today, in the enterprise. Their money was long gone.

So was Dr. Flower, who had moved on to other opportunities, leaving apprentice swindlers behind to recycle the Spenazuma mine. By that time it was called the Black Rock, using first the Graham County Mining Company and then the Advance Mining Company as fronts.[8]

The Julianna and the Silver Cliff

All of this subterfuge was old hat to Richard C. Flower, minis-ter, physician, faith healer, and mine promoter. He really didn't need any professional certificates for any of these followings in nineteenth-century America, but he graduated from Northwest-ern University in 1868, having studied law, medicine, and theol-ogy. As a young man, Flower was a dead ringer for the modern actor and comedian Steve Martin.[9]

He was raised in Albion, Illinois, a burg founded by a colony of Englishmen led by his grandfather George Flower and his partner Morris Birkbeck in about 1817.[10] Young Richard started his life as a preacher in the Christian Church, following his father's profession, but soon went on to medicine and faith healing. Prior to 1880, Flower traveled from town to town as a physician, but by that year he had established a clinic at Alliance, Ohio. Flower moved on to New York that year and Boston twelve years later, performing medical wonders with his staff of "electricians and magnetizers."

The key to Flower's financial success as a doctor was advertising. He promoted his medical skills in Boston, Chicago, Cincinnati, and smaller cities. He claimed to have cured 4,122 cases of cancer, with a success rate of 94 percent.[11] His ability to hold a patient's hand to diagnose and cure illness was advertised along with his ability to predict the rise and fall of stock prices.[12]

This financial genius claimed by Dr. Flowers brought him into the mining business—first at little Rosita, Colorado, a long-abandoned ghost town, once the headquarters of the Julianna Mining and Milling Company. Dr. Flower lost his initial investment there, but found a new avocation.

He simply purchased the Julianna in 1883 and put his father-in-law C. C. Manful in charge. Manful managed the mine, while Flowers sold shares in the enterprise back East. Despite amazingly rich finds reported by Manful, the Julianna continued to lose money.[13] Something had to be done—why not buy more worthless mines nearby and reorganize?

The Wet Mountain Valley surrounding Julianna was in a slump, which happens when mines don't produce commercial quantities of ore.

Undeterred, Flower and Manful assembled more distressed properties like the Julianna and capitalized the new Security Mining and Milling Company at ten million dollars, seeking to raise that amount by using advertising in Eastern newspapers such as the *Boston Traveler*.

Other swindlers were also at work pitching Wet Mountain Valley mines, which had often played out long before. These competitors included 1872 Diamond Hoax investor William Lent, who sold shares in his Bull-Domingo mine from comfortable digs in New York City. Flowers found professional help selling the Security Mining securities. The more flexible Consolidated Stock and Petroleum Exchange in New York accepted Security Mining for trading purposes even after the Boston Stock Exchange refused to list it.[14]

Flower added something new and unique to the Security Mining portfolio—a functioning mine purchased from James R. Keene, whom we met in the previous chapter. The Silver Cliff operation was somewhat typical of the mining swindles of the day. Rough, low-grade silver ore could be coaxed and wheedled from its mineshafts; the milling machinery functioned if necessary, but was rarely busy.[15]

This situation should have been perfect for Keene, who got rich on Comstock Lode speculation in San Francisco, but lost nearly everything when he tried to become a Wall Street operator.

The Silver Cliff was Keene's second chance. He capitalized a new company at $1.5 million, about $145,000 of which was actually used to develop the mine and build surface facilities. Keene paid $500,000 to the previous owner and kept the rest for himself and his partners; the mine itself was idle and forsaken when Richard Flower found it.

However, the Silver Cliff became golden after it was acquired by Security Mining, at least in the eyes of Will Orange, publisher of the *Silver Cliff Rustler.* Some of his competitors claimed he was Flower's nephew.

Profits were still but a dream for hopeful Security Mining investors in 1887, when Dr. Flower told them that the Silver Cliff milling operations needed a complete overhaul. Actually, Flower had decided to fix two problems. The Silver Cliff milling operation was revamped as he promised, but the price of Security Mining stock was also thoroughly scrubbed by a trick known as the "wash sale."

The good doctor simply sold Security Mining Stock to himself on the New York market, pumping the price up to nine dollars a share.[16]

Soon, however, the price of Security Mining stock collapsed, but Flower had not dumped it; since the company bylaws prohibited assessments against shareholders, he couldn't squeeze any more out of the operation. It was time for him to move on.

Despite persistent public announcements of rich ore discoveries, actual mining operations dwindled to nothing. A payroll was missed in April 1888, and the next month a creditor filed a lien to seize Security Mining. The creditor was none other than Richard C. Flower, who repurchased the assets at a sheriff's sale, renamed it Geyser Mining, then sold it to two cohorts to start the entire swindle again.

Twelve years later, the new management had deepened the Silver Cliff to 2,650 feet, then a record depth in Colorado. Perhaps the investors were proud of this achievement, at least until the Silver Cliff was sold to satisfy a piddling debt in 1901.[17] Dr. Flower had not been idle in the meantime. He faced three fraud charges by 1898, but soldiered on to the Spenazuma project.

Among the difficulties he then faced in his medical practice was a new-fangled state rule requiring that medical doctors obtain *licenses*. A New York County Medical Society undercover investigator sought treatment and prescriptions from Dr. Flower's office and then had him arrested, only to learn later in court that she had been treated by one of his associates.

None of this turmoil distracted Dr. Flower from beginning new mining ventures. This time, he purchased several unpromising, undeveloped copper mining properties from one of his former salesmen; Henry Clifford had done a road show for Spenazuma investors as the "commissioner of Arizona."

Flower purchased the marginal mines for next to nothing, made minimum payments on a smelter to be relocated from Spokane, Washington, and started raising money through his new shell operation, the Arizona Eastern and Montana Company. Although Henry Clifford was the Arizona Eastern manager, he retained the most highly promoted property—the Lone Pine—in his wife's name and began seeking other properties for himself.

When Flower discovered such underhanded dealing, he was

outraged. Flower forced Clifford out of Arizona Eastern, but recognized Clifford's control of the Lone Pine mine.

Clifford didn't miss much. Within a year, Arizona Eastern, which earlier had raised millions for mining, was auctioned off at a sheriff's sale for $5,000 to cover a debt of $130,000. Presumably, Dr. Flower had taken the investment proceeds.

Theodore Hagaman, who made a fortune selling Flower's mining stocks, died on September 11, 1900, at the Waldorf Astoria hotel in New York under mysterious circumstances. The treating physician, Dr. Richard C. Flower, signed a death certificate naming cirrhosis of the liver as the cause of death. When the family learned that Flower somehow had convinced Mrs. Hagaman to invest her husband's $600,000 estate with Flower before the patient had even died, they yelled, "Poison!" However, by 1903, when poor Hagaman was exhumed, any chance of proving murder was long gone.[18]

The Lone Pine Rebellion

That same year, some of Flower's victims from the Arizona Eastern swindle reorganized the company as the Lone Pine Mining Company and planned for a comeback. Flower tried to break up the effort by staging a corporate meeting; he freely apologized for his past mistakes in the Spenazuma and Arizona Eastern capers, then persuaded the shareholders present to replace the reform directors. Within a few weeks a compromise allowed Flower to name five of the twelve directors, but the reformed company also failed. Flower merely repackaged its assets as Pan-American Mining and Smelting Company for another scam.[19]

Some of the Eastern investors hired attorney Andrew Meloy to pursue Flower in the criminal courts. Meloy in turn hired young attorney George Mills to help with the case. Soon, he discovered that Flower's son, attorney Jewell Flower, had hired young Mills away. Eventually, Dr. Flower was arrested and charged with grand larceny, allegedly arising from false representations he had made to an investor about the Lone Pine Mining Company stock.[20] A female admirer bonded Dr. Flower out because she believed he saved her life, even though she had also lost $300,000 in his mining swindles.

Flower was in a vengeful mood. He had Meloy arrested for larceny, disclosing that Meloy had attempted to shake him down for bribery money allegedly being demanded by the police. Flower was arrested for attempted bribery, since he gave Meloy a check.

The good doctor then tried to have some grand larceny charges pending against him dropped. Young attorney Mills was sent to obtain the original grand larceny documents through bribery. Mills was arrested, convicted, and sentenced to fourteen months at Sing Sing prison.[21]

With serious criminal charges pending, Flower decided to run. He assumed new aliases and identities, but could not leave the swindler's life behind. He still owned the Sunset Mine in the Mexican state of Chihuahua. While in Juarez, Flower met with an attorney for Fanny Hagaman, then known as Fanny Delabarre, whom he had swindled out of about $600,000, about $15 million today, some three years earlier.

For what it was worth, and perhaps in hopes of returning to the United States, Flower offered to share the Sunset Mine profits with Mrs. Delabarre and his other victims. Soon, he had to flee again, hiding in Central and South America, Europe, and Passaic, New Jersey, and finally in Montreal, Canada, before disappearing without a trace.

He emerged as "Professor Oxford" in January 1907, with a new secret process designed to bilk some unwary Philadelphians out of their savings. New York City detective Barney McConville eavesdropped on Dr. Flower working the two suckers just long enough to identify his voice from previous surveillance and have two local detectives arrest him. The Philadelphia courts inexplicably allowed Flower to post bond, despite his record of jumping bail. Soon he had bilked some Pennsylvania investors out of $400,000.[22]

In September 1908, in Richmond, Virginia, police arrested

everyone in the Courtland gang except Richard Courtland himself. Afterward, his wife confessed that she was Fanny Delabarre, the widow of Theodore Hagaman. She claimed that Richard Courtland was really Dr. Richard Flower. Flower had created one last mining swindle, the Appalachian Mining and Smelting Company, before he was returned to New York where he pled guilty to larceny charges and was sent to prison.[23] There was a time when Buffalo Bill Cody might well have invested with Flower.

The Camp Bonito Swindle

Dr. Richard C. Flower never met Buffalo Bill Cody, but they shared interests in mining, patent medicines, and showmanship. Cody had invested thousands in the distribution of "White Beaver's Cough Creams, the Great Lung Healer" with Dr. Frank Powell, while Flower dispensed such liquid junk to individual patients between mining ventures.[24] And they each had a flair for convincing others to invest their savings in worthless mines, although Cody apparently did so innocently.

After investing in the Camp Bonito mine works, about forty-three miles from Tucson, Cody gave meticulous instructions to the mine managers preparing to entertain Cody's friends, who might also invest in the enterprise. "I wish you would have the Mrs. Thomas house whitewashed, also the store. It would help the looks greatly," he once requested.

The problem, of course, was the small quantity of good ore being extracted at Camp Bonito, rather than the appearance of the mining camp. His 1910 Wild West show season had produced a $200,000 profit for Cody. Two years later, he realized a more modest $62,500 profit, but that still would be a $1.4 million paycheck today.[25] Cody expected that his investments of these profits would provide him a comfortable retirement; had he not begun investing in the Camp Bonito mining operation ten years earlier he might have retired in luxury, but his financial losses at Camp Bonito virtually assured he would work the rest of his life.

Buffalo Bill (Western History Collection, University of Oklahoma)

Cody was intrigued by the mine fortunes being made all over the country. The frenzy that began with the California gold strikes in 1849 had been so intense that the government of the United States had even seized the Black Hills in the Dakotas from the Lakota Sioux in 1877 for gold and silver mining.[26]

Buffalo Bill was part of this frenzy. Colonel Daniel B. Dyer had approached Cody with the Camp Bonito opportunity in 1902. Dyer convinced Cody to join him mining for tungsten, gold, and lead in Pima County, Arizona, through the Cody-Dyer Mining and Milling Company. Colonel Dyer had served as an Indian agent at Fort Reno, Indian Territory, in present-day Oklahoma, but apparently knew little about mining.

They turned for expertise to Lewis W. Getchell, who according to one Cody biographer was "notorious for promoting worthless commercial properties." Apparently, he saw Buffalo Bill as an easy mark. Getchell used fake mining reports to trick Cody into making his initial Camp Bonito investment and then billed him for expenses that had not been incurred in mining operations.[27]

Beginning in 1903, gold began to appear in the ore samples produced by Getchell, but never enough to produce any significant return on Cody's investment. Estimates of the amounts Cody invested in the Camp Bonito mine have ranged from $200,000 to $500,000.

Cody was discouraged in November 1910. In one of his letters he urged Getchell to show some miners "where you thought the old workers lost the vein and let them start in and see if they can stake that silver vein . . . up would go our stock . . . *that vein is sure there someplace.*"[28]

But it wasn't. Discouragement slowly turned to despair. Six months later, Cody was dealing with a recent train wreck that cost his Wild West show $10,000, high-dollar promissory notes that were overdue, and the prospect of being driven to bankruptcy by the mining operation at Camp Bonito. "Your expenses this spring have been much heavier than I told you to spend . . . my old friend, I am nearly crazy."[29] Indeed.

A report by mining expert E. J. Ewing prepared the next year at the request of Colonel Dyer only confirmed what one engineer on a neighboring claim long suspected: "Getchell is playing him [Cody] for a sucker."[30]

During his investigation, Ewing encountered one of the few mine employees listed on the payroll who was actually working. He was salting the mill with ore much better than what Camp Bonito was capable of producing. Ewing also uncovered the kickback system Getchell had created. After Getchell was fired, the mining works were leased to E. J. Ewing to cut losses.

That December, Colonel Dyer, who had recruited Cody for the Camp Bonito debacle, died at Clarendon, his mansion high above the Missouri River at Kansas City, leaving a $600,000 estate. Cody died on January 10, 1917. The next year, his interest in the Camp Bonita mines was transferred to the heirs of Barney Link, a printer to whom Buffalo Bill Cody owed $10,000 when he died.[31] Cody at least outlived one mine swindler.

Dr. Richard C. Flower was out of jail on bond in 1916, when he collapsed and died at a Hoboken, New Jersey, theater, 2,400 miles away from the dream mine he had invented at Spenazuma.

CHAPTER 12

Albert Fall: The Art of the Bribe

—as typically Western as his black, broad-brimmed Stetson Hat and his love of fine horses.[1]

Deep in the Western wilderness, about thirty miles north of Casper, Wyoming, visitors can still see the Teapot Dome, marked by a tall craggy bluff jutting out of the ground. Until a 1962 storm damaged the spout, it really did look something like a teapot.

Some ninety years ago, in April 1921, President Warren G. Harding transferred control of the Teapot Dome, officially known as Naval Oil Reserve No. 3, into the grasp of Albert Fall, along with Naval Oil Reserves No. 1 and No. 2, located at Elk Hills and Buena Vista, California.[2] Fall claimed later it was Secretary of the Navy Edwin Denby who wanted to return the reserves to the Department of the Interior, where they had once been managed.[3] Fall even quoted Denby as saying of the politically charged oil reserve: "It is full of dynamite. I don't want to have anything to do with it."

On April 7, 1922, Fall leased the Teapot Dome Reserve to Tulsa oilman Henry Sinclair of Mammoth Oil Company. Soon, the California Reserves went to Edward L. Doheny, a longtime acquaintance whom Fall had known since their early prospecting days in Kingston, New Mexico. All three leases were exclusive, non-competitive, and secret.

Admiral John Robinson wondered out loud at the time whether the arrangement should be approved by Attorney General Harry M. Daugherty. Fall assured Robinson that he was an attorney and needed no other legal opinion.[4]

Mahlon T. Everhart was Fall's son-in-law. Within a month,

Everhart picked up $198,000 in liberty bonds in Harry Sinclair's private railway car, and then another $35,000 elsewhere. Sinclair also gave Fall a $35,000 loan. Despite Fall's efforts to keep these transfers a secret, New Mexico ranchers noticed improvements on Fall's Three Rivers Ranch and began complaining. Rumors about the leases began to surface.

Long before his son-in-law collected cash and bonds from Harry Sinclair in a private train car, Fall had asked his old New Mexico acquaintance Edward L. Doheny to loan him $100,000. He wanted to purchase the Harris Ranch, at the headwaters of the Three Rivers. Ownership of the Harris Ranch would assure water for the rest of his ranching operators.

And so, after a brief long-distance conversation, Doheny instructed his son Edward Jr. to deliver all that cash to Fall at his Washington apartment. The Harris Ranch purchase closed in early December 1921. In a sense, much of the Albert Fall tragedy to follow was about the Three Rivers Ranch.

Early Days and Rise to Power

Although Albert Fall was in every sense a son of the West, he had started life in Kentucky. His grandfather, Philip Slater Fall, was a Baptist preacher, but became a leader in the Christian Church. Reverend Fall was an educator who instilled young Albert with the habits of learning and reading, though not his religious beliefs. Later, Albert was the only member of Harding's cabinet to list himself as religiously unaffiliated.[5]

Much of his childhood was spent in Nashville, Tennessee, with his grandparents, although he had been born in Frankfort, Kentucky. His schoolteacher father served under Confederate General Nathan Bedford Forrest in the Civil War. His mother was born Edmonia Taylor. She came from a prominent Kentucky family, one branch of which produced Old Taylor whiskey.

His grandfather, born in England, refused to take the Federal loyalty oath and defiantly raised the Union Jack over his home.

Albert Fall (Library of Congress)

When Albert was fifteen, his grandfather moved back to Poplar Hill farm near Frankfort. The young man remained in Nashville briefly, working in a cotton mill before joining his parents, who were teaching school in Springfield, Tennessee. March 1881 found Albert in Morganfield, Kentucky, where he taught school while reading law at night. A year earlier he began efforts to apprentice with an established attorney, but never did. Finally, he was admitted to the New Mexico Territory bar in 1887.

Perhaps his brief employment in the Nashville cotton mill was responsible in part for his later lung problems and move west; perhaps debt was also a factor. Whatever the reason, he left Kentucky for Clarksville, Texas, in late 1881, after an earlier trip west to Eureka Springs, Arkansas, then a health spa, and present-day eastern Oklahoma.

His health was not good; Fall was a "lunger," so described by that indelicate Western term for a person who suffers from tuberculosis. He tried bookkeeping, but soon began working as a cowboy for Texas cattle operations, moving herds north to Kansas. While working on a ranch nearby, Fall wandered into the aftermath of the "Buffalo Gap War" and saw San Angelo, where three participants were lying dead on a sidewalk.

By 1883, he had moved on to real estate, insurance, and romance. He married Emma Garland Morgan, whom he pursued to Readyville, Tennessee, where the nineteen-year-old was living with relatives. He became a vagabond prospector traveling through Mexico; then he tried his luck at Silver City, New Mexico Territory, one boyhood home of Billy the Kid, before moving on to Kingston, in the spring of 1886, passing bullet-marked cabins that had been attacked by the Apaches as he traveled along.

He arrived in Kingston relatively well dressed but completely broke. Edward L. Doheny was among the prospectors he met there. Doheny was born in Wisconsin to a Canadian mother and Irish father; he would become a multimillionaire in mining and oil.

That was not in the cards for Albert Fall. He returned to Texas for his wife, who also had lung problems. Along the way, he had visited Mesilla Valley, a region extending from present-day Hatch,

New Mexico, to the west side of El Paso, Texas. It was "the garden of the world" as so he told his wife, since he was determined to settle in the heart of the Mesilla Valley at Las Cruces. And settle there he did. Albert Fall was admitted to the bar, became a judge, served as an army officer, and was elected a United States senator in 1912. He was re-elected to the Senate in 1918 and was appointed Secretary of the Interior by President Harding in March 1921. He owned the vast Three Rivers Ranch 125 miles north of El Paso, which he had first seen when it was owned by Patrick Coghlan, an Irish immigrant rumored to have brokered cattle rustled by Billy the Kid a few years earlier.

The Fountain Murders

Fall became a lawyer, rancher, politician, and even a statesman of sorts—a successful man from humble beginnings. Naturally, he had taken a few shortcuts along the way.

One might have involved his archrival Albert J. Fountain and Fountain's eight-year-old son, Henry, who disappeared with scarcely a trace on February 1, 1896, in the White Sands near Las Cruces. Fountain, a Republican, and Fall, then a leader of the Democrat party, were adversaries.

Fall defended the three men accused of the murder, and some suspected he was even more deeply involved earlier. Oliver Lee, Jim Gilliland, and Billy McNew all escaped punishment. Charges against McNew were dismissed, while Lee and Gilliland were acquitted because of Fall's legal abilities, despite the best efforts of former sheriff Pat Garrett.

The Fountains were apparently ambushed at Chalk Hill near where the White Sands began. A mail carrier noticed that some buckboard tracks drifted off the road there. The crime site evidence of possible murder was clear enough—three spent cartridges, a large pool of blood, and horse tracks indicating that Fountain and his son had been intercepted. About ten miles away, the buckboard and Fountain's briefcase were found later, both empty.

Some papers fluttered in the wind around the buckboard, but not the indictments that probably got the Fountains killed.

Fountain was an assistant U.S. district attorney when the southeastern New Mexico Stock Growers Association asked for legal help fighting local cattle rustlers. Fountain became their investigator and special prosecutor; he was carrying some thirty-two indictments against twenty-three accused rustlers when he, his son, and the paperwork disappeared.

One Pinkerton detective summarized Fall's suspected involvement. "I am thoroughly satisfied that Judge Fall was not at Chalk Hill, but I am not satisfied that he was not a party to the conspiracy. There is certainly a master hand in this whole affair, and the great legal point would be the proper disposition or disposal of these bodies so that they could not be found."[6] The detective pointed out that Fall was seven miles to the east at Sunol, in the San Andres Mountains, at the time of the murder and could have seen the whole thing with a good pair of binoculars.

Yet, there was never sufficient evidence of Fall's complicity in the Fountain disappearances. Also, he was involved in the decision to have Pat Garrett investigate the murders. Fall himself contended that the rumors accusing him of conspiracy to murder were all about politics.

Oliver Lee was a prime suspect, both as a rustler and the murderer of the Fountains. After Garrett was elected sheriff of Dona Ana County, Lee recalled how Garrett had ambushed Billy the Kid in a darkened room and declared he would not meet the same fate, just before he went missing, perhaps at Fall's instigation.

Eventually, Lee surrendered in brand-new Otero County, which was created for just that purpose, since Pat Garrett had no jurisdiction there. The trial began in May 1899 at Hillsboro, then a mining boomtown. The judge and lawyers ground through seventy-five witnesses. The eighteen days of testimony were often translated by a Spanish-speaking interpreter. During closing argument, Fall accused special prosecutor Thomas B. Catron of conspiring against Oliver Lee. It worked.

Years later, while a United States senator, Fall was asked for his recollections of the Fountain episode. "The old animosities have been buried and we must let them die" And that was all he ever said.

The Teapot Begins to Bubble

When rumors about Teapot Dome began to spread in 1922, the United States Senate passed Resolution 277, which requested the Secretaries of the Navy and the Interior to inform the Senate whether lease negotiations were pending and whether there would be competitive bidding.[7]

Fall was not in Washington, so Denby and acting Interior Secretary Edward Finney responded. They provided a copy of one lease and argued that the transactions had been appropriate, since the crude oil produced on the Teapot Dome lease was unsuitable as ship fuel and had to be exchanged. Also, they claimed millions of barrels of California oil had already been lost. Unless something was done, the remaining reserves would be drained by wells on adjoining lands.[8]

The Senate was not satisfied at all with this response.

The loudest complaints came from the oil industry, whose views were expressed by Progressive-Republican Robert M. La Follette of Wisconsin. La Follette argued that no such leases were necessary, because an abundant supply of oil was available. He also remarked that "turning over Government lands to the large pipeline interests for exploitation will have the direct result of depressing the price of crude oil without in any way relieving the people of the onerous and burdensome high prices of refined products."[9]

Within three months, President Warren G. Harding was dead. He had begun a cross-country "Voyage of Understanding" in June 1923, and collapsed suddenly on August 2 in the presidential suite of the San Francisco Palace Hotel built by San Francisco impresario William C. Ralston, whom we met earlier.

Harding probably died of a heart attack. During the speaking tour, he had complained, "I have no trouble with my enemies, I can take care of them. It is my . . . friends that are giving me trouble." And so they did—even after his death.

La Follette was chairman of the Senate Committee on Public Lands. He directed Montana Senator Thomas J. Walsh to conduct what was expected to be a fruitless search for wrongdoing.

The First Witness

Fall was the first witness when the Public Lands Committee Investigation began. He was a former Democrat turned Republican who then faced Thomas J. Walsh, one of the most ardent Democrats in the Senate. They both represented Western states and had protected their parochial mining interests, although Walsh was clearly more of a conservationist.

Walsh first questioned Fall about an exchange agreement between the Department of the Interior and Doheny for fuel to be stored at Pearl Harbor in Hawaii. United States naval authorities had worried about a Japanese attack in the South Pacific since the World War I era. Fall freely admitted that he had relied mostly on himself for legal advice during royalty-oil exchange agreements negotiations with Doheny for the construction work at Pearl Harbor.

After Fall concluded his remarks by emphasizing the importance of arranging a fuel supply for the Navy at Pearl Harbor, Harry Sinclair testified, but said nothing about purchasing a one-third interest in Fall's Three Rivers Ranch.

Most newspaper accounts of Fall's first appearance were favorable. In November 1923, Fall's situation seemed secure.[10]

That was before rumors of a big Fall-Sinclair land deal in New Mexico began to reach Walsh. The hearings adjourned for a month in early November, but Senator Walsh interviewed D. F. Stackelback, a *Denver Post* reporter who had discovered that supposedly the only rancher in New Mexico who could purchase the Harris Ranch then was Albert Fall.

Harry Sinclair (Library of Congress)

And there was more information available from Tulsa attorney-turned-journalist Carl C. Magee. The Tulsan became editor of the *New Mexico State Tribune* because his wife's health required a move farther west. Although Magee had purchased the *Tribune* from Fall and others, and had briefly worked in Fall's 1918 senatorial campaign, he testified to observing recent expensive improvements on the Fall place when he visited there in August 1923.

Magee became the star witness during the investigation hearing; his testimony provoked questions for Doheny, and necessitated a second appearance by Harry Sinclair. Doheny was asked whether Fall benefited either directly or indirectly from the Elk Hills leases and replied, "Not yet." Sinclair answered the same question by saying that Fall had not benefited by any transaction with Sinclair unless it was from some cattle that Sinclair had shipped to Three Rivers.

All serious hearing observers understood that Fall would be

recalled to testify. It was only a matter of time. Fall then decided to throw Walsh off the scent by developing what professional swindlers call a "legend."

He dispatched his son-in-law Clarence C. Chase to visit Pittsburgh steel magnate Price McKinney, who Fall hoped would testify that he provided the funds for all the recent improvements and expansions at Three Rivers.

Although McKinney said no, a witness arranged by Doheny said yes. During a December 23 meeting at the Atlantic City Ritz-Carlton, Edward L. "Ned" McLean, the publisher of the *Washington Post*, recalled that it was he, not Doheny, who had loaned Fall all that cash.

By this time Fall was in fact ill, and he used that illness to avoid testimony before the Walsh committee in Washington. Yet he could not avoid Christmas Eve visits from Republican politicos concerned about the potential adverse impact of bad publicity on the 1924 presidential election. Perhaps he also visited with Doheny and McLean, his newfound financial benefactor.

No matter, someone convinced Fall to come clean with the Walsh committee. And so, as Sinclair, his attorney, and a GOP dignitary watched, Fall solemnly composed a letter to the committee explaining that the money for the Three Rivers Ranch expansion came from Ned McLean, and not "one cent on account of any oil lease or upon any other account whatsoever." McLean verified the load in a message to the committee, but claimed he was too ill to substantiate this testimony under oath in a hearing room.

Pity then, that Walsh easily discovered McLean to be land rich and cash poor. Walsh confronted Fall and McLean in balmy Palm Beach, Florida, and turned up the temperature. They admitted that McLean had not loaned Fall the $100,000. Years later, Fall characterized this dunderheaded decision as a political calculation, concluding, "I thus made a bad matter very, very much worse." The McLean alibi was the only thing he later claimed to regret about the whole Teapot Dome affair.

Before leaving Palm Beach for New Orleans, Fall telegraphed Doheny that if the oilman would not tell the committee about the loan, he would. A Fall biographer has speculated that Ned McLean may have kept President Coolidge up to date on events at Palm Beach.[11] These disclosures made Albert Fall a perpetual target of the press. Even as his wife Emma shielded him from press intrusions, he met with Sinclair's attorney, Z. W. Zevely; Doheny and his lawyer, Garvin McNab, a Democrat fixer. Fall's former law partner, W. A. Hawks, also joined the meeting at the Roosevelt Hotel in New Orleans. They decided Doheny would testify about the $100,000 loan to Fall, who would sign a new note for the money. Doheny had torn Fall's signature off the first note, rendering it invalid. Despite the precaution, Doheny eventually showed the committee the original note for reasons that remain unclear. While Fall and Doheny traveled separately to Washington, futile efforts were made to stop the investigation.

In the meantime, two sons of former President Theodore Roosevelt had testified to the Walsh committee about the possibility that Harry Sinclair was planning to leave the country. After this news, on January 24, 1924, Doheny admitted to the $100,000 personal loan payment to Fall based on their shared experiences as young men in the New Mexico mining boom. He even offered to give up the leases and the Pearl Harbor project for no more than reimbursement of the costs he had incurred there.

Public disclosure that Fall had been paid by both Doheny and Sinclair brought a clamor for change. The Walsh resolution branded the leases corrupt and directed immediate court action by the first special prosecutors appointed by the Department of Justice.

At last, with subpoena in hand, Fall arrived at the hearings "aged, broken, and sick."[12] However, the old lawyer was well enough to claim that the committee's authority had expired with the last session of Congress; he also argued that the Walsh resolution removed the oil leases from congressional hands and placed the matter in the courts. Finally, he invoked the fifth amendment, refusing to testify on grounds of self-incrimination. And with that, the Teapot Dome became the most famous American scandal until Watergate.

Both parties faced repercussions. Democrat presidential nominee William G. McAdoo was also shown to be in the pay of Doheny, while

Coolidge had largely escaped public sanction by promptly appointing special prosecutor teams, perhaps assuring his 1924 election. By that time, even Republicans who had wanted the whole thing to go away began to reconsider their options. President Coolidge assured the public that any wrongdoing would be punished. After Fall appeared in February 1924 but invoked his fifth amendment rights, Congress passed the Walsh resolution, which called for the first ever appointment of a special prosecutor by the federal government.

Albert Fall had been living large when the hearings began in October 1923. He had resigned as secretary of the interior on March 4, 1923, perhaps hoping to defuse the various inquiries about Teapot Dome. But a few financial transactions came back to haunt him.

Fall always contended that he had not been bribed by Harry Sinclair, who had visited Three Rivers in December 1921; Sinclair had expressed an interest in purchasing one-third interest in the Three Rivers Ranch during the visit. Fall later contended there were no ranch sale discussions before Sinclair was awarded the Teapot Dome contract on April 7, 1922.

Although the sale of a one-third interest in the ranch to Sinclair was completed in May 1921, Senator Walsh considered the transaction a "shallow fable" covering a $233,000 bribery.[13] Soon the litigation began.

The Teapot Dome Lawsuits

The civil lawsuit to cancel Harry Sinclair's oil lease began in Cheyenne, Wyoming, in March 1925. During the preparation of the government case, the shadowy Continental Trading Company of Canada was uncovered. Sinclair and three other oilmen had formed Continental in 1921, apparently as a device to skim profits from their own companies. This was similar to the way inside shareholders of the Union Pacific Railroad used Credit Mobilier to reap extra revenues for inside investors during the construction of the Union Pacific Railroad.

Investigators found about $3,000,000 in liberty bonds parked at Continental Trading. Sinclair had transferred the $233,000 paid to Fall in bonds for the Three Rivers Ranch from his share of these bonds.

Although the federal trial judge in Cheyenne cleared Sinclair, a court of appeals reversed the decision and ordered the Teapot Dome leases canceled. The 1927 U.S. Supreme Court decision affirming the court of appeals spared no feelings, describing Albert Fall as a "faithless public officer."

Earlier in Los Angeles, Doheny lost both the Pearl Harbor arrangement and his United States Elk Hills lease; Doheny lost a United States Supreme Court appeal in 1927, as had Fall. By 1928, the full amount of Fall's compensation in the original Teapot Dome transactions was revealed to be $404,000. His modern biographer also estimated that Doheny and Sinclair reimbursed as much as $300,000 in legal fees and associated expenses for Fall, who was unable to cover them.

Fall and the two oilmen won the three-week Doheny criminal conspiracy trial that began in 1926, but this was virtually the last of their favorable court decisions.

Shortly after the Fall-Sinclair conspiracy trial began in March 1927, prosecutors learned that Sinclair had hired detectives to shadow the jurors. The trial judge promptly declared a mistrial, accused Sinclair of criminal contempt, and sentenced him to prison for six months, along with William J. Burns, former director of the Bureau of Investigation—now the FBI—who was eventually exonerated.

This development led to a separate conspiracy trial against Sinclair alone in April 1928. Earlier, in preparation for this trial, Fall gave a lengthy deposition at his home in El Paso. Fall emphasized again and again reasons why the leases to Sinclair and Doheny were legitimate and in the interest of the taxpayer. Fall insisted that payments he received from Sinclair had nothing to do with his official duties.

The jury agreed, despite damaging testimony from Fall's son-in-law Mahlon T. Everhart, who was a government witness. With these adverse court decisions behind them, the prosecutors turned to their last card, bribery charges against Albert Fall.

Fall weathered the earlier years of Teapot Dome turmoil, even as his health deteriorated. He was buoyed by friendships with Western writer Eugene Manlove Rhodes and Doheny, whom he frequently visited in Los Angeles. The Fall-Doheny friendship survived a brief July 1925 dustup after Doheny gave the *New York Times* an interview. Doheny was careful to say nothing negative about Fall.

However, a Doheny attorney told the reporter that Fall's letter to the investigating committee claiming *Washington Post* publisher Edward L. McLean rather than Doheny provided the $100,000 loan to Fall was the "one incident" in their friendship "that Doheny cannot excuse."[14] Fall was angered but eventually blamed only the Doheny attorneys.

Despite this flap, Doheny financed some efforts to tell the Teapot Dome story from Fall's perspective. He commissioned Las Cruces, New Mexico, attorney and aspiring author Mark B. Thompson to write an authorized biography. Doheny cancelled the project in 1926 after reading rough drafts of several sections of the work. Even so, Fall prepared his own version of these events for the use of his attorneys, and later co-authored a fifteen-article series with an *El Paso Times* editor, published just before prison doors shut behind him in 1931.

Fall was frustrated by the defense attorneys throughout the early phases of the Teapot Dome litigation. He was especially miffed because his own attorneys were constantly dominated by Doheny lead counsel Frank J. Hogan, undoubtedly with good reason. Hogan was flamboyant and beyond brilliant in the courtroom.

This resentment against Hogan did not prevent Fall from accepting Doheny's offer to have Hogan defend Fall at no charge during his bribery trial, which began in Washington in October 1929.

The prosecutors saw this trial as a good opportunity to finally get a conviction. Neither the national security issues pertaining to Pearl Harbor nor the threats of neighboring oil producers draining the Teapot Dome reserves would distract this jury. There was only one question to be answered: Did Albert Fall take any bribes?

Hogan began the defense with two character witnesses from the Old West. Oliver Lee was a successful rancher and businessman who made a good witness, despite continuing questions back in New Mexico about the Fountain case. Robert Geronimo, son of the famed Apache chief, also appeared for Fall.

Grandfatherly Edward L. Doheny patiently explained to yet another jury that he never bribed his old mining partner, Albert Fall. Doheny merely loaned Fall a small amount of money—$100,000—secured by the Three Rivers Ranch.

Hogan's closing argument urged the jury to return the wizened old-timer dozing in a wheelchair "to the sunshine and lung-healing climate of his beloved New Mexico." This affected one juror, if only for a tear-filled thirty seconds, before the trial judge somberly reminded them that this was not about New Mexico. He also emphasized that a verdict accompanied by a plea for a merciful sentence was entirely appropriate.

That response probably didn't help the juror whose wife called him "a miserable rat" once she heard the guilty verdict.

The very same judge instructed a March 1930 jury in the companion Doheny bribery trial that Fall's intent to receive a bribe did not necessarily prove that Doheny intended to give one. Doheny was found not guilty.

Fall's most recent biographer attributes the inconsistent verdicts to Doheny's appealing testimony in stark contrast to Fall, who did not testify at all; the absence of any testimony about Fall's acceptance of money from Sinclair; and the applicability of a different bribery statute in the Doheny trial—one that required clear proof of the bribe-giver's intent to bribe.[15]

When a court of appeals affirmed the jury verdict against Fall and the U.S. Supreme Court refused to review his appeal in June 1931, Fall could still hope for a presidential pardon or the possibility that the trial judge would suspend the one-year sentence. Neither happened, but the judge allowed Fall to do his prison time at the state prison in Santa Fe.

He was released after four months, but lost the Three Rivers Ranch to Doheny's heirs. The loan was foreclosed, the property sold to a third party, and the Falls evicted. The new owners would not even permit Fall's wife to take her flock of pet geese.[16]

They then struggled month to month on his small veteran's

pension from the Spanish-American war in an El Paso home that Fall had transferred to his wife years earlier.

The old politician spent hours in hospitals reading about politics before his death in November 1944 at El Paso. Perhaps in those final days, he pondered all that he had seen and done in his time, from the early days of the Old West until his downfall in the Roaring Twenties.

Yes, he had seen it all, yet remained stoically silent about two intriguing mysteries of the American West. Fall never revealed the complete story of the Teapot Dome scandal much less what had really happened to his nemesis Albert Fountain and an innocent young boy in the New Mexico desert so many years ago.

Notes

Prologue

1. DeArment, 279.
2. Hyde and Zanetti, 109.
3. "Cardiff Giant," Wikipedia.org/wiki/Cardiff_Giant.
4. Tozer, 7ff.
5. Maurer, 249.
6. Moore, 3-10.
7. Ibid., 160ff.
8. Brolaski, 281ff.
9. Irwin, 22-23.
10. Tozer, 138.
11. Ibid., 139-40.
12. Nash, *Hustlers and Con Men*, 77ff.; Hynd, *Con Man*, 130ff.
13. Nash, *Hustlers and Con Men*, 41.
14. Plazak, 20, quoting Mark Twain in *Roughing It*, originally published in 1871. New ed. New York: New American Library, 1962.
15. Plazak, 137.
16. Nash, *Hustlers and Con Men*, 37.

Chapter 1

1. Collier and Westrate, 28.
2. DeArment, 353.
3. Ibid.

4. "The Grafters Club," http://www.GraftersClub.com-http://www.BlongerBrothers.com.
5. *Denver Daily News,* April 19, 1882.
6. *Denver Republican,* April 18, 1882.
7. "Grafters Club," 7.
8. DeArment, 353.
9. Ibid., 101.
10. Ibid., 74.
11. Devol, 26.
12. Ibid., 18.
13. Ibid., 110.
14. Sir Gilbert Parker, *Tarboe, The Story of a Life,* quoted in DeArment, 332.
15. Devol, 190.
16. Ibid., 286; Long, 118ff.
17. Long, 121.
18. Devol, 285-86.

Chapter 2

1. Tarbeaux, *Adventures,* 173.
2. Clarke, 79.
3. Tarbeaux, *Adventures,* 47.
4. Miller, *Shady Ladies of the Old West,* 18-19.
5. Nash, *Look for the Woman,* 22.
6. Ibid., 336ff.
7. Ibid., 338.
8. Ibid., 321ff.
9. Van Cise, 350.

Chapter 3

1. See the J. Frank Norfleet entry in the bibliography.
2. Ibid., 112.
3. Ibid., 125.
4. Nash, *Hustlers and Con Men,* 219.

5. Ibid., 221.

Chapter 4

1. Robertson and Harris, 27-28.
2. Collier and Westrate, 22.
3. Ibid., 33-36.
4. Ibid., 38-39.
5. Robertson and Harris, 45ff.
6. Ibid., 56-57.
7. Collier and Westrate, 157-60.
8. 29 July 1889, quoted in Robertson and Harris, 72-73.
9. Robertson and Harris, 80-81.
10. Ibid., 93.
11. Ibid., 97.
12. Collier and Westrate, 99-100.
13. Ibid., 88-92.
14. James Wickersham, *Old Yukon*, quoted in Robertson and Harris, 196.
15. Irwin, 168.
16. Robertson and Harris, 174.
17. Ibid., 217.
18. Collier and Westrate, 203.
19. Ibid., 297.

Chapter 5

1. Nash, *Hustlers and Con Men*, 215.
2. Maurer, 158.
3. Nash, *Hustlers and Con Men*, 216.
4. *Rocky Mountain News*, October 18, 1892.
5. *Elbert County Journal*, November 14, 1902.
6. *Emporia Gazette*, August 6, 1906 (from Blonger Brothers Web site).
7. Van Cise, 104.
8. Ibid., 37.

9. Ibid., 314.
10. Ibid., 193.
11. Ibid., 208.
12. Ibid., 309.
13. Ibid., 308.
14. Ibid., 335-36.
15. Ibid., 342.
16. Ibid., 343-44.

Chapter 6

1. Dary, *Frontier Medicine,* 32, 245.
2. Ibid., 255.
3. Ibid., 278-79.
4. Ibid., 188-89, 192, 199.
5. Ibid., 31.
6. Ibid., 280-81.
7. Stross, 214-16; Brock, 20.
8. Dary, *Frontier Medicine,* 282.
9. Wilson, *Stanford Medical School History,* Chapter 26.
10. Dary, *Frontier Medicine,* 282.
11. Ibid., 283.
12. Ibid., 283, 285.
13. Ibid., 286, 348, n. 8.
14. Ibid., 288-89.
15. Brock, 1-5.
16. Ibid., 30.
17. Ibid., 40.
18. Fishbein, *History of the American Medical Association,* 953.
19. Brock, 48.
20. Mayo Morrow, a Los Angeles journalist, as quoted in Brock, 56.
21. Brock, 81.
22. Ibid., 89.
23. Ibid., 91.
24. Ibid., 113, 117.

25. Ibid., 123-24.
26. Ibid., 132.
27. Fowler and Crawford, 26-27.
28. Brock, 140.
29. Fowler and Crawford, 26; Fishbein, *History of the American Medical Association,* 514.
30. Fowler and Crawford, 33; Fishbein, *History of the American Medical Association,* 511.
31. Brock, 177.
32. Ibid., 183, 187-88.
33. Ibid., 199.
34. Ibid., 205.
35. Ibid., 224.
36. Fowler and Crawford, 61.
37. Ibid., 62.
38. Brock, 243.
39. Ibid., 261.
40. Ibid., 293.

Chapter 7

1. Magrath, 1, citing William Priest, *Travels in the United States of America* (London, 1782).
2. The next year he had acquired some 22,000 acres in Virginia, the Carolinas, and present-day Kentucky.
3. Smith, xiii, vvii, 297.
4. Nathan Miller, 118, citing Smith, 10.
5. Randall, 173.
6. Wilstach, 80-90. As early as 1870, one Edward A. Pollard questioned whether Henry had uttered these words in *Galaxy Magazine.* The authors express no opinion on this issue.
7. Wilstach, 90.
8. Unger, 2.
9. Randall, 452-53. George Washington himself elected to be addressed as "Mr. President."
10. *Webster's New Biographical Dictionary* (1983), 589.

11. Lindberg, 116.
12. Unger, 210.
13. Mayer, 118.
14. Sakolski, 5.
15. Lindberg, 117. Emphasis supplied.
16. Present-day Pittsburgh; Randall, 83, 215.
17. Randall, 55.
18. Mayer, 119.
19. Randall, 217.
20. Mayer, 119.
21. Lindberg, 117.
22. Sakolski, 44.
23. These tribes and the Seminoles comprise the Five Tribes, formerly called the Five Civilized Tribes because of the ease with which they adopted European laws and customs, regrettably including chattel slavery.
24. Magrath, 3-9.
25. Mayer, 467. One biographer described George Washington, Thomas Jefferson, and Patrick Henry as the Sword, the Pen, and the Tongue of the American Revolution. Wilstach, 78.
26. Magrath, 4-5, n. 11, 207. *Moultrie v. Georgia,* Supreme Court (1798).
27. Wilstach, 80.
28. Nathan Miller, 122-23.
29. Meade, 422-23.
30. Nathan Miller, 124-26.
31. Magrath, 213, n. 23.
32. Ibid., 8, 208, n. 14.
33. Ibid., 6.
34. Ibid., 7.
35. Nathan Miller, 126.
36. Magrath, 8, 213, n. 213.
37. Ibid., 9, 209, n. 25.
38. Ibid., 15, 210, n. 38. Emphasis supplied.
39. Ibid., 150, Appendix D.

40. Ibid., 10-12, 139. Eventually, Jackson's leadership in opposition to the second Yazoo land sale provided him a political platform to become governor of Georgia (1798-99) and return to the United States Senate.
41. Nathan Miller, 128.
42. Lindberg, 117, citing Sakolski.
43. Magrath, 29, 30.
44. Ibid., 31.
45. Nathan Miller, 120, citing Coulter, 197.
46. Magrath, 2.
47. Ibid., 41, 210, n. 41, citing Haskins, 87-88, Sakolski, 135-36, and Lindberg, 117.
48. "The ballad of Pretty Boy Floyd," *Encyclopedia of the Great Depression*, New York, MacMillan, USA.
49. Magrath, Appendix A, 170. Emphasis supplied.
50. Ibid., 30.
51. Nathan Miller, 24, 131.
52. Ibid., 132.
53. Magrath, 37.
54. *Fletcher v. Peck*, 10 U.S. 87, 6 Cranch 87, 3 L.Ed. 162 (1810).
55. Magrath, 54.
56. Ibid., 65-67.
57. Ibid., 69.
58. Hamilton provided a written opinion on March 25, 1795, which was followed by the Harper opinion provided in a pamphlet issued on August 3, 1796. The Supreme Judicial Court of Massachusetts declared the Georgia law invalidating the second Yazoo land sale a "mere nullity" in *Derby v. Blake*, 226 Mass. Reports 618, 1917. A 1795 federal circuit court case reached essentially the same decision in *Van Herne's Lessee v. Dorrance*. Magrath, 50, 140-48, 149-50.
59. Magrath, 74-78.
60. *Annals of Congress*, 13th Congress, 2nd Session (Washington: 1854), 209.
61. Nathan Miller, 133-34.

62. Unger, 210; Nathan Miller, 133-34. The successful litigant John Peck did not pay his lawyer Robert Goodloe Harper until the case had been concluded for more than a year.
63. Nathan Miller, 120.
64. Wilstach, 96. This version of events was not supported by his widow. Mayer, 472.

Chapter 8

1. Kunhardt, Kunhardt, and Kunhardt, 47.
2. Lindberg, 94.
3. Saxon, 336.
4. Werner, viii.
5. Saxon, 1.
6. Ibid., 77.
7. Ibid., 68-69.
8. Ibid., 69-70.
9. Albert Smith, "A Day with Barnum," as cited in ibid., 73, 356, n. 9.
10. Saxon, 119, 364-65, n. 19.
11. Ibid., 120.
12. Ibid., 123. In 1844, Barnum tried to buy the William Shakespeare birthplace in England for exhibition in New York, but was thwarted. Kunhardt, Kunhardt, and Kunhardt, 62, 108.
13. Saxon, 10-11, 15.
14. Mihm, 50.
15. Ibid., 35.
16. Ibid., 4. Emphasis supplied.
17. Ibid., 10.
18. Ibid., 9.
19. Ibid., 252-54.
20. Ibid., 6, quoting Ezekial Wiles, editor of the *Weekly Register,* a financial publication. Emphasis supplied.
21. Lindberg, 311, citing Nathan Miller, 164-65.
22. Mihm, 8.
23. Ibid., 186.

24. Ibid., 160.
25. Brodie, 195-97.
26. Mihm, 271-73.
27. Ibid., 180-81.
28. Ibid., 16.
29. Ibid., 10. Emphasis supplied.
30. Ibid., 167-68.
31. Brogan, 204.
32. Mihm, 204-7.
33. Sakolski, 233.
34. Lindberg, 118.
35. Ibid., 119-20.
36. Ibid., 118.
37. Ibid., 121. Emphasis supplied.
38. Mihm, 148.
39. Webb, 4, 138-39.
40. Dary, *Entrepreneurs*, 231-32, 337, n. 11.
41. Ibid., 235-36, 337, n. 14.
42. Ibid., 238, 337, n. 16.
43. Ibid., 242.
44. Ibid., 250.
45. Ibid., 255.
46. Greeley, 39.
47. Dary, *Entrepreneurs*, 252, 338, n. 14.
48. C. Peter Magrath, quoted in Morgan, 404.
49. Dary, *Red Blood and Black Ink*, 99.
50. Debo, *And Still the Waters Run*, 118-20.
51. Debo, *Tulsa*, 82.
52. Debo, *And Still the Waters Run*, 122, 203-5.
53. Thorne, 7.
54. Hogan, 154, 267-69.
55. Davis, 1-13; *Los Angeles Examiner*, August 24 and 28, 1905.
56. Tygiel, 34-35.
57. Debo, *And Still the Waters Run*, 196-200.
58. Debo, *Tulsa*, 78-80.
59. Lindberg, 120.

60. Dary, *Entrepreneurs,* 197.

61. Ambrose, 86, 92-93, 212.

62. Cochran, 388.

63. Josephson, 196-201.

64. Ambrose, 94. The Central Pacific Railroad with which the Union Pacific was competing had a similar relationship with the Charles Crocker Contract and Finance Company. Ambrose, 105.

65. Ambrose, 227.

66. John Adams (1735-1826) and John Quincy Adams (1767-1848); *North American Review,* (Boston), CVIII, January 1869, 147.

67. Ambrose, 320-21.

68. Ibid., 339-40.

69. Dary, *Entrepreneur,* 198, 336, n. 2.

70. Ambrose, 374.

71. Josephson, 87.

72. Ibid., 91.

73. Ambrose, 375.

74. Josephson, 204.

Chapter 9

1. Powell, 4.

2. *Arizona Gazette* (Phoenix), September 7, 1882.

3. *Phoenix Herald,* January 6, 1882.

4. *Arizona Daily Star* (Tucson), October 21, 1882.

5. Newton A. Johnson, "James Addison Reavis and the Peralta Claim," Appendix A; and James Addison Reavis, "Confession of Peralta-Reavis, the King of Forgers," *The Call* (San Francisco), March 26, 1899, as quoted in Powell, 14.

6. Powell, 14; Cookridge, 32. Neither text contains references supporting the Catron report.

7. Powell, 15.

8. Ibid., 19-20.

9. *Arizona Weekly Miner* (Prescott), March 20, 1874.

10. Sanchez, 49-62.

11. Powell, 10.

12. Ibid., 17, 24; R. A. Johnson, *Adverse Report*, 73-75; Cookridge, 12-13.

13. Powell, 20-26.

14. Ibid., 85, 87.

15. *Weekly Phoenix Herald*, July 12, 1883.

16. *Arizona Gazette* (Phoenix), January 15, 1883.

17. Powell, 49.

18. *Arizona Silver Belt* (Globe), August 4, 1883.

19. *Weekly Phoenix Herald*, November 15, 1883.

20. Powell, 52-53.

21. *Arizona Gazette* (Phoenix), January 24, 1884.

22. Powell, 43-44.

23. *Weekly Phoenix Herald*, February 14, 1884.

24. Powell, 49.

25. *Daily Examiner* (San Francisco), August 5, 1887.

26. *St. Louis Republican*, August 18, 1887.

27. *Arizona Silver Belt* (Globe), December 12, 1885, 28.

28. Powell, 71.

29. Ibid., 82.

30. *Daily Examiner* (San Francisco), August 1, 1887.

31. Powell, 84.

32. Ibid., 90.

33. The Hise document, entitled *Report of the U.S. Surveyor General for the District of Arizona as to the Validity of a Claim to Lands under the So-Called Peralta Grant,* bears the date February 1889.

34. R. A. Johnson, *Adverse Report*, 66. Emphasis supplied.

35. Ibid., 40.

36. Ibid., 28-32, 33-34.

37. Shortly thereafter, the Johnson report was received and affirmed by the Commissioner of the Land Office.

38. Petition of Claimants, 8-9.

39. Cookridge, 12-15.

40. Powell, 109.

41. Ibid., 109.

42. *Arizona, the New State Magazine,* Vol. X, Nos. 5-6 (September 1918).

43. *Arizona Gazette* (Phoenix), October 25, 1893; *Daily Examiner* (San Francisco), March 15, 1894, as cited in Powell, 112.

44. *Arizona Weekly Enterprise* (Florence), November 16, 1893.

45. *Daily Examiner* (San Francisco), March 13, 1894.

46. Powell, 118-19.

47. Cookridge, 165.

48. Ibid., 218.

49. Ibid., 233-34.

50. Powell, 124.

51. Ibid., 109.

52. Cookridge, 165.

53. Powell, 128-30.

54. Cookridge, 246.

55. Powell, 169-70.

56. Cookridge, 276.

57. Powell, 171-72; Cookridge, 281.

58. Powell, 173.

59. *Daily New Mexican* (Santa Fe), July 23, 1895, 50.

60. Powell, 109-10, 174.

61. Ibid., 174; Cookridge, 280.

Chapter 10

1. Plazak, 74.

2. Ibid., 89.

3. Ibid., 7-8.

4. Mark Twain, *Roughing It,* 231-32.

5. Mark Twain, *Mark Twain's Letters,* 245, 247, 253, 260.

6. Comstock was said to be so lazy he wouldn't make his own bread. Morris, 69-70.

7. Morris, 102; Powers, 104.

8. Drabelle, 15.

9. Makley, 64.

10. Ibid., 32. Punctuation modified to modern usage.
11. Drabelle, 113.
12. Ibid., 124.
13. Ibid., 78, 112; Plazak, 35-47.
14. Drabelle, 129.
15. Plazak, 95; J. L. Consodine, "The Great Diamond Swindle," *Sunset* 52 (February 1924): 49-58.
16. Elizabethtown: Hardin County Historical Society, 1979, 354-56.

Chapter 11

1. *Louisville Courier-Journal,* March 3, 1886.
2. *A History of Edwards County, Illinois,* I, 11-14.
3. *Arizona Bulletin,* March 17, 1899.
4. *New York Sun,* April 2, 1899.
5. *Arizona Republican,* May 17, 1899.
6. Plazak, 165.
7. *Arizona Republican,* May 27, June 6, June 30, July 8, 1899.
8. Plazak, 165.
9. Ibid., 154.
10. *A History of Edwards County, Illinois,* I, 11-14.
11. *Chicago Times,* February 10, 1884; *Cincinnati Enquirer,* April 17, 1886.
12. *Louisville Courier-Journal,* March 3, 1886.
13. *Rocky Mountain Mining Review,* June 5, 1884.
14. *Engineering and Mining Journal—Engineering and Mining Journal Press,* February 19, 1887, 128.
15. *Engineering and Mining Journal,* March 27, 1880, 224; December 10, 1881.
16. *Boston Globe,* June 14, 1887.
17. *Rocky Mountain News,* November 22, 1901.
18. *New York Times,* February 25, 26, 1903.
19. Plazak, 167.
20. Ibid.
21. *New York Times,* November 7, 1903.

22. Ibid., September 11, 12, 1908.
23. Ibid.
24. Carter, 377-78.
25. Shirley, 199.
26. In 1980 the Supreme Court of the United States ruled in *United States v Sioux Nation of Indians* that the Black Hills were illegally taken. The tribes refused to accept the $106,000,000 then awarded and still insist that the Black Hills should be returned as a matter of principle.
27. Warren, 534-35.
28. Carter, 420. Emphasis supplied.
29. Blackstone, 51.
30. Warren, 535.
31. Ibid., 633, n. 44.

Chapter 12

1. David Stratton, "Behind Teapot Dome: Some Personal Insights," *Business Historical Review* (Winter 1957), 386.
2. Executive Order 3474.
3. Stratton, 237.
4. Werner and Starr, 60-61.
5. Stratton, 12.
6. Ibid., 53-55.
7. S. Res. 277, 67th Cong. Rec.
8. S. Doc. No 67-191 (1922).
9. 62 Cong, Rec. 6893 (1922).
10. Stratton, 221.
11. Ibid., 292.
12. Ibid., 298.
13. Ibid., 269.
14. Ibid., 317.
15. Ibid., 331.
16. Perhaps this settled the question of whether Doheny paid a bribe or gave Fall a secured loan.

A Swindler's Dictionary:
The Argot of the Trade

The swindling profession has its own terms, largely unintelligible to the uninitiated, but used with good effect in *The Sting*, a classic movie about con men. Here are some of the common terms used in the confidence trade.

Ace—An arrangement with law enforcement, guaranteeing it will turn a blind eye to whatever con the fixer has in mind. See also *fix* and *fixer*.

Apple—The victim, also known as the dupe, sucker, or mark.

Autograph—A simple con to obtain a real signature, which is then forged onto a check.

Backup man—An accomplice used to steer the victim into the trap. See also *steerer, roper,* or *capper*.

Badger Game—The ancient swindle in which a female shill entices a generally married "respectable" man into bed. Then, when the couple is in a compromising position, the con man "husband" arrives, threatening to make the whole mess public. Unless, of course, he is properly paid off.

Banco—An old-time fixed gambling game.

Big con, or *big store*—A fake gambling parlor such as that portrayed in *The Sting*.

Bill wrapper—A swindler who appears to wrap bills in packages of soap or candy, and sells it to dupes eager to choose a cake of something with a bill inside. The only winners to guess which package contains the bill—and win—are the con man's shills.

Boiler room, also *bucket shop*—A secret room from which false or valueless stock is sold to legitimate investors.

Brace Game—Faro, crooked of course.

Broads—Three-card Monte.

Bunco—The generic description of a confidence game; once synonymous with bilk.

Burn—To hold out on a fellow grifter.

Capper, also *roper* or *steerer* —A con man's confederate who lures suckers into a crooked game or other con, or who is already in the "game" and wins big to encourage the suckers.

C.O.D.—In a "short-death" con, these are unordered items sent to the dead person in the expectation that heirs or the estate will pay for them.

Country Send—In a con directed at country people, sending the victim home for the money to "invest" in the con.

Depot worker—A swindler working bus, train, and aircraft terminals.

Drag Game—The con man—or woman—and victim are together when a second operator "discovers" a bag full of money, a wallet, or a purse. They are intent on finding the owner, of course, but agree that if he or she is not found, the mark and the cons will split the money. First, they must get some expert advice from somebody, or at least look for the owner. The mark coughs up some earnest money, and the cons go off to seek advice, or to find the owner. Before they go, they replace the precious bag, wallet, or purse with an identical one full only of cut paper. Also called *dropping the leather, drop-the-poke, the pigeon drop.*

Dukeman—A card cheat. Apparently derived from Duke, a playing card-based con.

Easy mark—The victim.

Envelope Switch—A con in which an envelope of money is deftly replaced by an identical envelope full of cut paper.

Eye—The Pinkerton Detective Agency.

Fence—A knowing receiver of stolen goods, as a crooked pawnbroker.

Fish—The victim.

Fix—An arrangement with crooked police. See also *ace.*

Fixer—The con who sets up the fix or ace.

Fleece—A con. Also called a *flim-flam.*

Flyflat—Victim.

Gaff—Three-card Monte.

Gaffed—Controllable. A game such as roulette "gaffed" with a controllable wheel.

Glim-Drop—A con game featuring a "lost" artificial eye.

Gold Brick—An ordinary brick, or one of brass, disguised as one of real gold. Sometimes with a plug of real gold in it, to reassure cautious marks who want a piece of the precious brick assayed before they buy.

Gouge—Three-card Monte.

Greek—A gambler.

Green Goods—An audacious con in which the con man advertises and sells "perfect" counterfeit money in exchange for the real thing.

Grifter—A con man. "Grift" is what he does.

Gull—To con or cheat.

Gypsy Blessing—A con in which a "gypsy" is paid by the credulous to confer future good luck on the victim.

Hang paper—To pass counterfeit currency.

Hawk—To entrap a mark into participating in a con game.

Hustler—A con man. What he does is "hustle."

Inside man—The con man to whom ropers and steerers bring a victim.

Jake—A victim.

Jamaican Switch—A simple play on sympathy, concern for an immigrant just arrived in America.

John—A mark; see also *jake*.

Juggins—Old term for a victim or mark.

Lookout—In a crooked card game, a "spectator" who watches the mark's cards and passes on his learning to the con man playing.

Magic Wallet, also *lost-and-found wallet*—A wallet stuffed with money and important papers "lost" by the swindler to gain acquaintance with the mark.

Match—A fraudulent game played by matching coins.

Mr. Goodman, also *Mr. Wright*—The victim.

Mush—An unusual con in which a con man takes bets at a track on a rainy day, then disappears—with the money—beneath his umbrella in a sea of other umbrellas.

Outside man—The roper or steerer who finds the victim and leads him into the con (see *inside man*).

Paper—A check, usually fraudulent.

Payoff—One of the elaborate big-store games, including phony horse-betting and stock-selling schemes.

Pennyweight—Substitution of cheap jewelry for real, expensive gems. One who pulls this swindle is a *pennyweighter.*

Peter-to-Paul—A big-store game in which early investors make huge profits paid for from the contributions of later investors; when the con man deems the time is ripe, he absconds with a big chunk of the latest money. A Ponzi scheme.

Pigeon Drop—See *drag game.*

Point-out—One con man points out another to the mark, identifying him as a man of status, wealth, or power.

Ponzi—The lure of astronomically high returns on investment powered this one. The brain child of one Charles Ponzi, who talked investors out of some $15,000,000 with promises of huge profits. Ponzi did pay some memorably high returns. Trouble was, he did it with money put in by later investors.

Pow-wowers—Con women who hold fraudulent séances with credulous victims.

Right, or *safe*—An accommodating or crooked cop.

Roper—An accomplice who guides dupes to the con man's racket.

Shake—Extortion.

Short con—A swindle intended to be brief and uncomplicated, relieving the dupe of whatever cash he may be carrying. In and out with no further contact.

Slave—A working man, a wage-earner, one of the herd of dupes waiting to be conned.

Slum hustler—A con man selling cheap jewelry, representing that it has been stolen.

Snitch—To inform on a criminal; an informer.

Soap Scam—Soapy Smith's great con. See his chapter, also *bill wrapper.*

Spanish Prisoner, also *The Prisoner*—The name for this swindle appeared during the Spanish Civil War in the 1930s, but this grift dates back to the American Civil War, if not earlier. A con in which the mark is convinced that a prisoner in some faraway dungeon will pass on the secret of his hidden wealth if the mark will take care of the prisoner's relatives or, sometimes, front money for his defense. In its simplest form, a plea for a thousand dollars or so to pay the fine and get the writer out of an awful jail.

Stake-player—A shill in a crooked gambling house who bets high and keeps raising, moving others to do the same. He splits the profits with the house.

Steerer—Accomplice of the con-man-in-chief, who "steers" likely victims to the scam. The first con man to contact the dupe. See also *capper* and *roper*.

Store—The phony bookie joint or stock exchange in which to fleece the mark.

Tear-Up—A reassurance to a mark who's skeptical. "Here," says the con man, "I'll just tear up your check." Only it's another check that is torn up. The original is quickly cashed.

Three-card Monte—Old and well known con game, in which the dealer uses three cards, generally two black suits, often aces, and a red queen. As the con man swiftly shuffles the cards back and forth, the idea is to identify which card is the queen. Often the game is won simply by the dealer's manual dexterity. But sometime there is a roper to help. After the mark wins a small bet or two, the roper, watching, whispers to the mark that the dealer has accidentally put a tiny crease in the queen, whereupon the mark bets high, only to find out that he has the wrong card. The dealer has smoothed the crease in the queen and put a tiny one in one of the black cards.

Throw—A newspaper or other object shoved under the nose of a dupe, distracting his attention and obstructing his vision of what the con men are doing.

Tiger—Faro, from the tiger often painted on wooden cases in which faro dealers carry their equipment. "Bucking the tiger" means playing against the bank at faro.

Top and Bottom—A simple scam in which the dupe bets that the top and bottom values of three dice will total twenty-one. And sometimes they might, if the dice were not crooked.

Wipe—A variation of the Spanish Handkerchief, in which a knotted handkerchief full of the dupe's money is swapped for a handkerchief full of cut paper.

Wire—A phony betting parlor in which the dupe bets heavily in reliance on advance news of racing results, allowing a last-second win. The wire comes complete with telegraph, odds-board, customer and staff shills, and lots of money visible. The dupe's "advance" notice is generally said to come from a tapped line or a confederate working for the telegraph company.

In the end, the success of most of these larcenies depends on the victim's credulous response to a man or woman who appears to be an honest human being. It is a tough way to learn about human nature.

Bibliography

Articles

Adams, John (1735-1826) and John Quincy Adams (1767-1848). *North American Review* (Boston), CVIII, January 1869.

Billington, Ray Allen. "The Origin of the Land Speculator as a Frontier Type." *Agricultural History,* Vol. 19, No. 4 (October 1945), 204-12.

Consodine, J. L. "The Great Diamond Swindle." *Sunset* 52, February 1924: 49-58.

"Queen for a Day," *Newsweek,* July 1, 1974.

Smith, Albert. "A Day with Barnum." *Bentley's Miscellany,* 21 (1847).

Stratton, David L. "Behind Teapot Dome: Some Personal Insights," *Business Historical Review* (Winter 1957).

Books

Adams, Henry Brooks. *History of the United States of America.* Vol. 1. New York: Penguin Books USA, Inc., 1889-91.

Ambrose, Stephen E. *Nothing Like It in the World: The Men Who Built the Transcontinental Railroad, 1863-1869.* New York: Simon & Schuster, 2000.

Balen, Malcolm. *The Secret History of the South Sea Bubble: The World's First Great Financial Scandal.* London and New York: Fourth Estate, HarperCollins Publishers, Inc., 2003.

Barnum, P. T. *Selected Letters of P.T. Barnum.* Edited by A. H. Saxon. New York: Columbia University Press, 1983.

Blackstone, Sarah J. *The Business of Being Wild Bill: Selected Letters of William F. Cody, 1879-1917.* New York: Praeger Publishers, 1988.

Blocker, Lawrence. *Gangsters, Swindlers, Killers and Thieves: The Lives and Crimes of Fifty American Villains.* New York: Oxford University Press, Inc., 2004.

Blum, Richard H. *Deceivers and Deceived.* Springfield, IL: Charles C. Thomas, 1972.

Bonelli, William G. *Billion Dollar Blackjack: The Story of Corruption and the Los Angeles Times.* Beverly Hills, CA: Civic Research Press, 1954.

Bridger, Bobby. *Buffalo Bill and Sitting Bull: Inventing the Wild West.* Austin: University of Texas Press, 2002.

Brock, Pope. *Charlatan: America's Most Dangerous Huckster, the Man Who Pursued Him and the Age of Flim/Flam.* New York: Crown Publishers, 2008.

Brodie, Fawn. *No Man Knows My History: The life of Joseph Smith.* New York: Alfred A. Knopf, Inc., 1971, First Vintage Books Edition, 1995.

Brogan, Hugh. *Alexis de Tocqueville.* New Haven and London: Yale University Press, 2007.

Brolaski, Harry. *Easy Money.* Cleveland: Searchlight Press, 1911.

Burrough, Bryan. *The Big Rich: The Rise and Fall of the Greatest Texas Oil Fortunes.* New York: The Penguin Press, 2009.

Cadle, Farris W. *Georgia Land Surveying History and Law.* Athens: University of Georgia Press, 1991.

Carter, Robert A. *Buffalo Bill Cody: The Man Behind the Legend.* New York: John Wiley & Sons, Inc., 2000.

Clarke, Donald Henderson. *The Autobiography of Frank Tarbeaux.* New York: Grosset and Dunlap, 1930.

Cleere, Jan. *Outlaw Tales of Arizona.* Guilford, CT: Two Dot Press, 2006.

Cochran, Thomas C. *Railroad Leaders 1845-1890: The Business Mind in Action.* New York: Russell and Russell, 1965.

Collier, William Ross and Edwin V. Westrate. *The Reign of Soapy Smith, Monarch of Misrule.* Garden City, NY: Doubleday, Doran & Co., 1935.

Cookridge, E. H. *The Baron of Arizona: The Great 12 Million-Acre Land Swindle.* New York: The John Day Company, Inc., 1967.

Coulter, E. Merton. *Georgia: A Short History.* Chapel Hill: University of North Carolina Press, 1961.

Crofut, W. A. *The Vanderbilts and the Story of Their Fortune.* Chicago and New York: Belford, Clarke & Company, 1886.

Dary, David. *Entrepreneurs of the Old West.* New York: Alfred A. Knopf, 1986.

——*Frontier Medicine: From the Atlantic to the Pacific, 1492-1941.* New York: Alfred A. Knopf, 2008.

——*Red Blood and Black Ink: Journalism in the Old West.* New York: Borzoi Books, Alfred A. Knopf, 1998.

——*Seeking Pleasure in the Old West.* New York: Alfred A. Knopf, 1995.

Davis, Margaret Leslie. *Rivers in the Desert: William Mulholland and the Inventing of Los Angeles.* New York: HarperCollins Publishers, 1993.

DeArment, Robert K. *Knights of the Green Cloth.* Norman: University of Oklahoma Press, 1982.

Debo, Angie. *And Still the Waters Run: The Betrayal of the Five Civilized Tribes.* Norman and London: University of Oklahoma Press, 1940, fourth printing, 1989.

——*Tulsa: From Creek Town to Oil Capital.* Norman: University of Oklahoma Press, 1996.

DeGrave, Kathleen. *Swindler, Spy, Rebel: The Confidence Woman in Nineteen-Century America.* Columbia: University of Missouri Press, 1995.

Devol, George H. *Forty Years A Gambler on the Mississippi.* Bedford, MA: n.d. Reprint of original title published in 1887 by Devol and Haines, Cincinnati.

Dobie, J. Frank. *Guide to Life and Literature of the Southwest.* Austin: University of Texas Press, 1943.

Drabelle, Dennis. *Mile-High Fever: Silver Mines, Boom Towns and High Living on the Comstock Lode.* New York: St. Martin's Press, 2009.

Dyer, Mrs. D. B. *Fort Reno or, Picturesque Cheyenne and Arapahoe Life before the Opening of Oklahoma;* with a new introduction by David Dary. Mechanicsburg, PA: Stackpole Books, 2005. Originally published by G. W. Dillingham, 1896.

Finch, Boyd L. *A Southwestern Land Scam: The 1959 Report of the Mowry City Association.* Tucson: Friends of the Library, University of Arizona, 1990.

Fishbein, Morris. *A History of the American Medical Association 1847 to 1947.* Philadelphia and London: W.B. Saunders Company, 1947.

——*The Medical Follies.* New York: Boni and Liveright, 1925.

Flower, George and Morris Birkbeck. *Combined History of Edwards, Lawrence and Wabash Counties, Illinois (1883).* Whitefish, MT: Kessinger Publishing, LLC, 2008.

Fogel, Robert W. *The Union Pacific Railroad: A Case in Premature Enterprise.* Baltimore: Johns Hopkins University Press, 1960.

Fowler, Gene and Bill Crawford. *Border Radio: Quacks, Yodelers, Pitchmen, Psychics and other Amazing Broadcasters of the Airwaves.* Austin: University of Texas Press, 2002.

Franklin, Charles. *They Walked a Crooked Mile: An Account of the Greatest Swindlers and Outrages of All Times.* New York: Hart Publishing Company, Inc., 1972.

Garcia, Frank. *Don't Bet On It.* 1978, n.d, n.p.

Gardner, Mark Lee. *To Hell on a Fast Horse: Billy the Kid, Pat Garrett and the Epic Chase to Justice in the Old West.* New York: William Morrow, 2010.

Gould, P. B. *The Irish Lord.* Congress, AZ: PBG Press, 2005.

Greeley, Horace. *An Overland Journey from New York to San Francisco, in the Summer of 1859.* New York: C.M. Saxton, Barker & Co., 1860.

Hall, Kermit L. *The Oxford Companion to the Supreme Court of the United States.* New York, Oxford: Oxford University Press, 1992.

Harding, T. *Fads, Frauds, and Physicians.* New York: Dial Press, 1930.

Harris, Neil. *Humbug: The Art of P.T. Barnum.* Boston-Toronto: Little Brown and Company, 1973.

Harte, Bret. *The Outcasts of Poker Flat.* Mattituck, NY: Amereoun House, 1982.

Haskins, C. H. *The Yazoo Land Companies.* New York: The Knickerbocker Press, 1891.

Hogan, Lawrence J. *The Osage Indian Murders: The True Story of a Murder Plot to Acquire the Estates of Wealthy Osage Tribe Members.* Frederick, MD: AMLEX, INC., 1998.

Hyde, Stephen and Geno Zanetti, Ed. *Players*. New York: Thunder Mouth Press, 2002.

Hynd, Alan. *Sleuths, Slayers and Swindlers*. New York: A.S. Davis & Co., 1959.

——*Con Man*. New York: Paperback Library, 1958.

Irwin, Will. *The Confessions of a Con Man*. New York: B.W. Huebsch, 1909.

Johnson, R. A. *Adverse Report of the Surveyor General of Arizona Royal A. Johnson Upon the Alleged Peralta Grant, a Complete Exposure of its Fraudulent Character*. Phoenix: Arizona Gazette Book and Job Office, 1890.

Josephson, Matthew. *The Robber Barons: The Great American Capitalists, 1861-1901*. New York: Harcourt, Brace and World, 1962.

Klein, Alexander. *The Double Dealers*. Philadelphia: J. B. Lippencott Co., 1958.

Krakauer, Jon. *Under the Banner of Heaven: A Story of Violent Faith*. New York: Doubleday, 1993.

Kunhardt, Phillip B. Jr., Phillip B. Kunhardt III, Peter W. Kunhardt. *P.T. Barnum: America's Greatest Showman*. New York: Alfred A. Knopf, Inc., 1995.

Lears, Jackson. *Something for Nothing: Luck in America*. New York: Penguin Putnam Group, 2003.

Leff, Arthur Allen. *Swindling and Selling*. New York: The Free Press, 1972.

Lindberg, Gary. *The Confidence Man in American Literature*. New York, Oxford: Oxford University Press, 1992.

Long, Mason. *The Life of Mason Long, the Converted Gambler*. Fort Wayne, IN: Mason Long, 10th ed., 1887.

McCartney, Laton. *The Teapot Dome Scandal: How Big Oil Bought the Harding White House and Tried to Steal the Country*. New York: Random House, Inc., 2008.

McClure, Daniel E. Jr. *Two Centuries in Elizabethtown and Hardin County, Kentucky*. Elizabethtown, KY: The Hardin County Historical Society, 1979.

McIver, Stuart B. *Dreamers, Schemers and Scalawags*. Sarasota, FL: Pineapple Press, 1994.

Mackay, Charles. *Memoirs of Extraordinary Popular Delusions and the Madness of Crowds*. London: Office of the National Illustrated Library, 1852.

Magrath, C. Peter. *Yazoo: Law and Politics in the New Republic, the Case of Fletcher v. Peck*. Providence, RI: Brown University Press, 1966.

Makley, Michael J. *The Infamous King of the Comstock*. Reno: University of Nevada Press, 2006.

Maurer, David W. *The Big Con*. New York: Anchor Books, 1940.

Mayer, Henry. *A Son of Thunder: Patrick Henry and the American Republic*. New York, Toronto: Franklin Watts, 1986.

Meade, Robert Douthat. *Patrick Henry: Practical Revolutionary*. Philadelphia and New York: J.B. Lippincott Company, 1969.

Mehling, Harold. *The Scandalous Scamps*. New York: Henry Holt & Co., 1959.

Melville, Herman. *The Confidence Man: His Masquerade, an Authoritative Text, Background and Sources, Reviews, Criticism*. Edited by Herschel Parker. New York, London: W. W. Norton, 1971.

Mihm, Steven. *A Nation of Counterfeiters: Capitalists, Con Men and the Making of the United States*. Cambridge: Harvard University Press, 2009.

Miller, Nathan. *The Founding Finaglers*. New York: David McKay Company, Inc., 1976.

Miller, Ronald Dean. *Shady Ladies of the Old West*. Los Angeles: Westernlore Press, 1964.

Moore, Dan Tyler. *Wolves, Widows and Orphans*. New York: World Publishing Co., 1966.

Morgan, George. *The True Patrick Henry*. Philadelphia, London: J.B. Lippincott Company, 1907.

Morris, Ray Jr. *Lighting Out for the Territory: How Samuel Clemens Headed West and Became Mark Twain*. New York: Simon and Schuster, 2010.

Moulton, Candy. *The Writer's Guide to Everyday Life in the Wild West from 1840-1900*. Cincinnati: Writer's Digest Books, 1999.

Myers, Gustavus. *History of the Great American Fortunes*. New York: The Modern Library, 1936.

Nash, Jay Robert. *Encyclopedia of Western Outlaws and Lawmen*. New York: DaCapo Press, 1994.

———*Hustlers and Con Men*. New York: M. Evans & Co., 1976.

———*Look for the Woman*. New York: M. Evans & Co., 1981.

Norfleet, J. Frank. *Norfleet*. Fort Worth: White Publishing Co., 1924.

O'Connor, Richard. *Bret Harte: A Biography*. Boston: Little, Brown and Company, 1966.

Partnoy, Frank. *The Match King: Ivar Kreuger, the Financial Genius Behind a Century of Wall Street Scandals*. New York: Public Affairs, 2009.

Plazak, Dan. *A Hole in the Ground with a Liar at the Top: Fraud and Deceit in the Golden Age of American Mining*. Salt Lake City: University of Utah Press, 2006.

Powell, David M. *The Peralta Grant: James Addison Reavis and the Barony of Arizona*. Norman: University of Oklahoma Press, 1960.

Powers, Ron. *Mark Twain: A Life*. New York: Free Press, 2005.

Randall, Willard. *George Washington: A Life*. New York: Henry Holt and Company, Inc., 1997.

Raynor, Richard. *Drake's Fortune*. New York: Anchor Books, 2002.

Recko, Corey. *Murder on the White Sands: The Disappearance of Albert and Henry Fountain*. Denton: University of North Texas Press, 2007.

Robertson, Frank C. and Beth Kay Harris. *Soapy Smith: King of the Frontier Con Men*. New York: Hastings House, 1961.

Russell, Don. *The Lives and Legends of Buffalo Bill*. Norman: University of Oklahoma Press, 1960.

Sanchez, Joseph P. *Between Two Rivers: The Atrisco Land Grant in Albuquerque History*. Norman: University of Oklahoma Press, 2008.

Sakolski, A. M. *The Great American Land Bubble: The Amazing Story of Land-Grabbing, Speculation and Booms from Colonial Days to the Present Time*. New York and London: Harper & Brothers Publishers, 1932.

Saxon, A. H. *P.T. Barnum: The Legend and the Man*. New York, Oxford: Columbia University Press, 1989.

Shirley, Glenn. *Pawnee Bill: A Biography of Major Gordon N. Lillie*. Albuquerque: University of New Mexico Press, 1958.

Smith, Frank E. *The Yazoo River.* New York, Toronto: Rinehart & Company, 1954.

Spence, Clark C. *British Investments and the American Mining Frontier, 1860-1901.* Moscow: University of Idaho Press, 1995.

Stratton, David H. *Tempest over Teapot Dome: The Story of Albert Fall.* Norman: University of Oklahoma Press, 1998.

Stross, Randall E. *The Wizard of Menlo Park: How Thomas Alva Edison Invented the Modern World.* New York: Three Rivers Press, 2007.

Sutherland, Edwin H. Ed. *The Professional Thief.* Chicago: University of Chicago Press, 1973.

Swierczynski, Duane. *Frauds, Scams and Cons.* (n.c.) Alpha, 2003.

Tarbeaux, Frank. *Adventures.* London: John Long Ltd., 1933.

Thorndike, Jonathan L. *The Teapot Dome Scandal: A Headline Court Case.* Berkeley Heights, NJ: Enslow Publishers, Inc., 2001.

Thorne, Tanis. C. *The World's Richest Indian: The Scandal Over Jackson Barnett's Oil Fortune.* New York: Oxford University Press, 2005.

Tozer, Basil. *Confidence Crooks and Blackmailers.* London: T. Werner Laurie, 1929.

Twain, Mark. *Mark Twain's Letters.* Edited by E. M. Branch, et al. Berkeley and Los Angeles: University of California Press, 1988.
————*Roughing It.* Pleasantville, NY: Reader's Digest Association, 1994.

Tygiel, Jules. *The Great Los Angeles Swindle: Oil, Stocks and Scandal During the Roaring Twenties.* New York: Oxford University Press, 1994.

Unger, Harlow Giles. *America's Second Revolution: How George Washington Defeated Patrick Henry and Saved the Nation.* Hoboken, NJ: John Wiley and Sons, Inc., 2007.

Van Cise, Philip S. *Fighting the Underworld.* Cambridge, MA: Riverside Press, 1936.

Wallace, Irving. *The Fabulous Showman: The Life and Times of P.T. Barnum.* New York: Alfred A. Knopf, 1959.

Wallis, Michael. *Oil Man: The Story of Frank Phillips and the Birth of Phillips Petroleum.* New York: St. Martin's Griffin, 1995.

Walsh, Dr. James T. *The Story of Cures That Fail.* New York: Appleton, 1923.

Warren, Louis S. *Buffalo Bill's America: William Cody and the Wild West Show.* New York: Alfred A. Knopf, 2005.

Webb, James H. *Born Fighting: How the Scots-Irish Shaped America.* New York: Broadway Books, 2004.

Webster's New Biographical Dictionary. Springfield, MA: Merriam-Webster, Inc., 1983.

Werner, M. R. *Barnum: The Story of the Greatest Showman of Them All.* New York: Grosset and Dunlap, 1923.

Werner, M. R. and John Starr. *Teapot Dome.* New York: Viking Press, 1959.

Wilstach, Paul. *Patriots Off Their Pedestals.* Indianapolis: The Bobbs-Merrill Company, 1927.

Wood, Gordon S. *Empire of Liberty: A History of the Early Republic, 1789-1815.* New York: Oxford University Press, 2009.

Young, James Harvey. *The Medical Messiahs.* Princeton, NJ: Princeton University Press, 1992.

Zuckoff, Mitchell. *Ponzi's Scheme: The True Story of a Financial Legend.* New York: Random House, 2005.

Government Publications

Fletcher v. Peck, 10 U.S. 87, 6 Cranch 87, 3 L.Ed. 162 (1810).

Report of the Committee to the Georgia House of Representatives, dated December 9, 1794.

Internet Sources

Wilson, John Lung. *Stanford University School of Medicine and the Predecessor Schools: An Historical Perspective.* Stanford University School of Medicine, 1918. Accessed 27 November 2009. Available from http://elane.stanford.edu/wilson.

Newspapers

Arizona Bulletin
Boston Globe
Chicago Bulletin

Engineering and Mining Journal-Engineering and Mining Journal Press
Louisville Courier-Journal
New York Sun
New York Times
Rocky Mountain Mining Review
Rocky Mountain News

Other Sources
Annals of Congress, 13th Congress, 2nd Session (Washington, DC: 1854)
62 Cong. Rec. 6893 (1922)
Executive Order 3474
S. Doc. No. 67-191 (1922)
S. Res. 277, 67th Cong. Rec.
United States v. Sioux Nation of Indians, 448 U.S. 371 (1980)

Acknowledgments

Nobody writes alone. We have had unlimited help from the following people and institutions who responded not only accurately but with tolerance for our sometimes unclear inquiries. If we have omitted anyone, the omission is inadvertent, and we much regret it.

Mr. John Lovett, the University of Oklahoma Western History Collection

Ms. Jennifer Karr, the University of Oklahoma Western History Collection

Ms. Lisa Bowles, the Donald E. Pray Library of the University of Oklahoma College of Law

Ms. Jennifer Hawk, Reference Assistant, the Donald E. Pray Library of the University of Oklahoma College of Law

Ms. Judith Munns, Curator, the Skagway Museum, Skagway, Alaska

Ms. Jennifer Vega, Photo Librarian, History Colorado, Denver

Kansas State Historical Society, Center for Historical Research, Topeka

The Library of Congress

The Oklahoma Historical Society Research Center, Oklahoma City

Mr. John R. Waggener, Associate Archivist, American Heritage Center, the University of Wyoming, Laramie

Denver Public Library

Western History Collection, the University of Oklahoma

Ms. Susan Jellinger, Librarian, State Historical Society of Iowa, Des Moines

Rocky Mountain News

Denver Times
The National Archives
Tulsa City-County Library

Index

Powell, Frank, 243
Preissnitz, Vincent, 124
Preston, John, 151
Pretty Billy, 31
Prevost, Severo Mallet-, 210
Promontory, Utah, 163, 192
Pueblo, Colorado, 123, 221

R
Raburn, Thomas, 155
Ralston, New Mexico, 217
Ralston, William C., 217, 228-29, 231, 253
Randle, Les, 116
Randolph, John, 157, 159, 161
Readyville, Tennessee, 250
Reavis, James Addison, 195-96, 203, 216
Reavis, J.A. Peralta-, 206
Reid, Frank, 102
Rhodes, Eugene Manlove, 260
Richmond, Virginia, 242
Riverside, California, 208
Roberts, George D., 217, 219, 223, 232
Robinson, John, 247
Rodgers, Jimmie, 140
Rosita, Colorado, 238
Round Rock, Texas, 85
Rudabaugh, Dirty Dave, 93

S
Sacramento, California, 47
Salomen, Edith, 63
Salpointe, John B., 214
San Bernardino, California, 209, 228

Sandoval, Andres, 209, 215
Santa Anna (Gen), 197
Santa Fe, New Mexico, 209
Sapulpa, Oklahoma, 110
Savannah, Georgia, 155
Schulz, Jonas, 224
Schurz, Carl, 200
Scott, Winfield, 225
Sewell, Samuel, 162
Seymour, Silas, 192
Sharon, William, 33, 228-31
Sheeny Sam, 109
Sherman, John, 190
Sherwood, Alfred, 208, 212-13, 215
Sherwood, A.T., 215
Shew, Joel, 124
Short, Luke, 46
Silver City, New Mexico, 250
Simpson, Sockless Jerry, 95
Sinclair, Harry, 248, 254-55, 257-58
Sinclair, Upton, 135
Sister Mary, 64
Sitting Maude, 96
Skagway, Alaska, 14
Slack, John, 217-21
Smalley, George, 236
Smith, Albert, 165
Smith, H.M., 41
Smith, Jeff, 85, 98, 100
Smith, Joseph, 171
Smith, Soapy, 14-15, 30, 36, 39, 43-46, 51, 85, 102, 104-5, 109, 112
Snowball, John, 208, 213
Sorenson, Andrew, 113